The Preacher

AND HIS AUDIENCE

The Preacher

AND HIS AUDIENCE

Webb B. Garrison

FLEMING H. REVELL COMPANY

To Mary

loyal listener
and
inspiring helpmate

CONTENTS

ACKNOWLEDGMENTS

This volume owes its genesis to an experience during a preaching mission at Craig Field, Alabama. Chaplain Harvey Holland, Jr., was responsible for the invitation—so played a significant role in my ensuing study of the audience as a major variable in preaching.

Miss Marella Walker, circulation librarian, Emory University Library, extended many courtesies without which the research involved would have been impossible.

Chapter XII was originally published in *Religion in Life* (New York) and a portion of Chapter III appeared in *Interpretation* (Richmond) as part of an article entitled, "The Necessity and Relativity of Biblical Interpretation."

Scripture quotations are from the Revised Standard Version, Copyright, 1946 and 1952, The National Council of the Churches of Christ in the United States of America. Special thanks are due the publishers for permission to quote from this version, and to the Fathers of the Church, Inc., for permission to quote from various volumes of their splendid new translations of early Christian classics.

The Preacher

AND HIS AUDIENCE

Chapter I

A NEW LOOK AT PREACHING

THERE IS LITTLE DOUBT THAT THE MOST CHARACTERISTIC
aspect of contemporary civilization is *uncertainty*.

Few observers agree as to the exact causes, and none has
offered a generally accepted cure. But almost without exception analysts concur in the diagnosis of the illness. Evap-
orating from currents of change as vapor rises from a
mountain river on frosty mornings, uncertainty swirls through
every area of modern thought and action.

"Since the Renaissance," said a recent Gifford lecturer,
"there has been no such upheavel of thought, no such revalu-
ation of values as in the century upon which we have entered.
Now as then, within about fifty years, within the span of a
single lifetime, all the old conceptions, the previous beliefs in
science, in religion, in politics have been wholly transformed;
a change has taken place, we might almost say, in the incli-
nation of the earth's orbit."[a]

That statement was made when the atomic bomb existed
only in the minds of physicists. It may take the perspective of
several centuries to assess correctly the extent and intensity

[a](1), 26.

of the uncertainty that now grips mankind—panting through the birth pangs of the atomic age.

Meanwhile, we who are in it must make the best of it and do our small part to guide the turbulent stream. That is part of the preacher's rôle. He would not stand in his pulpit if he did not expect to touch and change individual lives. But he cannot move men without to some degree moving mankind.

Sitting as he does in a driver's seat, the preacher—of all men—needs to know where he is going. More, he must have a profound certainty that he is not merely moving, but is moving in the right direction.

No sense of sureness hovers like a halo over contemporary Protestant pulpits. Bombarded by many streams of thought, the preacher is tempted to abandon thinking. Like the devout Mohammedan, he may turn toward some ancient Mecca, closing his eyes to the here and now. Or he may turn his back upon the past and stride boldly toward some vague future, oblivious of the fact that he has left his compass behind.

Torn between sacred traditions and radical new ways of thought, it is as though the preacher turns on his radio and twists the dial rapidly. He alternates between two stations. One of them is broadcasting a religious service, in which the speaker is leading in prayer. Station No. 2 is broadcasting a popular science program, transmitted directly from a laboratory where an experiment is in progress. This is the message that comes into the preacher's study:

Let us lift our hearts to God, then take ten grams of radioactive silver nitrate and place in a retort. . . . We are grateful for thy favor, Our Father, and clean our test tubes with scrupulous care. . . . As thou didst shelter Abraham, Isaac, and Jacob, we now adjust the flame of the Bunsen burner. . . . So care for us and watch over us, Great Jehovah, that the products of the laboratory will cause mankind to enter a new era of comfort and abundance. Amen.

Time was when the servant of God faced no such difficulties. During that period sometimes called "the long night of Europe," the parish priest lived in comparative calm. He had problems, of course. But they were about the same problems that had been met and solved by his fellows for a thousand years. Political transitions there were from time to time. But there was no single instance of a radical transformation of culture within a generation. Not once between the fall of Rome and the adoption of the experimental method did Western civilization turn a corner in three seconds—as G. Ray Jordan has said of the Wright Brothers' first flight at Kitty Hawk, N. C.

Today the preacher faces one radical transformation after another. Guided by empiricism—the philosophy of experiment—natural science has proved as prolific as the cod. Her wonders are spawned in prodigal hordes. Such is their nature that each new find accelerates the process of discovery itself. No staid arithmetical progression, inventions and processes accumulate in a geometrical progression. Within the ever-mounting total, any single discovery may set off a chain reaction that lashes out with ungoverned speed, sometimes blinding those who unleash it, and ending no one knows where.

It is inevitable that Christianity should be affected. Flowing like the Amazon into the ocean of human culture, religion does not at once yield to pressures from the environment. But at length other currents do their work, and the stream once clearly defined begins to lose its individuality.

That such a process has been taking place for quite some time it is hard to deny. It is proverbial that the preacher seldom finds difficulty in discovering a crisis. There are those so callow as to intimate that the prophet who cannot find a crisis will manufacture one.

But the instability of Western culture, mounting with increasing tempo since the Reformation, has affected the roots as well as the branches of Christianity. As early as the decade before the outbreak of World War II numerous observers sensed an impending crisis. In 1933, an exhaustive survey produced the conclusion that "half of all the business men, lawyers, and writers listed in *Who's Who in America*, two thirds of practically all the men and women having the slightest right to be called 'scientists,' and the same proportion of the students of the intellectually superior colleges are unable to profess belief in the God worshiped in the churches."[b]

Coming as they did from a professed foe of traditional religion, these findings are not to be taken at face value. No matter how unscientific the study and dogmatic the conclusions, preachers must regard the final indictment as startling. Were this a single leaf driven by a mild May zephyr, it might be discounted but not ignored. One year after the study was made, Reinhold Neibuhr published a volume with the significant title, *Reflections on the End of an Era.*[c] Twelve months later, C. G. Jung described the period as characterized by "the greatest restlessness, nervous tension, confusion and disorientation of outlook."[d] That was not a surprising statement from a psychiatrist, but it was news when Jung interpreted the condition as "one more indication that our religious truths have somehow or other grown empty."

As a layman, Jung perhaps hesitated to speak as bluntly as he might have. Not so two contemporary Christian thinkers, who boldly point to "the obvious maladjustment of traditional religion to the modern world."[e]

It does not require a prophet or a son of a prophet to see

[b] (2), 20.
[c] (3).
[d] (4), 268.
[e] (5), 22.

that the pulpit has declined in prestige and power. Gone are the days when every village preacher was a man of weight in the community, when men crowded to hear the preached word, regardless of who was preaching.

Of course, preachers had no monopoly in those "dear, dead days." Men had no automobiles to take them to theaters and sports arenas. They had no radios or television sets to bring distant events into their homes. So they were not particularly discriminating; they went to hear political orators, preachers, and, later, Chatauqua lecturers—with almost equal fervor.

Once, after Daniel O'Connell, a noted Irish patriot, had addressed a great crowd, a member of the audience was asked, "Could all of you hear?" "Certainly not," he protested. "Only 30,000 of us could hear. But the rest of us kept very quiet."

How rare are the speakers—laymen or preachers—who regularly create seating problems! Public address systems make it possible for us to speak to more and more, yet the majority of speakers are addressing fewer and fewer. Even a Billy Graham must lean heavily upon the services of that ubiquitous symbol of modern aggressiveness, the public relations man.

Preaching has entered upon a period of hard times. Not since the post-Nicean Age have the demands been so heavy. If that statement seems unduly vehement, consider the history of preaching. Beginning in Apostolic times, it rose gradually in power and influence. A peak was reached in Chrysostom. Thereafter, preaching gradually declined for a period of more than ten centuries. There was no particular function left for the pulpit; dogma was settled, and all questions were referred to the infallible authority of Rome.

Reborn with the Reformation, preaching entered upon

a period of great vitality. It was the pulpit that gave unique and original direction to the political ideas which produced American democracy. Especially in the New World, where there were no ties with the state, preaching became a mighty force. This hard-won position is by no means lost. Yet there are many indications that the preacher is no longer an automatic candidate for commander of American society's advance scouts. Your man of the cloth is usually too busy fighting a rear-guard action to be discovered anywhere near the front lines.

It is this dilemma, more than any other single factor, which provides the basis for another book in the already crowded field of homiletics.

This volume attempts to provide "a new look at preaching" in three important respects:

(1) Primary emphasis is upon principles rather than methods.

(2) Preaching is studied here as a special form of communication, in which the rôle of the hearer is as significant as that of the speaker.

(3) There is a determined effort to develop an objective study, as opposed to the subjective analysis of a pulpit giant who looks at preaching primarily from his own experience.

These emphases are designed to shape a study which will help the modern preacher speak with greater authority and effectiveness—to lift his voice so that it will be heard even above the babel of competing ideologies.

PRINCIPLES TAKE PRECEDENCE

Tradition has it that an old Irish cook book includes a detailed recipe for rabbit stew. Each step in the process is listed in precise order. None is unusual except the first, which reads: "Step 1—Catch your rabbit."

Here is the first requisite in preaching: Have something

to say! It is part of the thesis of this volume that any television clown can excel preachers in entertaining an audience. Tricks and gadgets cannot give lasting power to a sermon. They are like the fancy tail-pipes which young sports like to put on their cars. Such gadgets are merely ornamental; they put no more power under the hood of the automobile.

Preaching has a claim over other forms of communication, not in skillful manipulation of shiny gadgets, but in its basic purpose. St. Paul was no mean student of psychology, and he certainly recognized the central rôle of the spoken word. But he insisted that the Christian orator speak "not with eloquent wisdom, lest the cross of Christ be emptied of its power" (I Cor. 1:17).

Charles T. Brown, writing in *Education*, has voiced a plaintive lament: "It is a pity that so many speech books are designed to teach people how to be effective."[f] His is a voice crying in the wilderness, for that emphasis simply represents a concession to popular demand. Dangerous as it is in relation to the secular speaker, it confronts the preacher with a momentous decision. Recognizing the importance of methods, shall he cast principles aside as of secondary moment?

To do so may produce popularity. There is a well-worn saying to the effect that people are hungry for God but do not know it. Rather, the masses suffer from a spiritual vitamin deficiency. They do not recognize their own condition, and "crave something." But instead of going to a reputable physician for a prescription, they attempt to satisfy the craving by stuffing with chocolate-covered cherries. Many popular sermons, especially of the self-help type, are gobbled up avidly and the multitude clamor for more.

Methods are important; this volume is devoted chiefly to such practical matters as attention, persuasion, literary style, and a fresh analysis of that significant sermonic device,

[f](6), 10.

the illustration. But we must not lose sight of long-range goals in our enthusiasm for short cuts to personal power.

A builder may set out to erect either a lean-to or a cathedral. Both structures have legitimate functions, but society does not judge them of equal significance. In order to build the former, one needs nothing more than rudimentary skill in using a few tools. That is essential for the latter, too. But no amount of dexterity with trowel and plumb line, hammer and saw alone can produce a Chartres. If one would build it, he must first master architectural theory. So it is with preaching which is to have more than a brief functional value.

Movie sets sometimes employ great castles made of wire and papier-mâché. Such an edifice, imposing in its baroque splendor, may be a delight to the eye. It stands up nicely under the mock storms of Hollywood's make-believe world. But for real living it would prove a very poor shelter indeed. Its majestic battlements would crumple before the first gale. Its storied roof would sag into shapelessness at the first downpour.

Methods, though important in their own right, must remain subsidiary to principles. Mere use of techniques can produce popular speakers, but not great ones. More than a thousand years ago St. Augustine put it like this: "Do we not see how few attain to great eloquence, while throughout the world the rhetorical schools are noisy with throngs of young men?"[g]

There can be no real eloquence without great ideas. One may master all the methods and still fail to move men. And woe to the world when an orator gains great skill in use of techniques, but has no constructive message to convey. It is inevitable that he should become a dictator or a demigod, en-

[g](7), 411; Sect. 7.16.

ticing multitudes toward emptiness or destruction like a modern Pied Piper.

A SPECIAL FORM OF COMMUNICATION

Given only a pulpit and a preacher, it is possible to have a monologue, but not a sermon. Preaching cannot exist without the listener as well as the talker.

That conclusion is so obvious that it may seem trite. Yet a glance through the literature on preaching indicates that most of it is preacher-centered. As with the church, so with the world. An inquisitive student investigated numerous courses in public speaking. Said she: "I found that in all of them, from Dale Carnegie's to the college subject known as Classical Oratory and Rhetoric, there was plenty of mention of what public speaking would do for the speaker, but an almost total disregard for what it would do for the hearers."[h]

Clearly, the conventional approach to homiletics assumes that the preacher will do the hearer good. In cynical moments one sometimes wonders whether that broad assumption is justified. But there is another phase of the matter that deserves attention—the listener's rôle in the communication process itself.

"Communication between man and man is a two-way process. The hearer may work as hard as the speaker . . ."[i] When one preaches, language symbols originate in the vicinity of the pulpit and are transmitted to the ears of each individual hearer. Though he is a member of an audience, the listener is also an individual. His listening is as real and essential a phase of the communication as is the preaching.

In spite of considerable attention to "psychology of the audience," there has been little emphasis upon communica-

[h] (8), 332.
[i] (9), 176f.

tion problems in relation to preaching. Phillips Brooks recognized that "preaching is the communication of truth by man to men,"[j] and Edwin DuBose Mouzon has said that "the preacher is a communicator."[k] Neither attempted to analyze the problem of communication, but by so much as recognizing that it exists, they placed themselves among a small group of specialists.

Chapter III deals with basic problems in the communication of meaning. And throughout this study there is an attempt to approach preaching as a communication situation. This involves the realization that the effect of a sermon is not due to the persuasive power of the preacher alone. That is but one of several elements in a highly complex situation. Granted that it may be, and often is, one of the most significant of the variables, it cannot be treated as standing alone. Preaching may be reduced to a diagram somewhat like that on page 23.

Preacher-centered studies tend to minimize, even ignore, all factors other than those included in the italicized line (1) in the diagram on page 23. Throughout this volume, an attempt is made to recognize multiple factors and to give the listener approximately as much attention as the preacher.

AN EFFORT TO ATTAIN OBJECTIVITY

Most books on preaching are written by men who have achieved what we usually term "success in the pulpit." Since this writer has not the slightest claim to such distinction, it is impossible for him to share any secrets of personal success, and futile for him to offer profound advice stemming from experience before great audiences.

Any authority that this study may claim grows out of a survey of many authorities. In its basic approach it does not

[j] Quoted in (10), 238.
[k] (10), 244.

The Sermon: A Single Variable in a Complex Context of Situation

$$\textit{Variation in}\begin{cases}
\text{1. } \textit{Persuasive power of preacher} \\
\quad \text{(a function of his authority, pur-} \\
\quad \text{pose, logic, style,} \\
\quad \text{and many other} \\
\quad \text{elements)} \\
\text{2. The occasion} \\
\text{3. Hearer's purpose} \\
\text{4. Established beliefs} \\
\quad \text{of hearer} \\
\text{5. Polarization of the} \\
\quad \text{audience} \\
\text{6. Response of other} \\
\quad \text{hearers} \\
\text{7. Temperature} \\
\text{8. Distractions: audi-} \\
\quad \text{tory and visual} \\
\text{9. Other factors}
\end{cases} \textit{influences}^{1} \begin{cases}
\textit{Response of} \\
\textit{congregation} \\
\textit{and} \\
\textit{Response of} \\
\textit{each individ-} \\
\textit{ual hearer}
\end{cases}$$

[1]This scheme is freely adapted from an analysis of coffee as a stimulant. For the original, see (11), 46. Note that where Stevenson used "determines," I have substituted the term, "influences." This is in order to avoid any implications of rigid behaviorism. At the same time, this language leaves room for the undefined but significant possibility that the "work of the Holy Spirit" may be an integral factor in the effect of a particular sermon.

If this scheme has no other value, it will at least prove a source of some consolation in time of apparent failure. One can always conclude that failure was occasioned by some factor beyond the preacher's control. So minor a variable as temperature (No. 7), may play a very significant part in the response of an audience and the individuals who make it up.

fit neatly into any established category set up by philosophers of religion. It is essentially eclectic—at points, frankly synthetic. Its philosophy of religion lies close to the heart of the "liberal" movement, whose proponents are labeled "ethical intuitionists" by Wieman and Meland.[m]

There is one important departure from "liberalism" in its usual sense. Empiricism is here repudiated as a self-sufficient ground for the discovery of truth. This study claims to be empirical only in the special sense employed by William James—i.e., "contented to regard one's most assured conclusions concerning matters of fact as hypotheses liable to modification in the course of future experience."[n]

Much of the source material has come from areas outside the traditional boundaries of homiletics. Accepting Plato's principle that "cross-questioning is the greatest and most efficacious of all purifications," there has been no hesitation in citing the ideas and indictments of irreligious—even anti-religious—thinkers.

This approach is based upon the conviction that, though more difficult, it is in the end more rewarding. With Josiah Royce, we shall insist upon "the right to criticize as fearlessly, as thoroughly, and as skeptically as may be, the foundations of conduct and faith . . . for doubt on religious questions is for a truth-seeker not only a privilege but a duty."[o]

Numerous source references are included, not only to give credit where it is due, but also to afford some direction to those who wish to plow where this writer has used only a spade.

It will be readily apparent that few final answers are proposed. Indeed, it is likely that most chapters will raise more questions than they will answer. Cicero held it easier to be a military genius than an orator—and the task of the political orator is simple compared with that of the preacher.

Our search for a satisfactory philosophy with which to undergird the preaching of the Word places us in the posi-

[m] (5), 149-210.
[n] (12), vii.
[o] (13), 14.

tion of a worshiper seated behind a woman wearing a huge picture hat. Every time he discovers a peephole through which to glimpse the preacher, the woman moves. We shall not succeed in digging all the stone from the quarries of certainty. As Sir Isaac Newton suggests concerning the pursuit of knowledge in the field of natural science, we shall be fortunate if we manage to discover "a few pebbles on the shore of the great ocean."

In the end, it is good that this should be the case. If the New Eden were to come tomorrow mankind would soon be completely miserable. Change and struggle—both personal and group—are conditions without which manhood cannot develop or continue. Perhaps the *working for* God's kingdom is the only realization of it in this life. Preachers will never find formulas to solve all the problems involved in writing and delivering sermons. That could be done only in a society so ordered that no sermons would be needed.

That enigmatic statue which Athenians erected to the Unknown God had at least this merit: it mocked man's presumption in attempting to know all. If man could attain all the truth of God, he would cease to be man. We must be content with some tentative explanations, some hypotheses, and above all, some mysteries.

So with Oliver Cromwell on the night before he plunged into the battle of Dunbar, we must admit that "we are upon an engagement most difficult." Enter the fray we must, taking hope and courage with us. Recalling some of his most difficult periods in the struggle to produce something worthy of his age, Keats said: "I leaped headlong into the sea, and thereby have become better acquainted with the soundings, the quicksands and the rocks than if I had stayed upon the green shore, and piped a silly pipe, and took tea and comfortable advice."[p]

Let us, in turn, leap into our own sea.

[p]Quoted in (1), p. 298

Chapter II

⊓⎽⊓⎽⊓⎽⊓⎽⊓⎽⊓⎽⊓⎽⊓⎽⊓⎽⊓⎽⊓⎽⊓⎽⊓⎽⊓⎽⊓⎽

MOTIVATION OF PREACHER AND LISTENER

RECENT PSYCHOLOGICAL STUDIES HAVE MADE IT CLEAR, beyond any doubt, that human purpose is extremely complex in nature. There are occasional periods when an individual is bombarded by stimuli of a particular type, and is dominated by a single purpose. For example, a man intensely hungry tends to judge every element of a situation in terms of food; "the desire to eat divides things only into the edible and the inedible."[a]

In general, however, purpose is neither so single nor so clear. One's total set of purposes at a given instant, sometimes termed his "set," may include elements that are actually in conflict with one another. St. Paul was neither the first nor the last to recognize himself as a field of battle, with war raging "in his members."[b]

Preaching, like every other situation involving human attention, provides a constant stream of complex stimuli. These stimuli bombard the listener and play a significant part in his response. But there is no simple and direct causal

[a](45), 71.
[b](52), 369, gives a clear discussion of multiple set.

relationship here. Any stimulus acts as "a starting point from which thought may leap, like a knight in chess, in many different directions; and the direction of the leap is determined by interest (purpose)."[c] In view of this situation, it is necessary to examine the purpose of the listener— recognizing that an individual's purpose on a particular occasion is likely to be made up of several wants, with one holding temporary dominance.

PURPOSE OF THE LISTENER

"Crowd psychology" has emphasized the tendency of the individual to identify himself with what he believes to be the spirit of a group. Yet even in the most highly organized group—the mob in process of carrying out a clearly defined course of action—each member retains some degree of individuality.

Congregations are made up of individual listeners, each of whom is guided by an elaborate complex of purposes. Some of the more significant motives that lead persons to listen to sermons are here considered briefly.

(1) *Loyalty to an institution.* A listener with strong ties to a local church tends to be very keenly interested in its success./He defines such success, however, in terms of his own standards. Contemporary emphasis upon material values leads many loyal churchmen to be chiefly interested in those phases of church life which may be expressed in statistics.

"The churches are troubled," says John Oman, "but it is about their numbers, their finances, their enterprises . . ."[d] A listener who has consciously or unconsciously joined the success cult wishes to hear sermons that sparkle. He considers a message to have achieved its goal if it is of the nature to

[c](21), I, 187.
[d](43), 15.

draw crowds, fill the church, build up the congregation, and increase the offerings.

An officer of a local church tends to retain his special viewpoint when he sits in the congregation as a listener. If he has responsibility for the affairs of the institution, he is likely to feel: "We have an important program that must be maintained. Our expanding plant is a tribute to our wise leadership. Since the sermon is the standard by which many persons measure us as an institution, we must have messages that will attract the masses. We are not particularly interested in theology; it makes no great difference what approach the preacher takes, so long as he continues to pack the house."

Such a purpose may be dominant. It is inherently dangerous, for a listener who holds it is not likely to be greatly concerned about either information or inspiration. His mind may be like concrete—all mixed up and permanently set.

Few sermons are preached to congregations which are free from such listeners. "A mixture of worldly and spiritual policy is to be found in all religious societies. It addresses itself partly to man's deepest needs and partly to his hastiest fears and his shallowest appreciations. Every religious society is a mixture more or less pure of the Divine and the human, of the true and the customary, of the ideal and the expedient."[e]

Denominational organizations tend to foster and accelerate the growth of institutional loyalty, centered first in a local church and then in the denomination. A revealing contemporary trend is the movement toward physical examinations for young preachers. Without a shadow of a doubt, it shows that the group adopting the practice is moving toward a relatively static state. There is no relation between physical health and prophecy at its best. But in order to be efficient

[e] (44), 274.

the institutional servant must be strong and healthy; he must be able to perform well those tasks most closely related to the growth and progress of the institution.

(2) *No recognized purpose.* Habit provides a strong motivation for many listeners. From childhood, Sunday morning has been associated with church attendance. Unless a stronger purpose asserts itself on a particular occasion, the habitual churchgoer will make his way to the sanctuary with no more thought than he devotes to putting on his shoes in the morning.

Such a listener is not likely to be critical. He has a mild desire to be entertained and to be made to feel comfortable. But he will listen even when, upon analysis, he feels that the preacher gives him little or nothing in return for his investment of time.

Let a cynical observer describe some qualities of the habitual noncritical listener: "He enjoys *any* sermon, no matter what the moral principles recommended, no matter how poorly organized or developed, so long as it is delivered in an impressive tone of voice with proper (i.e., customary) musical and physical settings. . . . Because listeners of this kind are quite numerous, intellectual shortcomings are frequently no barrier to a successful career in public life, in the ministry, or on the lecture platform."[f]

There are no statistics on the subject, and it is doubtful that any analysis could yield accurate results. So, in the absence of factual evidence, it is easy to hazard the guess that "habitual listeners" form a considerable part of most congregations.

At the same time, we see here an important factor related to non-attendance. A careful survey made by a minister-psychologist has led him to conclude that the greatest

[f] (45), 66.

decline in church attendance is among "the less educated classes." He found that few persons stay away because of rank skepticism, and that few have clear reasons for not going. They simply have not acquired the habit.

Modern society offers comparatively weak motivation for forming such a habit. "With the liberalization of popular religious opinion which is breathed in from the social atmosphere," this analyst concluded, "the old fear compulsions lose their power and the old belief in the efficacy of going to church as a means of salvation is challenged by the assertion, 'I'm as good as Smith and he goes to church.' "[g]

(3) *Fellowship.* Some listeners are strongly motivated by the gregarious instinct. Such a person may actually attend church primarily for the pleasure of seeing friends and acquaintances. When one attends his usual church, this motive is not likely to be dominant. But when he visits the church where he attended Sunday school in childhood, or where he was a member in the past, fellowship may be his chief goal.

In many sections of America the urge for fellowship has contributed to the spread of the "all-day singing." Semi-religious in character, such gatherings give some of the satisfactions associated with church attendance. Hence, it is not unusual for an individual to transfer his loyalty from a church to a band of singers.

(4) *Worship.* Especially in those communions which give strong emphasis to ritual, any congregation is likely to include some persons who come primarily to worship. An individual of this type tends to regard the sermon with indifference. He neither likes it nor dislikes it as a phase of his worship, but simply tolerates it. He tends to be a passive hearer rather than an active listener.

(5) *Desire for information.* This purpose is included,

g (46), 232.

with the frank recognition that it is rarely dominant and often absent. During the hectic decades of the Reformation men crowded to hear the preacher explain doctrinal formulas. There was a keen desire to know how the teachings of a particular body differed from those of others.

This purpose has largely disappeared. One has the feeling—again unsupported by data, but nevertheless real—that the contemporary listener seldom sits through a sermon in order to gain information. He is not particularly interested in hearing analyses of what he considers dead issues in religion. And if he wants information about matters which he judges of vital concern he is likely to consult a physician, a psychiatrist, a lawyer, or some other expert in a secular field.

This very condition may, however, point to an opportunity. Men are still interested in the primary and vital issues of life. Not one such matter is foreign to the concern of Christianity. Perhaps it is time to begin preaching more sermons which deal with the basic assumptions of various schools of thought. Clothed in new language and studied against the background of natural science, there should be a real place for vigorous preaching about human freedom, the soul, the nature of knowledge, and allied topics.

(6) *Respect for traditional authority.* This is another purpose that is becoming rare among educated listeners. Certain persons of naïve outlook go to church in order to get ultimate answers on all questions. Fostered by the "fundamentalist" view of the Bible, literal exponents of this purpose are now largely confined to sectarian movements. Within the major denominations, however, there is a large residue of persons who consciously retain fragments of the authoritarian view and have unconsciously rejected large portions of it. A listener of this type is likely to become indignant, if

not angry, when anything said by the preacher may be construed to throw doubt on his particular interpretation of the authoritarian position.

(7) *Curiosity*. It is safe to say that few persons attend an ordinary church service in order to satisfy their curiosity. But in every local church there are occasions which tend to attract the curious and to magnify that interest in the minds of habitual worshipers. This purpose may be strong—even dominant—on the occasion of a trial sermon or during a minister's first month in a new parish.

Again, curiosity may lead persons to hear a strange or noted speaker. Jesus himself undoubtedly had many such in his audiences—even Herod was eager to meet this strange young prophet—"he had long desired to see him, because he had heard about him, and he was hoping to see some sign done by him" (Luke 23:8).

A desire to "see some sign" is a major element in the purpose of those who flock to hear a noted evangelist or other highly publicized preacher. Though not easily isolated for analysis, this purpose is doubtless present in any congregation assembled to hear a visiting preacher on any occasion.

(8) *Exhibition*. So many stories are in circulation about Easter hats and Easter congregations that little need be said on that score. Individual members of a congregation may be affected by the desire for exhibition on occasions other than Easter, however. A new dress or a permanent wave may be the factor that tips the scales on a particular Sunday, leading one to attend church services rather than sit at home.

This element is by no means limited to the distaff side of the house. Especially in rural areas, candidates for political office sometimes develop great interest in worship, there being some intangible connection between the devotional life and the approaching election. Some business and professional men are aware that it may be advantageous to be seen at church.[b]

(9) *Emotional outlet*. Especially among sectarian groups that emphasize extreme and distinctive doctrines, there are those who attend church in order to enjoy an emotional orgy.[c] Since such an emphasis on the part of the preacher may attract large crowds, it is clear that many listeners actually want to have their emotions stirred. Manifestations of emotion tend to vary somewhat according to the social and intellectual stratum to which an individual belongs.

But no person is immune from feeling. There is some reason to believe that middle- and upper-class churches are losing heavily because of their failure to provide any opportunity whatever for emotional release on the part of individual worshipers.

(10) *Personal problems*. In spite of numerous charges that "the churches are failing in their task," there are many persons who still bring their problems to church. Especially when one is actively seeking a way out of a dilemma the preacher has a great opportunity.

A listener who has a strong set toward help from religion will seize upon and use elements that make no impression upon individuals dominated by other purposes. For example, John Wesley was wrestling with personal problems on the historic evening when he attended a prayer meeting in Aldersgate Street, London. Guided by a strong purpose, he selected a few phrases from those read by the leader. His attention centered upon one aspect of Luther's interpretation of "justi-

[b] This is no careless indictment. It is readily illustrated from personal experience. To mention just one case, I recall a conversation with a successful undertaker in a Southern town. He had a virtual monopoly, and wished to keep it. Himself a prominent Methodist, he had persuaded his son and partner to become a Baptist. And when he took his new son-in-law into the business, the latter became an active worker in the local Presbyterian church. "I'm a steward," explained the head of the establishment. "Son is a deacon, and my son-in-law will soon be elected to the session. Then we'll have key places in every church in town."

fication by faith," and in it Wesley found an answer to his problem. He left the little meeting room a different man. It is significant that we have no record that others who heard the same words by the same speaker were affected in like fashion. Here is a clear instance in which the purpose of the listener was a major element in his own response to the spoken word.

Individuals may wrestle with a particular problem over a period of years. Or one's problems may wax and wane like the moon, one after another alternating in a position of temporary dominance. In any case, conscious attempts to reach a solution play a vital part in the listener's reactions. A man who is a problem to himself is a ready-made opportunity for the preacher. Conversion may be described as problem-solving on the basis of religious motivation. It is a high-level synthesis, enabling a person in some sort of trouble to move out of it by moving God-ward.

Hence, problem-centered listening tends to help produce those transformations of personality that are closely associated with Christianity at its best.

Some aspects of personal conflict are discussed in Chapter X. At this point, one practical suggestion is in order. Preaching that is more or less closely related to actual problems known to exist in the congregation usually tends to be fruitful.

Some preachers will find it helpful to use questionnaires at intervals. In practice it is readily discovered that some cultivation may be necessary in order to get significant numbers of returns. And it goes without saying that personal confidences must be respected. Careful use of questionnaires with definite groups within a congregation—Sunday-school classes, the youth fellowship, and other groups—will yield more returns than indiscriminate circulation.

Even when the return is relatively low, however, a listener who spends even a few minutes with a personal analysis sheet tends to clarify his own thinking. Thereby he gains new purpose in listening.

A typical questionnaire is printed on page 36. Modified to meet the needs of a particular congregation, it will help the preacher to discover problems with which he should deal directly or by implication. (Certain emphases are deliberately repeated in this particular questionnaire. This is in order to see whether answers are made carefully and consistently or in haphazard fashion.)

PURPOSE OF THE PREACHER

If preaching were ideal, every sermon would be prophecy of the first order. Noble as such a goal may be, it is not readily attained. "Let us have prophetic utterances, by all means; *but* first catch your prophet. The supply of Isaiahs and Jeremiahs that God affords to the world is strictly limited."[1]

Sparkling though that observation is, it lies nearer half-truth than truth. God does indeed give the world its Isaiahs, but not without the conscious striving of the Isaiahs themselves. Man's rôle in revelation is not to be minimized. And if the preacher is to discover rare moments when he deserves to stand among God's prophets, he must deliberately cultivate high purpose.

While such a purpose is here accepted as the norm, it would be less than honest to ignore other motives that sometimes cause one to stand behind the pulpit.

(1) *Loyalty to an institution.* Closely related to the same purpose on the part of some listeners, this motive comes to focus in a local church or a denominational program. At best,

[1] (47), 407.

PERSONAL PROBLEM SHEET

DIRECTIONS: Indicate sex, and age to nearest multiple of 10 years. Then study the list of personal problems: in each case encircle the *x* in the column which applies to *you*. Please be honest with yourself: DO NOT PERMIT ANYONE TO SEE THIS SHEET; DO NOT SIGN YOUR NAME. If you have personal problems not listed, please use the blank spaces to write them in, and to indicate how serious they are to you.

PERSONAL PROBLEMS	No Problem	Minor Problem	Regular Problem	Serious Problem	Critical
1. Personal relations in the family	x	x	x	x	x
2. Unsatisfied desire for money	x	x	x	x	x
3. Recognition of self-centeredness ...	x	x	x	x	x
4. Temptation to drink	x	x	x	x	x
5. Personal relations on job or in school	x	x	x	x	x
6. Sense of guilt from using tobacco ..	x	x	x	x	x
7. Problems related to sex	x	x	x	x	x
8. Worry about international affairs ..	x	x	x	x	x
9. Temptation to gamble	x	x	x	x	x
10. Sense of guilt from using alcohol ..	x	x	x	x	x
11. Worry about a future depression ..	x	x	x	x	x
12. Sense of guilt from having broken laws of the Bible	x	x	x	x	x
13. Worry about attitude of friends	x	x	x	x	x
14. Worry about health	x	x	x	x	x
15. Temptation to sexual sin	x	x	x	x	x
16. Sense of guilt from dishonesty	x	x	x	x	x
17. Unsatisfied desire for recognition ..	x	x	x	x	x
18. Worry about attitude of relatives ..	x	x	x	x	x
19. Sense of guilt from using profanity	x	x	x	x	x
20. Sense of guilt from failure to live up to Christian ideals	x	x	x	x	x
21. _____	x	x	x	x	x
22. _____	x	x	x	x	x

DEGREE OF SERIOUSNESS IN MY OWN LIFE:

SEE BACK OF SHEET FOR ANY COMMENTS YOU CARE TO MAKE

Age _____   Sex _____

loyalty to an institution does not give the same power as possession by a great idea.

At worst, this purpose tends to degenerate into "going through the motions." While himself a patient in a mental hospital, Anton Boisen recognized the futility of the usual preaching in the chapel. He tells of one "kindly old minister who gave us a series of sermons on missions—missions in China, missions in Africa, missions in Japan." Another, who was more vigorous if not more intelligent in his support of institutional Christianity, once expounded on the text, "If thine eye offend thee, pluck it out." Observed listener Boisen: "I was afraid that one or two of my fellow patients might be inclined to take that injunction literally."[j]

Even when it does not produce such obviously faulty fruit, sheer loyalty to a program may be a dangerous motive. One impelled by such a purpose is subjected to many temptations. He is not content merely to temper the wind for the benefit of shorn lambs; he may go so far as to withhold any blast of righteous indignation that might annoy one of the old rams. William Peter King used to tell preachers about the brother who spent all the week writing a good sermon. On Saturday night he become fearful of the results and extracted all the teeth. "Next morning," said King, "he went gumming his way through the congregation."[k]

Any preacher has burden enough trying to decide what his people really need. He can build an institution, but not the Kingdom, by attempting to give them what they want as a substitute for what he believes they need. This procedure brings the church and the world into harmony by knocking out the partitions between the rooms. Some observers are cynical enough to say that the larger room so obtained bears

[j] (46), 6.
[k] (48).

more semblance to the market place than to the sanctuary.

Hear another salvo from the trumpet of one who peers at the church through what we are tempted to denounce as jaundiced eyes. According to language-analyst S. I. Hayakawa, the chief purpose of a spoken message may be, "not to give the audience information they did not have before, nor to create new ways of feeling, but to reaffirm feelings already held. . . ." When one attends a high-school pep-rally he does not come out "any wiser or better informed than he was before he went in. To a great extent this is also true of religious ceremonies. The priest or clergyman in charge utters set speeches, frequently in language incomprehensible to the congregation . . . and communicates no information whatever."[1]

(2) *Material gain.* There are occasions on which the preacher's chief goal is the honorarium or purse he expects to receive from his listeners. Even when not a primary motive, this may be a contributing factor affecting his larger purpose.

(3) *Personal triumph.* It is ridiculous to accept the verdict of those Freudians who declare that the libido is the spring from which all preaching flows. But it is equally foolish to claim that self-display is wholly absent from every preaching occasion.

Certain situations actually tend to magnify and accentuate such purpose. Trial sermons provide notable examples. Different in quality but not in kind is the occasion when a preacher has word that members of the pulpit committee from First Church will be among his listeners on a particular Sunday morning.

Perhaps it is not straining the meaning of the gospel passage to suggest that success as a public speaker was the prize offered Jesus by the prince of darkness. Any gifted preacher who is willing to pay the price can still gain "all

[1] (45), 30f.

the kingdoms of the world and the glory of them" (Matt. 4:8). For, as Aristotle has suggested, a speech may be a "success" even though it is spurious in its logic and unjust in its purpose. As a significant purpose, personal success is not to be repudiated, but used.

Some preachers are recognized as superb actors by everyone except themselves. Somewhere in the writings of Soren Kierkegaard there is a brief passage which he calls "A Parable of the End of Time." Its action takes place in a great theater, crowded with eager patrons. Just at curtain time, fire breaks out in the rear of the building. Wishing to avoid a panic, the manager sends a great and popular actor to make an announcement. He tells his story and urges his hearers to leave in quiet and orderly fashion.

They think him acting a part, and give him a round of applause. Now genuinely alarmed, he repeats his warning with new emphasis. Again, his listeners thunder approval at the emotional quality of his acting. Once more, the great man lifts his hands for silence. This time, he shouts out a message of quick doom. Dropping to his knees, he pleads that his audience heed his warning. There is no time to go slowly now; all must run.

Unable to take seriously the man whom they have known only as an actor, the patrons cry their delight at the artistry of his make-believe. He concludes his impassioned plea. Then, simultaneously, the audience breaks into new applause and the walls of the theater collapse upon the crowd.

Any preacher who becomes typed as an actor has great difficulty in ever persuading his hearers that he is in dead earnest. If his real purpose is to move men toward himself rather than the Kingdom; if he loves the praise of men more than the praise of God, his personal triumphs cannot cover the nakedness of his real failure.

In order to be used for the highest ends, the element of

ambition must be recognized. One cannot dam a destructive stream and turn its waters into irrigation ditches until he discovers that the problem exists. There is only one way to use ambition best. That is by attaching it to a new goal, outside the self. Such a goal is suggested in the last purpose here analyzed.

(4) *An agent of an absolue authority.* Within evangelical Christendom, infallible authority is associated only with the Bible. Given new impetus by some interpretations of Barthian theology, there is still a strong movement to regard the preacher as a relatively passive agent—an organ yielding melodies that are not his own.

A contemporary European theologian declares, "The Word of God is given; the minister does not create it."[m] Something of the same viewpoint is implied by a writer in *Religion in Life.* "The preacher," says he, "is neither a teacher nor a lecturer. He is the minister of the Word."[n] For some men all the time and for most men some of the time preaching is motivated by a more or less certain conviction that the message is grounded on "given" truth that is beyond question.

(5) *Dispensing information.* Relatively few sermons are wholly didactic. Indeed, the message that conveys information but lays down no challenge may not deserve to be called a sermon at all. Ronald Colman, speaking on the "Halls of Ivy" radio program, once commented: "Just because a man stands up in a pulpit and talks, he isn't necessarily delivering a sermon—any more than if your cat had kittens in the oven they'd be biscuits."

That witticism conceals a fallacy—that there is a universally accepted and readily recognized characteristic setting

[m] (49), 8.
[n] (50), 263.

a sermon off from every other type of discourse. Yet it does point to the fact that the sermon actually is a distinctive form of communication, having qualities that are more or less clearly exhibited.

Persuasion alone does not make a sermon—the salesman and the political orator are also seeking to produce action on the part of the listener. But without persuasion toward moral and spiritual ends there is no preaching. There are occasions when the sermon should be used for educating and informing the hearer; indeed, when such purpose is entirely absent, the message may consist only of "sound and fury, signifying nothing." Yet the desire to dispense information must always be linked to persuasion.

(6) *Changing lives for the better.* Preaching has no higher purpose than that of persuading listeners to change their lives for the better.

Even when this "better" is by definition related to moral and spiritual values, it is quite apparent that no ready-made norms exist. This factor has large bearing upon the diversity of preaching; each man who aspires to be a prophet must devise a scheme of values before he can urge men to accept them. That this process is often unconscious in no way reduces its paramount significance.

Here is the central problem of preaching: What shall a man preach, and why? Before this question, all matters related to methods of delivery and handling of the audience fade into insignificance.

In "the desire to make known what obsesses and hypnotizes," a contemporary analyst sees "the driving force to good speech." "When this force is behind speech," says he, "we have unmistakable vigor, incontrovertible sincerity. Here is the key to great speech for here is its driving force."[o]

°(61), 43.

Penetrating though it is, this analysis fails to recognize that one may be obsessed and hypnotized by error, passion, or a false scale of values. There is no doubt that Hitler was among the most forceful speakers of all time. Even a brief glance through *Mein Kampf* affords conclusive evidence that he was indeed driven by a desire to make known those ideas which obsessed and hypnotized him.

So the preacher must not merely be gripped by dynamic beliefs and purposes; they must be directed toward the highest and best goals that may be selected. Such selection involves a discriminating survey of contemporary culture, in addition to an effective devotional life.

Keen mind and warm heart complement one another. Neither is to be magnified at the expense of the other. No amount of intellectual development can compensate for spiritual anemia, but no degree of zeal is sufficient to cover intellectual nakedness.

Thus the ideal of preaching is beyond literal attainment: "You, therefore, must be perfect, as your heavenly Father is perfect" (Matt. 5:48). In order to be effective in changing the lives of his listeners for the better the preacher must himself be constantly moving toward that ideal on which he may fix his eyes, but never quite clasp his hands.

There is glory in an impossible goal. It is the moving toward such a goal that this volume seeks to examine.

CONCLUSIONS

A typical congregation is like a tree loaded with apples. Each fruit represents an opportunity, but some are easier to shake down than others. A few are ready to fall at the first quiver of the limb. Others may cling to the branch no matter how violently it is agitated. Some are rosy and mellow. Others are green and sour. There is an occasional magnificent specimen, suitable for exhibition at the county fair. But along with it one finds many that are misshapen and wormy.

No matter what his purpose in listening to a sermon, each member of a congregation represents a challenge to the preacher. There is always the possibility that one who came to scoff or preen may remain to pray. But neither the successes nor the failures in preaching are to be attributed to the speaker alone. One listener seeking an answer to a problem can raise the level of the preaching situation; a few completely dominated by ignoble purposes can pull so many feathers from the wings of the preacher that he finds it all but impossible to soar.

Few men who take the vows of the church are impelled by ignoble purposes. It is the high ideal of every preacher to stimulate his listeners to change their lives for the better. But because this invariably demands the best that one can give there are occasions when other motives strive for mastery. In order to be transformed, such motives must be recognized.

Hence a suggested exercise. At least three months out of every twelve, keep a "preaching analysis chart." Each time that you are to preach, before going into the pulpit list the occasion, subject of the sermon, primary purpose in preaching, and any contributing purposes that you can recognize by introspective examination. Absolute honesty in keeping such a record may sometimes lead to a reappraisal of personal values and will certainly afford incentive to form a more precise philosophy of preaching.

Chapter III

THE COMMUNICATION OF MEANING

MEANING IS ESSENTIALLY PRIVATE AND INDIVIDUAL. IT CAN be made public and common only with great difficulty and to a limited degree. In the case of either a speaker or writer, meaning is prior to communication. It is held in a single mind before being imparted to numerous minds.

Ideas are formed first; these ideas are then offered to others through the medium of symbols. Without symbols which have approximately the same meaning for speaker and listener there can be no communication whatever. That is why John Dewey terms the development of symbols "by far the greatest single event" in the intellectual history of the human race.[a] Without such symbols it would be impossible to share knowledge or to form social institutions. Stuart Chase goes so far as to declare that were language to be wiped out, "man would cease to be a human being."[b]

That judgment is valid only if the term "language" is used in the widest possible sense to include numerous non-verbal communication forms.

[a] (14), 151.
[b] (15), 72.

Words are the most important devices employed in human communication. But the mind's relentless tendency to create vehicles to convey meaning is not limited to words.[c] In a worship service meaning is conveyed by liturgy quite apart from the words employed; in preaching, tone, emphasis, rhythm, and bodily movement communicate subtle shades of meaning.

Music is an important medium of communication. Emotions in the mind of the composer may be conveyed to a listener by means of music which employs no words whatsoever. In the same way, sculpture, paintings, and photographs are vehicles by which meaning is conveyed from the mind of a creative genius to those who are exposed to the symbols he uses.[d] Michelangelo, Rubens, Raphael, and a host of others conveyed religious meaning in their masterpieces. Though seldom utilized in Western civilization, perfume is also a medium of communication.

Modern man has developed an important communication device unknown in ancient times: the scientific chart or graph which expresses some types of complex meaning far more efficiently than can words alone. It should be noted, however, that the graph is merely a special form of map—which seems to have been in use since the earliest civilized times. Mathematicians and scientists rely heavily upon special symbols, often given exceedingly complex meaning.

[c] Samuel Butler, in (16), 235, maintains that we may have a sentence without even one word. He cites the famous story of the method by which Mrs. Bentley used to send for beer. Wife of the great scholar of Trinity College, Cambridge, she sometimes wished to order beer when guests were present. So, instead of sending an oral message to the college buttery, she would send her snuff box. It always brought the beer, for Mrs. Bentley and the steward had agreed that the snuff box should mean, "Please send beer." Hence they were using an object rather than a word as a symbol of communication.

[d] Philip B. Ballard, in (17), 240, interprets Tolstoy to make a "clear-cut distinction between language, whose function it is to transmit thought, and art, whose function it is to transmit feeling." But this distinction will not hold water. Feeling is a kind of meaning. It is the function of both language and art to transmit "facts" and/or "feelings."

But for the preacher the most important non-verbal medium of communication is the gesture. W. A. Sinclair goes so far as to declare that "speech is simply gesture made audible. Speech is simply gesture that can be listened to, instead of watched."[e]

Such a view makes the problem unduly simple. Gesture, like speech, is but one means of communicating. There is no reason to believe that one developed independently of the other. It is significant, however, that man could not learn to use words without gesture—pointing of some sort—to indicate what conventional sound forms the name of a particular object.

THE PROBLEM OF LISTENING

Preaching relies chiefly upon two classes of symbols: words and gestures. A sermon is not simply a message prepared by one person and impressed upon the minds of his hearers like a rubber stamp on successive sheets of blank and passively responsive paper.

Rather, there is an extremely complicated group of processes involved. Groups of meanings arise in the mind of the preacher. He chooses words and gestures which he judges suitable to convey his meanings. These symbols are presented to a congregation. Simultaneously, each listener is required to translate the speaker's gestures and words into meanings. Thus the process is as follows:

A		B		C
Meaning in the mind of the preacher	becomes	Words and gestures, which serve as aural and visual stimuli. These are	translated into	Meaning in the mind of the hearer

Many complex problems are involved in the double transition. It is difficult, if not impossible, for "C" to be identical with

[e] (18), 113-19.

"A" except in the most elementary acts of communication —such as simple pointing. We must, therefore, give serious attention to the problem of listening.

As early as 1917, it was noted that one reading or listening to a single sentence must go through "a very elaborate procedure involving a weighing of each of many elements, their organization in the proper relations one to another, the selection of certain of their connotations, and the rejection of others."[f]

Listening is thus a far more complicated matter than *hearing*, though the terms have become virtually synonymous. Purposeful attention is implied in the former, while the latter may be nothing more than the organism's reception of aural stimuli. And no matter how significant a preacher's meanings, he fails unless he at least approximately succeeds in arousing his own meanings—ideas and emotions—in the minds of those who listen to him.

Here is an analysis by an alert layman: "The average person in the pew is more mentally lazy than he is spiritually indifferent. He will not make the effort to take a long intellectual leap. He must be led gently around a chasm rather than be expected to leap across it. He must be led carefully from thought to thought."[g] Though less apparent, the problems of language itself are even more vexatious than those of logic.

Of course, communication difficulties may serve as consolation in time of apparent failure. It is always possible to conclude that a particular sermon misses the mark because of the audience, not the preacher. Simply because a particular group of persons do not understand a preacher does not prove that he is incoherent. Brand Branshard points out that Hegel

[f] (19), 323.
[g] (20), 114.

suffered a great deal from the demand that he speak plainly. Nettled by what he considered an unreasonable standard, the philosopher commented: "If a hero is not a hero to his valet, that may be rather because the valet is a valet, than because the hero is not a hero."[h]

Comfortable though this view may be in time of communication failure, it does not solve the problem. "It is the speaker's task to study his audience," says a modern analyst, "for an audience cannot be expected to endure unintelligible noises."[i]

Clearly, the burden is upon the speaker. He must be aware that a communication problem exists. He must recognize the inadequacies of words, and do all in his power to minimize the difficulties of those who sit and listen. He must remember that, unlike readers, hearers cannot go back and ponder about the meaning of difficult passages.[j]

NEW LIGHT ON AN OLD PROBLEM

Active interest in the philosophy and psychology of communication is quite recent. Not until 1948 did *Psychological Abstracts* establish a special section on language and communication.

But such ancient thinkers as Aristotle, Socrates, and Zeno recognized that language is imperfect. So did St. Paul, who spoke of "sighs too deep for words" (Rom. 8:26), and

[h](21), I, 71.
[i](9), 200.
[j] Various investigators, working independently of one another, have found experimental evidence to support the conclusion that listening is more difficult than reading. Paul S. Yates (22) and W. E. Young (23) found that at the fifth-grade level, reading comprehension begins to exceed hearing comprehension. Their studies show that after the fifth-grade level, reading ability begins to exceed hearing ability, the differential increasing at an accelerated rate. From tests made with 175 high-school seniors, (24) concluded that there is a significant difference between reading vocabulary and listening vocabulary —in favor of reading. This verdict was confirmed by (25). None of these studies attempted to measure more than word-recognition. As is shown below, this matter does not exhaust the problem.

warned Timothy against "disputes about words" (I Tim. 6:4-5).

Francis Bacon gave some attention to the nature of words, and reached a conclusion that has a strangely modern ring:

> Men converse by means of language; but words are formed at the will of the generality; and there arises from a bad and unapt formation of words a wonderful obstruction to the mind. Nor can the definitions and explanations, with which learned men are wont to guard and protect themselves in some instances, afford a complete remedy; words still manifestly force the understanding, throw everything into confusion, and lead mankind into vain and innumerable controversies and fallacies.[k]

There are a few scattered comments on the problem of communication in the works of Hobbes, Kant, and Hegel. Jeremy Bentham recognized the significance of legal interpretation, and in his *Theory of Fictions* laid the basis for a new science —that of semantics.

No definition of the discipline surpasses that of a contemporary physicist: "General semantics is concerned with the pervasive problem of the relation of language to reality, of word to fact, of theory to description, and of description to data—of the observer to the observed, of the knower to the knowable."[l]

One of the youngest major disciplines, semantics was born as a science in 1923—the year C. K. Ogden and I. A. Richards published *The Meaning of Meaning.* Enormous activity has followed. Irving J. Lee, a pioneer in the field, points out that the contemporary press has produced hundreds of discussions of "the nature and rôle of language in its relation to fact and evaluation in the writings of mathematicians, logicians, physicists, anthropologists, lawyers, physi-

[k](26), sect. 43.
[l](27), 159.

cians, psychiatrists, philosophers, sociologists, educators, artists, rhetoricians, literary critics, grammarians."[m]

Granting that some of the discussions have gone to extremes, it is highly significant that this exhaustive list mentions neither preachers, Biblical scholars, nor theologians. So far (1952), except for two or three brief articles in *The Christian Century*, I have been unable to discover that the religious press has manifested any interest whatever in general semantics.

Linguists dealing with the literature of two or more languages were first to grasp the extent of the problem. Names —which make up the simplest class of words—depend upon the value-system of the culture. Identical objects, assigned different values by different peoples, are classified in quite dissimilar fashion. This classification has tremendous effect upon the language structures.

For example, coffee is a major factor in the economy of rural Brazil and automobiles are of negligible significance. But in the United States, automobiles are far more important than coffee. This produces two sets of classifications, in which Brazilian words and Yankee words are not even approximately equivalent.

North Americans use a single word, *coffee*, to stand for: the coffee plant, its green bean, the dry bean, the dry bean after being pulverized, powdered extract of the bean, frozen extract of the bean, a hot beverage, a cold beverage, and a stock-market commodity.

Rural Brazilians have no name for coffee extract or for coffee as a stock-market commodity. But for the other meanings covered by the single Yankee term they have separate and distinct names.

Conversely, the Brazilian peasant has only one word for a gasoline-propelled land vehicle. His scale of values

m (28), xviii.

does not lead him to be keenly interested in what he regards
as minute distinctions between automobiles. But his Yankee
customers have adopted an elaborate system of classification,
which distinguishes between the sedan and the coupé, the
convertible and the pick-up, as well as trade names of makers.
This means that the Brazilian farmer has no equivalent words
for "Buick convertible." Nor do Americans have an equivalent for the single Brazilian term which means "green bean
of the coffee plant, spread for drying."

A modern anthropologist once spent fourteen months in
the Solomon Islands trying to pin down the meaning of a
single word—*mumi*—which has no English equivalent.[n]
Examples might be multiplied endlessly.[o] Even this brief
examination leads to the conclusion that "language does not
exist in isolation from the culture of which it forms the chief
vehicle. . . . One really acquires a language only insofar
as he acquires a culture."[p]

Bronislaw Malinowski has reached the reasoned conclusion that absolutely accurate translation is impossible.[q] Without identical value-systems, there can be no identical words.

This conclusion has tremendous implications for students of the Bible. Important as it is in that field, however,
its most significant effect is to make clear the fact that there
is a communication problem even when two persons belong
to the same cultural and lingual group. For every person
has his own system of values. To the extent that his values
differ from those of others in his culture his language is individual and private.

[n] (29).
[o] Note that as early as 1786 Goethe observed that "northerners" say "Good
night" at any hour of parting in the dark—while Italians say "Felicissima notte"
only once; at the parting of the day and night, when the lamp is brought into
the room. Americans and Eskimos have no equivalents for names of carbonated
beverages and snow formations. Nor is it possible to translate the hundreds of
Arabic terms related to the date palm into English, or to translate the terminology of radio and television into Arabic.
[p] (30), 555-8.
[q] In (31); Appendix, p. 303. Cf. (32) and (33).

Consequently, all the problems of inter-language communication are involved—though in miniature—in intra-language. Stuart Chase puts it like this:

> When a Russian speaks to an Englishman unacquainted with Slavic, nothing comes through. The Britisher shrugs his shoulders and both comprehend that communication is nil. When an Englishman speaks to an Englishman about ideas—political, economic, social—the communication is often equally blank, but the hearer thinks he understands, and sometimes proceeds to riotous action.[r]

Certainly the problems of religion are as complex as those of economics. Terminology is equally specialized and emotional connotations are probably more numerous. It is clearly impossible for a preacher to communicate exact shades of meaning to any considerable number of listeners. Success in this attempt is approximated only when all the words used mean the same thing to both speaker and hearer.

ABSTRACTION WITHOUT END

Much of the difficulty is due to the abstract nature of language. Individuals inherit most or all their words from the supporting culture. Humans learn speech gradually, over a period of many years, and may achieve considerable skill in the use of complex abstractions without being aware of their nature.

This is not strange; many other skills are acquired in the same way. Ability to see objects is perhaps the best example. Persons born with cataracts, and subsequently given sight by surgery, frequently require months to learn how to distinguish between visual stimuli which present no problem to those who learned to see in infancy.[s]

It is clearly possible to use language without having first

---

[r] (9), 14.

[s] M. von Senden, a noted European surgeon, concluded that "to give sight to a blind-born person is more the task of an educator than a surgeon." He is quoted in (34), p. 217.

analyzed its nature. Were this not so, no child would learn to communicate with its parents. But to shrug away the problem on this score is to miss its great significance.

Semantic study has brought new understanding of the abstractive nature of communication. No description is complete. Rather, the observer selects certain aspects of a stimulus-situation and interprets them in the light of his past experience and present mental "set."

Let me give an example—the brief experience that awakened my own interest in the field. In the Spring of 1952 I was speaker for Religious Emphasis Week at Emory Junior College, Oxford, Ga. Three students stood with me on the campus one morning, chatting. We constituted Observers A, B, C, and D.

We walked under a tree and noticed a swarm of bees hanging from the limb of a small oak. At 12:50 P.M. on March 20, 1952, all four of us were exposed to the same complex of sensory impressions, of which some elements were:

Visual stimuli

> an oak tree with tender young leaves
> violets, grass, and tiny yellow flowers on the ground
> blue sky (exact shade undetermined)
> brown leaves from last winter, scattered irregularly
> a torn cigarette paper (Lucky Strike)
> dogwood in bloom behind the oak
> a red fireplug in extreme right edge of visual field
> a swarm of bees on a limb of the oak, approximately
>> eight feet from the ground
> three humans, observing the complex of stimuli

Visual stimuli

> hum of bees
> distant, faint calling of three or four crows

nearer, but still faint crowing of a rooster
symbolic noises, constituting conversation of the
    observers

Tactual stimuli

warmth of mid-day sun
gentle play of a Spring breeze (direction unde-
termined)

From this complex of stimuli, the observers abstracted
four distinctly different meanings.

Observer A noted that the bees were the 3-banded
Italian variety. He smacked his lips and stated that he would
like to have some hot biscuits, butter, and honey.

Observer B brought his attention to focus upon the torn
cigarette paper. "I think I'll walk up to the dormitory and
get a cigarette," he said.

Observer C made a futile attempt to estimate the wing-
beat of the bee nearest the ground. He commented that he
"would like to have the flight control of a bee."

Observer D tried to note the more prominent factors in
the complex of data. He overlooked many features, and from
the experience abstracted as its meaning the conclusion that
all perception is relative to the organism that perceives.

It should be noted that hypothetical observers E, F, and
G could abstract yet other meanings from the same complex
of stimuli. Observer E, an artist, would attempt to catch the
beauty of the scene on canvas. Observer F, a machinist, would
note the rusty condition of the fireplug and wonder how long
it could stand without replacement. Observer G, an employe
of the school, would be led to conclude that he should get his
rake and clean up the remainder of last winter's fallen leaves.

These hypothetical observers point to the conclusion that

what one sees in a particular moment is greatly affected by his total past experience and present set of wants. Brief analysis showed this to be the case with the actual observers. We may note that Observer A had been running around the track and was hungry; B was an habitual smoker who had left his cigarettes in his room; C was a candidate for military service, and was eager to enter the Air Force; D was in the process of reading Bertrand Russell's *Human Knowledge*. It is clear that another observer from, say Alaska, would have abstracted meaning quite different from that of any person cited.

For no observer has achieved anything like a complete analysis or a meaningful synthesis of all factors involved in the brief experience. In order to achieve such a result, it would be necessary to note and relate every datum, microscopic and macroscopic. That would involve a complete catalogue of individual types of grass and weeds, with their chemical and physical constituents. It would also require analysis of the atomic structure of every "object" in the complex. And the synthesis would not be complete without relating the observer's position in space and time to the earth's movement about the sun, the sun's movement in respect to the Milky Way, and the known universe to no-one-knows-what unobserved stellar system. Even this would not touch the *why* of the universe, or the problem of the destiny of those humans who played the rôle of observer.

Now, lingual abstraction is quite similar to visual. It is not merely convenient; it is a necessity in communication. If each object in human experience had to be described in terms of every datum related to it, the process would never end. There would be no communication at all.

For example, take what appears to be a simple symbol, the word "tablecloth." It conveys meaning instantly, and with some degree of precision. Yet in order to describe its object completely, the word would have to include all the confining qualities involved. The cloth is white. Light rays reflected from it are of a particular wave length. It is a particular size, and made of a particular fabric. This fabric is woven in a particular manner. It is decorated with an orderly and recognizable pattern. It is located at a unique point in time and space. In order to complete the description, the descriptive modifiers must be interpreted. This means that complete analysis of a single tablecloth would have a mushroom growth, eventually including all knowledge.

For practical purposes no such analysis is needed. In order to speak of a particular datum we require merely a concept, or idea, that deals with a few distinctive features of the object we wish to name.[t] "The name is what abstracts the conception of the horse from the horse itself, and lets the idea recur at the speaking of the name. This permits the conception gathered from one horse experience to be exemplified by another instance of horse, so that the notion embodied in the name is a general notion."[u]

It is necessary at this point to note that names like "horse" and "tablecloth" have no connection with reality as humans experience it. That is, there are no universals except in thought. The only real horses are particular animals, each of which differs in some respects from every other. This in spite of the fact that one label, "horse," is used to designate them all.

"Whoever humbles himself like this child, he is the greatest in the kingdom of heaven" (Matt. 18:4). But there is no such creature as *child*; there are only particular children: Isaac and Rufus, Thomas and Billy. By abstracting

[t] For a more detailed discussion of this matter, see (35), 33-8.
[u] (36), 140ff.

some of the more prominent characteristics of individual children, we arrive at the concept "child." But each person who reads or hears this symbol will interpret it in terms of his own most frequent and vivid contacts with children.

Let us take another example. There is no such entity as *father*; there are only particular fathers. Each particular father conditions the "father idea" of each of his children. It follows that every listener or reader interprets "Our Father, which art in heaven . . ." in a somewhat different manner.

Son_1 grows up in a small village in China. His father ($father_1$) is a carpenter whose shop is an integral part of the home. Son_2 grows up in Minneapolis, Minnesota. His father ($father_2$) is a traveling salesman who seldom spends more than two or three days a month at home. $Father_1$ differs from $father_2$ in appearance, personality traits, and attitude toward the family. Hence, son_1 and son_2 are *incapable* of reaching identical meaning from encounters with the abstract symbol, "father." Their meanings are necessarily relative to experiences of $father_1$ and $father_2$.

So far, we have examined only one level of abstraction —that which gives names to objects susceptible to sense-perception. Words on this level deal with clusters of stimuli which affect the sense organs.

There are two higher levels of abstraction which are even more complex in nature. At the second level, we find words which stand for both formal and informal human relationships. Thus, we speak of family, church, nation, labor, management, and numerous other groups within society. Obviously, the meaning of a term like "labor" is far more susceptible to variety of meaning than that which refers to a single object or organism, as "horse" or "child." Yet more problems are encountered on the third level of language— which consists of words designating abstract qualities.

Considerable difficulty would be involved in an American's attempt to teach the meaning of "apple" to a Japanese, neither having any knowledge of the other's language. By pointing to an apple, however, it would be possible to lead the Oriental to attach the usual occidental meaning to the symbol. At first, it is true, he might think the sound to mean "redness" or "roundness" or "firmness" or "something to eat." But repeated trial and error, using objects other than apples and having qualities of redness and roundness, will convey the unique meaning of "apple."

No amount of pointing to objects can convey the meaning of words like "truth," "honor," or "justice."

Helen Keller has given a vivid account of the tremendous difficulties involved in grasping non-physical names. Until Miss Sullivan had been with her for some weeks, she did not realize that every object has a name. She learned the names of a few things, then made a great leap of imagination and connected running water with water in a cup.

Next she mastered the spelling of "L-O-V-E," but could not imagine its nature. She thought it strange that her teacher could not put her hand on love in order that she might feel its shape, texture, and temperature.

One day she was stringing beads, making many mistakes. Miss Sullivan took the girl's hand and traced on it the word "T-H-I-N-K." Then she touched her forehead. "In a flash," Helen Keller later explained, "I knew that the word was the name of the process going on in my head. This was my first conscious perception of an abstract idea."ᵛ

Word symbols which stand for abstract ideas represent the most complex of all instruments used in verbal communication. They are particularly numerous in the vocabulary of religion; consequently, communication between preacher and

ᵛ(37), 29-30.

audience is far more complicated than that between an architect and a crew of builders. Indeed, some students of communication hold that there can be no exact exchange of information except in words that refer to physical objects.[w]

MEANING SUPPLIED BY HEARER

Regardless of whether a word refers to a physical object or an abstract quality, no insuperable problems arise until we begin to treat the symbol as having only one proper meaning—and that an inherent one. In its essence, such a view regards a word as having necessary and inflexible connections with the thing it names. Thus, one might be tempted to declare, "The hog is called a hog because he is such a dirty animal." In 1937, State Senator John McNahoe of New York waged bitter opposition to a bill for the control of syphilis. His argument was based upon the contention that the word itself was contaminated, and would serve to corrupt the innocence of children.[x]

The Rev. Charles Dodgson, given insight by his study of non-Euclidian geometry, knew that words are only sounds to which arbitrary meaning becomes attached. In *Through the Looking Glass* he makes a classic statement on the relativity of language:

"When I use a word," Humpty Dumpty said, in a scornful tone, "it means just what I choose it to mean—neither more nor less."

"The question is," said Alice, "whether you *can* make a word mean so many different things."

"The question is," said Humpty, "which is to be master, that's all."

Humpty was right. No word has a "correct" meaning. Dictionary definitions simply point out conventional usages

[w](38), 64ff.
[x](9), 63.

in terms of broad areas of meaning. Each time a word is used in a sentence both the context of the word and the background of the reader or hearer limit and direct its exact meaning.

Words which designate things are somewhat like the names of persons. A single name stands for a multitude of different phases in one's growth. Thus, "David Livingstone" designates a new-born baby in the arms of his mother, an African trail-blazer dying in the jungle, and every intermediate personality. Obviously, the name "David Livingstone" does not designate precisely the same person every time it is used. In order to know whether it refers to a schoolboy or a missionary hero, we must examine the context.

Words often have been compared with stones. It is said that they may be fitted together to build sentences and paragraphs, which become the foundations and walls of language-houses.

This analogy is far from accurate. Words are not at all like stones. They are more like sponges. No word has the rigidity of granite; rather, it takes its shape in a sentence as a result of pressure placed upon it by other words. And like sponges, words soak up fluid from their environment. Lifted out of one phrase and placed in another, a particular word will take on a new shape and absorb different meaning.

Adjectives and adverbs afford especially clear examples. Let us attempt to determine the precise meaning of "big." Here are a few phrases in which we seek its meaning:

> a big grain of sand
> a big diamond
> a big apple
> a big elephant
> a big hotel
> a big galaxy

Obviously, "big" has no exact meaning. In each case that it is used, the word represents a value-judgment based on comparisons. And even within a definite phrase there is no stability in the word. To John Jones, buying an engagement ring, a diamond that costs $125 is "big." But to DeBeers Syndicate a stone worth $5,000 does not begin to deserve the title. To Bill Smith, whose experience with hotels is limited to small towns in South Carolina, the Wade Hampton in Columbia is big. But to the New Yorker who has seldom been in a hotel outside Manhattan the Wade Hampton is small.

Jesus made many references to the dangers of wealth. How much property must a man own in order to be wealthy? In rural Palestine, a shepherd with twenty sheep might have been termed "rich." In Cartersville, Georgia, a person who owns twenty pieces of business property is considered wealthy. But legend has it that among the millionaires of Houston, Texas, no man is considered wealthy unless he owns at least twenty oil-fields.

It seems absurdly simple to analyze a statement like, "John saw the cat." But until that sentence is placed in a descriptive and limiting context it is impossible to determine its meaning. Space prevents listing the twenty-eight recognized meanings of *cat*; they range from small tame animal to big wild animal, and from caterpillar tractor to quart pot. A person hearing, "John saw the cat," will interpret *cat* in terms of his own most common experience of the symbol.

That is why Borden P. Bowne says, "One who does not know how to read would look in vain for meaning in a printed page. And in vain would he seek to help his failure by using strong spectacles. Language has no meaning except for one who furnishes the meaning out of himself. Where the mental insight is lacking, eyeglasses and ear trumpets are of no avail."[y]

[y](39). 52.

In order to understand any word, the listener or reader must interpret it in the light of its context and his own total experience. "Until it gets into a mind, a word is only puffs of air or streaks of ink."[z]

Meaning of the sound "eagle" is quite different, depending upon the background of the hearer. To an American it means a large predatory bird which has a place in national symbolism. But to a German the identical combination of syllables means a hedgehog. Again, the meaning of the sound "war" varies with the hearer. To a revolutionary it means joy. To a merchant, anxiety lest a ship be lost. To a manufacturer it may mean satisfaction from certainty that prices will rise. And to a mother it always means fear.[a]

Like a field of perception, a sermon is a complex of stimuli. Each word and group of words used by the preacher, and each group of words in relation to the total context, brings about a response that is affected by the word, the word group, and the total message. In each case meaning is supplied by the listener in terms of his total experience and present set of wants.

CONCLUSIONS

Listening is an extremely elaborate process that includes analysis of simple and complex symbols, plus synthesis of their individual and total meanings. These meanings are not taken over bodily from the mind of the speaker, but are supplied by each hearer.

No wonder the preacher is frequently misunderstood!

Try as he may, no preacher can gain complete success in

[z] (40), 613.
[a] Even conventional meaning is frequently implied rather than expressed. A native of New Guinea, brought to America, would easily learn the meaning of "shop" by visiting, say, a dress shop, coffee shop, and stationery shop. In the light of his understanding of the term, he would, however, be completely astonished to see a sign, "Baby Shop."

producing desired meaning in the minds of all his hearers on even one occasion. Human communication is limited in its effectiveness, for meaning does not attach to words in the same way that a message is fastened to a carrier pigeon.

At this point, we may be in danger of despair. We are tempted to agree that, "especially in its imperative and hortatory modes, language is so impressively vague that it seems to say nothing at all clearly, but only darkly to mutter in the name of an untutored 'will' or an unenlightened 'sentiment.' "[b] Abstract language dealing with symbolism of religion is particularly susceptible to gross differences in interpretation.

No matter how exalted the thoughts of the preacher, he moves no single life until he communicates with a high degree of skill. So we must gird up our loins and go forward. "Language may be compared with the spear of Amfortas," Ernst Cassirer reminds us. "The wounds that language inflicts upon human thought cannot be healed except by language itself."[c]

Even by earnest application we shall not succeed in healing all the wounds. But by recognizing language to be a major element in human misunderstanding we shall place ourselves in a position to see our task in a new light. Throughout the remaining chapters of this study the fundamental problem of communication forms part of the background.

[b] (41), 545.
[c] (42), 327.

Chapter IV

ATTENTION OF THE LISTENER

A SPEAKER WHO HOLDS THE ATTENTION OF HIS LISTENERS DOES not necessarily succeed—but no speaker can succeed unless he does hold their attention. H. A. Overstreet puts it like this: "The person who can capture and hold attention is the person who can effectively influence human behavior."[a]

In view of its crucial rôle in the preacher-audience situation attention has been given surprisingly little consideration by writers in the field of homiletics. Spurgeon devoted a chapter to the matter in his *Lectures to My Students* (1875).[b] He notes that few earlier writers in the field even mentioned the problem of attention, and emphasizes its extreme importance. Though he has some surprisingly modern opinions, he does not approach the subject from the standpoint of psychological findings.

Rooted in the idea "at tension," *attention* implies definite focus of the perceptual system. Such directed reactions involve motor-muscular as well as mental effort. Unless a speaker succeeds in commanding the attention of those who

[a] (201), 11.
[b] (202), Vol. I.

make up his audience, they will yield to the incessant bombardment of other stimuli and direct their attention away from the message.

Everything in the perceptual field bids for attention. Eyes, ears, nose, and organs of touch are receptors which are constantly catching stimuli. Each sensory organ is like a radio in a taxi. It is turned on and waiting; as soon as the dispatcher speaks into his microphone the stimulus is picked up. Unlike the radio, however, the human receptor has an automatic screening mechanism. During every waking moment, impulses rain upon the organism. Many of them never reach the brain. Such sensations as the touch of a shoe, the odor of a familiar room, and routine background noises are screened out. Only when attention is directed to such matters do they loom into consciousness.

Any impression or group of impressions can be dominant. A man riding a trolley and reading can ignore noises and odors. A fellow passenger with a headache notices only his own discomfort. Another, suffering from upset stomach, concentrates on a disagreeable odor. Still another listlessly reads the car cards; having no dominant want at the moment, he directs his attention to the most striking feature of his environment.

For the preacher it is significant that every such stimulus is a competitor. A listener can direct his attention to an outside noise, to itching skin, the wriggling of a near-by child, the hum of an insect, the blonde two pews ahead, or to the hymnal in the rack before him. "Perception is a selective process. At any moment, the organism experiences only a fraction of what is potentially available for perception."[c] Someone has said that the human mind is like the office of a Tammany ward leader on the day after winning an election

[c] (203), 369.

—the place is crowded with applicants for favors, and he has only a few to bestow.

When a person is fully awake he is incapable of achieving a state in which attention is absent. Eating breakfast, he reads the label on the cereal box if no other stimulus is stronger. Sitting in church, he examines the pattern in his clothing or counts rafters if the preacher does not offer a more commanding stimulus. Unlike canines, humans do not drop the outer ear when they cease attending to an auditory stimulus. But communication is effectively blocked when the man in the pew ceases to listen to the preacher and, after re-reading the bulletin, turns his attention inward.

Such turning inward is possible because of the extreme complexity of the human mental organization. Not only is every person subjected to a ceaseless barrage of stimuli upon his sensory organs; he is also affected by memories and wants, fears and hopes. Consequently, each listener is to some degree a Walter Mitty. Any stimulus—external or internal—can cause him to focus upon fulfillment of some wish. Anything seen or heard—any word in the sermon—can send the listener off on trails of thought. This condition is not limited to persons of average capacity; Herbert Spencer is said to have had difficulty in reading because any page of any book suggested so many problems that he could hardly refrain from closing the book and turning his attention to one of the problems suggested by it.

Duration of attention. It is a fallacy to think of attention as a single total response to a sermon. Attention must be captured, held, and recaptured many times in twenty-five minutes.

Analysts vary in their estimates of the duration of an act of attention. But as early as the pioneer days of experimental psychology, it was known that the period is very short. Hyland made numerous measurements, concluded that "a perceptual element could probably not be retained continuously for nearly a second."[d] Pillsbury was more cautious, estimating that "the duration of a single act of attention is from 3 to 24 seconds; most usually 5 to 8 seconds."[e]

Recent studies indicate that these early estimates were entirely too liberal. Scientific measurement of eye movements has shown that brief inspection of a stimulus field, such as a painting, involves 40 to 250 separate fixations, each measured in terms of fractions of a second.[f] Laboratory tests indicate that the center of clear vision normally shifts at a rate of at least 100 times a minute, and that the rate is much greater when one reads or drives a car.[g]

There are no corresponding studies concerning the duration of attention to sounds. But the preacher must face the fact that "some people with the best will in the world cannot be good listeners. They really *do* listen very hard for as long as they are able—which is a very brief period."[h]

Every student of attention comes to recognize that any type of perception is subject to satiation, that no matter how hard one tries to focus on a given stimulus, there are limits to static attention. One of the most obvious illustrations is that of the classic ambiguous cube, reproduced below. After very brief fixation, attention fluctuates and the observer sees a new pattern:

(In studying this and the following figures, cover the printed text with blank sheets of paper in order to prevent interference from stimuli outside the figure.)

[d] (204), 61.
[e] (205), 83.
[f] (58).
[g] (34), 155.
[h] (206), 110.

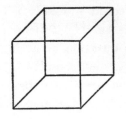

An even more dramatic example is given below. When attention is focused upon the center of this figure it will remain static for a few instants, then suddenly seem to reverse itself. After extensive experiments with this pattern, Wolfgang Kohler concluded that no subject is able to prevent "a sequence of abrupt transformations."[1]

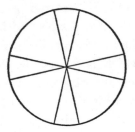

Psychologists have no generally accepted explanation for the fact that attention seems to shift against the will of the observer; yet the fact of the shift is beyond dispute. Take any familiar word, such as *sermon*. Isolate that word from distracting stimuli and concentrate upon it; within a matter of seconds the word begins to lose its meaning and to appear as a mere visual sign—a shape. Prolonged attention will result in actual disintegration of the word into separate elements; at length it will appear to be nothing more than a combination of black marks on white paper:

sermon

[1] (158), 68.

NEED FOR POLARIZATION OF THE AUDIENCE

Every veteran speaker has had the experience of delivering the same message to several audiences, with group response varying all the way from complete apathy to vigorous enthusiasm. Given a message that is virtually identical, it is obvious that the variable here is the audience. One group of listeners forms a compact mass, so coherent that every individual hangs on the speaker's words; another is nothing more than a collection of individuals, each relatively impervious to the speaker's stimuli.

H. L. Hollingworth lists five types of audiences:*

Pedestrian—the audience of the street preacher
Discussion group and passive audience
Selected audience
Concerted audience
Organized audience

Speakers need give little time to catching the attention of an organized audience; but in the case of pedestrian listeners that is his chief task.

Some clues to these differences, and how to treat them, are to be found in psychological analysis of crowds.

A review of the history of psychology shows definite change in doctrines concerning crowds. Munsterberg, Tarde, and Ross thought of a crowd as an entity; Le Bon borrowed this notion and extended it to such a point that it became commonplace to speak of "the crowd mind."

More recent investigation has shown that such a view is untenable; it represents an overemphasis comparable to that of Freud upon the rôle of the *libido*. There is no such thing as a crowd—even a mob—which forms an organic whole.

*(213).

No matter how skillfully organized, a group of persons is made up of individuals. These individuals may approximate, but never actually achieve, complete uniformity.

Nevertheless, there are many degrees to which an individual may "lose himself in the mass." An audience may vary all the way from a collection of persons acting entirely as individuals to a mob in which individuality is at a minimum. F. W. Lambertson lists these traits as characteristic of a middle state which he labels "homogeneous crowd":

1. Feeling of expectancy;
2. Narrowed focus of attention;
3. Increase of emotional response;
4. Decrease of rationality;
5. Impulse to act.[j]

Of these factors, we are at present chiefly concerned with (2), "narrowed focus of attention."

Obviously, if the preaching situation is to produce any impact upon the audience, individual listeners must unite in giving their attention to the preacher—rather than to a multitude of diverse personal interests. Impact of a sermon—or any other form of public address—is greatly affected by the degree to which members of the audience become one in their attention to the speaker.

"Polarization of the audience" is, therefore, a twofold process. It involves leading the listener both to focus his attention upon the speaker and to inhibit other influences. Such a dual movement is involved in all states of high attention. Rosett points out that a person cannot attend to two diverse stimuli simultaneously. Thus, "While a person's attention is on tasting a certain food, he either does not feel the inconvenience of a tight shoe at all, or feels it very slightly;

[j] (207), 124.

but the moment he feels it clearly, he either does not taste the food at all or tastes it but slightly."[k]

In the same fashion, a chess player may be so absorbed in the game that he inhibits his response to outside stimuli; "the universe has contracted to the dimensions of the game; his mind is a cloud of proposals and possibilities hovering anxiously over the pieces, responsive to the shift of a pawn, but dead perhaps to thunderstorms."[l] A high-school football hero aches from the pounding he received on the gridiron. But when he is hailed by the father of his sweetheart, his attention is redirected and his aches are pushed out of the domain of consciousness.

There are obvious dangers involved in producing a highly polarized audience. As attention is narrowed, the listener becomes less critical and more susceptible to suggestion. Infected by the contagion of group enthusiasm, he can be persuaded to accept ideas or to perform acts that would be refused in other psychological states. This is both a danger and an opportunity. Abused by the office seeker or the callously professional evangelist, great harm can result. But no group is really swayed until individuals yield to the personality of the speaker.

Though condemning his goals, the preacher can learn from the methods of even a monster like Hitler. One of the greatest orators of modern times, Hitler said of his own techniques: "I have been reproached for making the masses fanatic and ecstatic. . . . I can lead the masses only if I tear them out of their apathy. Only the fanatic mass can be swayed. . . . Apathy is to the masses a defensive form of rejection. They hide behind apathy."[m]

There is no doubt that members of many a middle-class

[k] (208), 219.
[l] (21), I, 195.
[m] (207), 129.

congregation actually do hide behind apathy. In general, it is the dictator and the demagogue who, among modern speakers, sin by a too-sweeping use of methods that create a strongly polarized audience. Perhaps one other type speaker should be added to that list: the exponent of the more lurid forms of Christian evangelism. Among the great middle-class Protestant denominations of America no such condition prevails. For every preacher who follows Hitler in "playing the crowd like a giant organ," there are hundreds who seldom succeed in getting even a feeble squeak from the human instrument. Under-use, rather than overuse of psychological methods is the rule in the contemporary pulpit.

Consequently, it is necessary to give attention to some specific methods by which the preacher can direct the attention of his listeners.

Physical setting plays a significant part. Social facilitation—the effect of the audience upon the individual listener —exerts its most powerful influence in a large audience.[a] But there is considerable evidence that this is due largely to one factor: when a crowd jams a lecture hall, football stadium, or church, actual physical contact between individuals increases with reduction of average square feet of space per person.

Beecher was among the first to recognize (but not measure) this effect. "I can speak just as well to twelve persons as to a thousand," he declared, *"provided those twelve are crowded around me and close together, so that they touch each other.* But even a thousand people, with four feet of space between every two of them, would be just the same as an empty room."[b]

Entertainers are keenly aware of this factor. Radio and

[a] (209), 649ff.
[b] (210), 73.

television programs frequently originate from small studios in which every seat is occupied. Musical comedies sometimes use a runway from the stage to the audience, permitting the performers to get very close to their listeners.

Some preaching situations yield all the advantages of a closely, packed audience. Many others do not. Indeed, it is not unusual to be confronted by an audience in which the space occupied by listeners amounts to only one-third or one-fourth the total seating capacity. In such cases, listeners are likely to be bunched into two or more distinct groups, separated by chasms of empty seats. To make matters worse, the front seats usually are empty, creating a yawning gulf between the preacher and his two or more audience groups.

What may be done about such a situation?

There is only one remedy: get the listeners as close together as possible, and reduce the distance between speaker and audience to a minimum. This involves a procedure that requires bold action: simply ask the listeners to move together in a clearly designated manner. This is best accomplished by a confident mood coupled with a light, even jocular, approach. Here is a routine that I have used many times, usually with good effect:

Sitting here on the rostrum, I've been struck by a problem, I can't quite decide whether we have too many pews or too few people. . . . And I'm not quite sure whether we have one audience or three! Since I'm not very good at using scatter shot, I'd like to ask you to demonstrate your sympathy for me by moving together into the center section. And just to make it unanimous, I'll step down to the edge of the rostrum to meet you.

Before you move, though, let me tell you one of my favorite stories. I borrowed it from Dr. Pierce Harris, pastor of First Methodist Church, Atlanta. Dr. Harris says that talking to a congregation scattered like this is like trying to chat with a woman who has false teeth—and forgot to put in her lower plate.

You don't want to let her see that you notice anything unusual, but you can't keep your eyes off her mouth to save your life! Now let's move over and close these gaps. . . .

Decision to use such a plea involves several factors. Obviously, it is an emergency measure, to be employed only when dead air space insulates listeners so effectively that no real communication is possible. And there is always the possibility that your appeal will be wasted, that members of the group will refuse to move. Such an outcome is usually the result of lack of skill in making the appeal; it should be timed to a natural movement, such as rising to sing a hymn. But even if it fails, little has been lost; if it succeeds, much may be gained.

By patient and sympathetic leadership a pastor can frequently train his people to form the habit of filling some designated portion of the sanctuary rather than scattering all the way through it.

In addition to the physical distribution of the listeners and placement of the audience in relation to the speaker, there are other important factors in the situation itself. These include architecture, lighting, and temperature.

Before the turn of the century Hyland observed that attention includes at least the dimensions of time, intensity, and direction. Time is short and intensity high in periods of excitement; time is long and intensity low in "vacant," listless periods.[p] The latter effect is produced by some types of physical setting for the preaching situation.

A Gothic cathedral is designed to produce an atmosphere of hushed reverence; every aspect of the building magnifies the individual's sense of dependence. To the degree that this effect is actually created, motor-vocal responses of the listener are inhibited. Social facilitation is thereby reduced, and

[p](204), 62.

each listener tends to remain completely individual rather than becoming a part of a group.

Bright lights reduce this effect, while it is heightened by subdued lighting. Under extreme conditions, it becomes almost impossible to secure such overt response as laughter, nodding of the head, or acceptance of an evangelistic invitation. Only the most skillful of speakers can overcome such obstacles to polarization.

Temperature is not often a dominant factor in the response of the listener, but it may be. Humans are comfortable and efficient only within a comparatively narrow temperature range. If the upper limits of that band are exceeded, the listener begins to give undue attention to his body. He squirms, twists, mops his brow, and fans. To the degree that his attention is brought to focus upon the temperature he is unable to attend the preacher. On the other hand, when temperature falls below a comfortable level, blood goes to the skin. No longer getting a maximum volume of oxygen, the brain ceases to function at its peak. Both speaker and listener become mentally sluggish; active attention is inhibited, and the audience disintegrates into many individuals.

Group action is a factor of such importance that it can overcome the negative effects of all but the most extreme physical disadvantages. Given a reasonably compact group in a well-lighted sanctuary with comfortable temperature, group action can weld lethargic individuals into a sensitive and responsive mass.

Again it is significant to note that Beecher anticipated the findings of experimental psychology. "If I can bring the congregation, before I come personally to handle them, into a triumphant, jubilant state, a cheerful, hopeful, genial state, my work among them will be made easier by one half than if they were in a very depressed, sad state."[q] That "triumphant, jubilant state" is most readily produced by group singing—using songs that have spirited melodies and cheerful emphases.

Members of an audience are like free-swinging steel pointers. So long as they are permitted to remain completely individual they will point in many directions. But once the tips are magnetized, each will swing toward magnetic north. Just so, listeners who have acted vigorously as a group will point toward a single center of attention. A hearty song service creates a polarized—or magnetized—audience.

Singing is not the only effective device, but it is the most convenient and suitable one available to the preacher. When persons laugh together, weep together, or shake their fists together they move toward psychological unity. Uniforms, badges, and pins help create a sense of oneness. Persons sitting on one side of a football stadium, alternately shouting and moaning together, sometimes achieve a remarkable degree of integration.

Persons gathered in a place of worship are comparatively restrained and inhibited. Group action is usually limited to standing and bowing, repeating a creed, and singing. This raises a very important question concerning the rôle of the choir.

If the purpose is to permit passive spectators to enjoy as good music as possible, there is no doubt that the church should employ the best professional musicians available. But if the purpose is to form a cohesive and responsive audience through group action, such a choir may be actually harmful. One good song leader can do more to condition the attention of an audience than any number of highly paid singers who simply put on an exhibition.

[q](211), 120.

Audience-speaker relationships are always significant and may be crucial. Preaching is best regarded as extended conversation. But it is a special type of conversation, in which the response of the listener is likely to be quite limited. In contrast to informal conversation, discussion groups, or question-and-answer sessions, the listener is unusually passive.

In the typical preaching situation, there is no applause, no argument with the speaker, no asking of questions, no shouting of approval, no taking of notes. Convention prohibits alike vigorous expression of agreement, or violent objection to the preacher's statement. This means that the conversation is nearer monologue than dialogue.

Anything that tends to set any listener apart as a spectator and outsider rather than as a participant should be scrupulously avoided. Consider the typical announcement: "*We* are glad to have *you visitors* with *us* today. *We* welcome *you* back to worship with *us* at any time." While this statement may be made with the best of intentions, it tends to emphasize the visitor's awareness that he does not belong to the "we group." To a small but important degree he is given negative psychological conditioning. Every possible effort should be exerted to create a "we" relationship between the speaker and every member of the larger conversational group that is the preaching situation.

Finally, *a few responsive individuals* can affect the response of an entire audience. When a group has become polarized, the process of social facilitation has maximum effect. A chuckle or a sob, originating with a single listener, tends to sweep through the whole group. Every comedian knows that one person with a "contagious laugh" can greatly increase the total response of the audience. European dramatists used to accuse one another of hiring *claquers*. A few of these fellows, scattered through a theater and instructed to clap at strategic moments, could generate applause from almost any audience.

Children and youth are less inhibited than adults. When several youngsters sit in a compact group this group can act as a fuse to set off reactions in the surrounding mass of adults. Many evangelists, therefore, make a practice of forming a youth choir or reserving a section of front pews for adolescents. Total response of the audience may be greatly affected by such procedure.

HOW TO HOLD ATTENTION

Given a strongly polarized, homogeneous audience, the preacher must still maintain that situation for the duration of the sermon. Great as may be the advantages gained by physical setting and group action prior to the sermon, a vigorous state of attention will not prevail under adverse conditions.

It is therefore essential to prepare the sermon in the light of the fact that persons are fundamentally interested in four things: (1) basic human wants, and methods by which to satisfy them; (2) people; (3) activity; (4) conflict. These matters will be developed in some detail in Chapters V and X.

In addition to emphasis upon subject matter of inherent basic interest, attention grows out of skillful use of contrast. Indeed, it is safe to say that *the most important single element in commanding attention is contrast,* or ordered change.

Highway engineers have discovered that a broken center line holds attention much more effectively than a solid line— no matter what its color or width. In the same fashion, a blinker is more effective at intersections than a light that shines without interruption. After a short train ride, a passenger becomes oblivious to the noise of the train. Whimpers from a baby, though only a trifle more intense than outside noises, at once grip attention. So trivial a noise as a repeated cough may be a source of intense irritation. Meanwhile, the continuous and constant roar of the train goes unnoticed.

Hollingworth, one of the few scientists to devote an entire book to psychology of the audience, declares that

> Attention is like a bird. Unless there are several branches to its perch, from which it can flit to and fro while yet remaining on its perch, it is likely instead to flit to some foreign object. Well organized diversity is therefore one of the conditions of sustained attention.[r]

Though he could not cite scientific evidence, Charles G. Finney knew that "if a minister means to preach the gospel with effect he must be sure not to be monotonous. . . . Any monotonous sound, great or small, if continued, disposes people to sleep."[s]

There is ample evidence in support of Finney's conclusion. On the basis of laboratory experiments Rosett decided that "persistent sway of the scope of consciousness by the same one or few sensations is an effective method of inducing sleep."[t] Munsterberg found the state of boredom to derive from an apparently inborn aversion to uniformity.[u] Hoche made a much more detailed analysis, and concluded that monotony is linked with irritation at failure to receive sufficient stimuli to inhibit consciousness of time.

"The crux of the monotonous condition," according to his studies, "lies in this *disproportion between the temporal duration and the actual content offered*."[v] Thus the listener who does not receive sufficient stimuli to command and direct his attention becomes bored. He begins to wriggle, tap his fingers, or sigh at intervals. He is too polite to get up and

[r] (213), 59.
[s] (214).
[t] (208), 192.
[u] (215).
[v] Cited in (216), 229.

leave, so, unless his attention is recaptured, he retreats into reverie or even sleep. A sermon which has little variety in content or delivery may be compared with such preliminary hypnotic techniques as directing the attention to a metronome, motionless coin, or source of light.[w]

Even a train of thought or a type of action that is inherently interesting fails to hold the attention in the absence of comparatively sudden change.[x] Mere intensity of stimulus is not enough; it is contrast-value that counts. Witness the famous incident of the last experiment on Preyer's frog. Having had its brain removed by an operation, the animal continued to live. It was capable of responding to a variety of sudden stimuli, but showed no reaction to slow change. Consequently, when the water in which it was living was heated very slowly the poor animal permitted himself to be cooked to death without making a movement!

That master of audiences, Charles H. Spurgeon, had this advice for young preachers: "Keep on, on, on, on, on, with commonplace matter and monotonous tone, and you are rocking the cradle, and deeper slumbers will result; give the cradle a jerk, and sleep will flee."[y] It is contrast, not mere force, that provides the stimulus. A listener can go to sleep almost as easily when the preacher shouts in a monotone as when he murmurs monotonously. "The lighting of a candle in a dark room has vastly more power to attract us than the continuous glare of the sun to which we have been long exposed."[z]

Even physical perception of jet black is not obtained by placing a subject in total darkness; rather, the effect is derived from weak illumination of a small part of the retina.

[w] See (217), 71.
[x] (158), 39.
[y] (202), I, 224.
[z] (205), 28.

This causes the unlighted background to stand out vividly; "the deepest black results from contrast."[a]

Of course, such vivid contrast must be ordered. If presented too suddenly and violently, it defeats its own purpose by producing an effect of incoherence. Contrast must always remain subordinate to the message. Wendell White credits an orchestra with having ideal elements of change. While the drum beats out a single rhythm and so gives continuity, other instruments provide a high degree of variety.[b]

Total contrast in a sermon should be like a smart woman's clothing: distinctive enough to give individuality and attract attention, yet not so extreme as to create an impression of eccentricity or deliberate display.

Check-list on variety. Here is an exhaustive list of the different types of change which may be used to give attention-value to the sermon. Obviously, no twenty-five minute message should—or could—have a high degree of change in every respect. But the sermon that has a low degree of change in each category is likely to fall flat on its face. Use of the following check-list will yield two values: (1) it will help the preacher develop habitual use of change; one element at a time may be mastered until all become second nature; (2) particular sermons can be analyzed and scored in order to be sure that they contain sufficient contrast-value. Detailed discussion of some of these categories will be found in Chapters V, VII, VIII, IX, X and XI.

Any sermon may be tested against this list before it is delivered for the first time. It will also prove helpful to prepare copies of the check sheets and arrange for listener-evaluations of your sermons as preached. In most cases the preacher's wife will prove to be the ideal person to score

[a](218), 19.
[b](219).

the sermon. But any intelligent and sympathetic adult in the congregation can serve. A consistently low rating in one or more areas should provide stimulus for greater effort in the affected categories.

Types of Change

1. Change in interest content, through appeal to:
   - ( ) interest in persons
   - ( ) interest in activity
   - ( ) interest in conflict
   - ( ) interest in basic human wants
   - ( ) curiosity
   - ( ) suspense
   - ( ) the unusual—given an application connecting it with the familiar
   - ( ) the very familiar—given an unusual application

2. Variety in direct appeal to the senses of the listener:
   a. Appeal to the ears
      - ( ) use of silence—an important and neglected aural symbol
      - ( ) variety in rate, or speed—from the very slow to very fast
      - ( ) variety in emphasis—from the very soft to the very loud
      - ( ) variety in tone
   b. Appeal to the eyes of the listener
      - ( ) variety in facial expressions
      - ( ) gesture—including the body, as well as hands and shoulders
      - ( ) visual aids and illustrations

3. Change through indirect appeal to the senses of the listener—using words which arouse memories of sensations actually experienced:

( ) visual—recollection of things seen (as dew trembling on blue Morning Glory)

( ) auditory—recollection of sounds heard (whine of power saw biting into seasoned oak)

( ) motor—recollection of muscular effort (yanking on steering wheel)

( ) tactual—recollection of things felt (cold, wet nose of dog)

( ) gustatory—recollection of things tasted (hot cinnamon toast)

( ) olfactory—recollection of things smelled (musty odor of an unused house)

( ) thermic—recollections of sensations of heat and cold (diving into a spring-fed lake on a hot summer day)

( ) kinesthetic—recollection of sensations of motion, speed, dizziness (first ride on roller-coaster)

This appeal to attention is closely related to use of specific words; see Chapter V, Style.

4. Variety in content of sermon:
   a. Type of material used—
      ( ) prose argument (logical presentation)
      ( ) illustrations
         ( ) description
         ( ) dialogue
         ( ) verse
         ( ) statistics
      ( ) drama
   b. Quality of contents:

( ) solemn	( ) reverent	( ) comical
( ) serious	( ) shocking	( ) ludicrous
( ) grim	( ) surprising	( ) use of satire
( ) earnest	( ) amusing	( ) use of invective
( ) fervent	( ) whimsical	

5. Change through appeal to various emotions—including emotions touched in illustrations:

( ) anger ( ) grief ( ) pity
( ) anxiety ( ) hate ( ) pride
( ) contempt ( ) hope ( ) regret
( ) disappointment ( ) jealousy ( ) relief
( ) fear ( ) joy ( ) remorse
( ) gratitude ( ) love ( ) shame

6. Variety in sentence construction and type:
   a. Change in sentence structure—
      ( ) short sentences
      ( ) long sentences
      ( ) declarative sentences
      ( ) interrogative sentences
      ( ) exclamatory sentences
   b. Change in style through use of special types of sentences—
      ( ) proverb   ( ) paradox
      ( ) witticism   ( ) antithesis

7. Variety in use of words:
   ( ) personal words (names of persons, personal pronouns)
   ( ) concrete words (names of things which can be seen, felt, heard)
   ( ) specific words (rather than general words)

8. Careful and consistent use of major figures of speech:
   a. Figures resting upon sounds—
      ( ) alliteration
      ( ) onomatopoeia
   b. Figures resting upon comparisons—
      ( ) metaphor ( ) fable   ( ) hyperbole
      ( ) simile   ( ) parable   ( ) irony
      ( ) allegory ( ) personification

Attention-value of various types of change: Gain general familiarity with the above check-list. Then score each category separately in evaluating a particular sermon, and add the individual scores. A sermon with total attention-value of 30 or under is likely to be monotonous; 30-60 is the range of interesting and stimulating material; a well co-ordinated sermon with score of 60 or over is extremely high in attention-value.

Type of change (above)	No change	Very little	Consider- able	Much
(1)	−10	4	10	15
(2)	−10	4	10	15
(3)	−5	2	5	8
(4)	−5	3	7	10
(5)	−5	3	7	10
(6)	−5	2	5	8
(7)	−5	3	7	10
(8)	−5	2	5	8

In scoring a particular sermon mark the proper column for each type of change, then add the values.

THE PROBLEM OF DISTRACTIONS

Use of a manuscript is frequently condemned as tending to draw attention from the message. Clarence E. Macartney is voicing a common opinion when he declares that "in season and out of season, year after year, and to the average congregation, there can be no question that the sermon that does the most good is the sermon that is preached without notes."[c] By this he means without any manuscript whatever.

Though such a verdict is echoed in many books on

[c] (220), 145.

homiletics, it has not been substantiated by actual tests. On the contrary, Alan H. Monroe measured the reaction to numerous student speakers and found that more "good" speakers used notes than "poor" ones.[d] Similar results were reported by F. H. Knower.[e] On the basis of limited data it appears that moderate use of notes is not an appreciable source of distraction.

Personal mannerisms in voice and gesture tend to distract from the attention of listeners who are relatively unfamiliar with the speaker. Except for such habits as staring at the ceiling and dropping the voice below audible levels, personal mannerisms are quickly taken for granted by listeners. After hearing a particular speaker a few times, a mannerism of normal dimensions is ignored. It is important to be aware of one's habits, and to correct them if they are serious. Trivial eccentricities should not occasion worry, however, for they drop into obscurity when a speaker's message holds the strong attention of his listeners.

Noises and movements inside or outside the preaching place are usually beyond the control of the speaker. Stimuli of this sort are far more distracting to the listener than to the speaker—whose attention is concentrated upon his message.

There can be no precise rules for handling these situations. A disturbance of mild intensity, which soon comes to an end, should probably be ignored. Experimental tests indicate that minor distractions do not affect test results when a group listens with definite attention-focus.[f]

A disturbance of great intensity is likely to command so much attention that the preacher will need to recapture his listeners when the disturbance ceases. One of the most effective devices in such emergencies is silence. Remember

[d] (221), 34.
[e] (222), 87.
[f] (223), 376; (204), 11.

that it is contrast, not intensity of a given stimulus, that commands attention. It may be impossible to shout loudly enough to catch the minds of persons diverted by a noise; an interval of silence tends to reorder the scattered group. In using silence bear in mind that the interval is likely to appear much longer than it actually is.

One other problem remains to be mentioned: crying babies! Any mother will testify that when her baby is noisy she can't possibly attend the speaker. Neither can anyone else within the effective stimulus radius of the child. If the mother does not have the good taste to leave, most of us will be forced to endure the distraction. A few preachers with great reputations, not serving as pastors, have dared to ask that noisy children be taken from the place of worship.

While this procedure secures silence, it may initiate an adverse reaction on the part of many listeners—effectively blocking good communication. Sometimes it is possible to induce the mother to act without a direct request. Instead of trying to outshout the disturbance the speaker can deliberately lower his voice. This makes the child seem even more noisy, by contrast. For a brief period many listeners will be unable to hear. But if the mother is startled into action, after she leaves the preacher can take steps to recapture lost listeners. In such emergencies it is always helpful to use a humorous story that is in keeping with the theme. Laughing together, the listeners are reformed into an attentive audience.

CONCLUSIONS

Good preaching depends upon careful use of every technique that will help command the active attention of every listener. Mere bodily presence within the preaching situation does not guarantee communication between speaker and listener.

Emphasis upon polarization of the audience will vary

with the purpose of the particular occasion. Pure and passive worship does not demand polarization; active audience response does. Physical setting, preliminary group action, audience-speaker relationships, and the presence or absence of particularly susceptive individuals are important factors in polarization.

It is not enough to gain attention; the preacher must hold it for the duration of the sermon. This involves a constant process of recapturing each listener, for the duration of a period of attention is very brief. There is strong evidence that persons actually cannot maintain sustained attention upon a single stimulus, no matter how hard the effort to do so.

Change is the most important element in holding attention, for this provides contrast-value which serves to magnify the impact of stimuli. By use of the foregoing check-list on variety, it is possible to get an approximate indication of the attention-value of any sermon. In practice the list is most useful when actual listeners score the sermon while it is being delivered.

Distractions tend to break the listener's attention, so should be reduced or overcome whenever possible. Contrary to general opinion, casual and moderate use of notes does not appear to be a major source of listener distraction. Neither are personal mannerisms serious, unless they are of extreme intensity. Noises and movements are more serious than either notes or mild mannerisms; when attention is momentarily lost it may be necessary to inject new resources into the message in order to reattract the minds of listeners.

Chapter V

PROBLEMS AND OPPORTUNITIES OF STYLE

STUDENTS OF RHETORIC FREQUENTLY DIVIDE THE SUBJECT
into two parts: "what is said" and "how it is said." W. H. D.
Rouse frames a typical definition when he holds that "style
is the manner, as distinct from the matter."[a]

Such division is completely arbitrary, for in any form
of communication ideas are inseparable from the vehicles
by which they are transmitted. Just as water is molded by
vessels in which it is frozen, so ideas are shaped by the
style or manner in which the communicator presses them into
his chosen medium. In the case of preaching, language is the
major vehicle; in the case of painting, pigments transmit
ideas. So the preacher's style is largely concerned with the
use of words, the artist's with the use of pigments and brushes.

HOW TO BE UNDERSTOOD

One Sunday morning a middle-aged man ushered his
mother into a pew and sat down beside her. Early in the
sermon he scribbled on the edge of his bulletin and passed
her a note: "Can you hear?"

[a] (224), 52.

She shook her head.

An alert member of the official board happened to be sitting behind the visitors and saw the note. He presented the matter to his associates, and they promptly decided to install expensive public address equipment. It was simply unthinkable that anyone should miss the preacher's messages because of a physical handicap.

Those church officials are to be commended. It is right and proper that hearing aids should be provided for those who need them. But, somehow, many a preacher who takes mechanical hearing aids for granted has failed to recognize that there is no listening when his language conveys no meaning to the hearer. Communication is as effectively cut off by language failures as by deafness. Studying the problem of incoherent speech—and any speech that is not understood by the listener is incoherent for him—a great preacher concluded that

If even lifeless instruments, such as the flute or the harp, do not give distinct notes, how will anyone know what is played? And if the bugle gives an indistinct sound, who will get ready for battle? So with yourselves; if you in a tongue utter speech that is not intelligible, how will anyone know what is said? For you will be speaking into the air (I Cor. 14:7-9).

St. Paul was, of course, dealing with the problem of ecstatic witness. But his analysis applies equally well to the matter of a style and/or vocabulary that makes the speaker's message seem "a foreign tongue" to the listener.

At least nine Yale lecturers have held that clearness is the most significant single element necessary for good style.[b] However, this is one more instance of a matter about which preachers have done more talking than studying. Classic works on homiletics pose the problem but offer no solutions

[b](225), 134ff.

based on data more substantial than personal impressions.

A group of lay scholars, concerned chiefly with readability of the printed word, have recently made monumental contributions at this point. Readability is far easier to measure than "listenability"—for gesture, tone, and force shade and complicate the oral communication situation. Consequently, most modern scientific studies of clarity have come to focus on the written rather than the spoken word. Conclusions reached through such studies are, however, obviously valid for preachers and other students of social speech.

Much of the pioneer work in study of readability has been done by Rudolph Flesch and his associates. He has produced more than one formula purporting to afford a means of making exact measurement of the readability of any printed passage. There is at least one weakness in any attempt to achieve such precision; this factor is discussed below. In general, however, the conclusions of Flesch and his coworkers may be regarded as both valid and helpful. Much of the discussion in this section is directly or indirectly indebted to the findings of this group of communication analysts.

In order to be understood, the preacher must adapt his style to his listeners. A sermon that would prove unintelligible to a group of adolescent boys might well be regarded as lucid, even elementary, by a convention of theological professors. Recognizing the relativity of the speaker-listener relationship, there are nonetheless a number of principles that govern "listenability" of any sermon.

(1) *Short sentences* are always easier to understand than long ones. No matter what the cultural level of the listener, the brief, direct statement scores high in clarity. Beecher put it like this:

Involved sentences, crooked, circuitous, and parenthetical, no matter how musically they may be balanced, are prejudicial to a facile understanding of the truth. *Don't whip with a switch that has leaves on, if you want to tingle.* A good fireman will send the water through as short and straight hose as he can.[c]

There are only two major reasons for habitual use of long and tortuous sentences in mass communication.

Sheer laziness is the first, and probably the major, factor. It is far easier to be obscure than to be lucid. Dealing with a difficult and complicated subject, any tyro can tie himself in verbal knots. Theological and scientific books are often dull, principally because the writer did not care to work at the task of making himself clear.

There is a persistent legend to the effect that certain devout followers of Klopstock assembled about his deathbed. After an awkward silence, a bold spirit ventured to ask the master to explain a particularly difficult passage in one of his poems. He read the offending lines, reread them, then spoke: "My dear children," he said, "I myself cannot be quite sure of what I meant when I wrote this passage. But I distinctly remember that it was one of the finest things I ever wrote. You can do nothing better than to devote your lives to discovering just what it means!"

Take the problem of describing a grindstone to a person who has never seen one. Hard work is required to translate mechanical terms into everyday language; any first-year student of mechanical engineering could put it like this:

A grindstone is a mechanical device, or apparatus, which operates by means of a pedal attachment through which a fulcrum lever converts a vertical reciprocal motion into a circular movement. Power so transmitted is applied through the axis of a large disc which revolves in a vertical plane; work is done on the periphery of the disc, whose physical constitution is such that surface contact with metal produces friction of such nature that particles shear off, permitting the operator to shape the metal without resorting to high-range thermal conditioning.

[c] (210), 229.

Any first-year theological student can be obscure; it takes ability and effort to present complex thoughts in simple sentences.

Pride is the second major factor producing obscure sentence structure. At first look, such a pronouncement may seem absurd. But it will bear closer examination.

No matter what their field, ambitious writers without reputation tend to be stilted or even pompous. Thus, the first sentence in Ruskin's first book—*Modern Painters*—contained 18 clauses and 153 words. Near the end of Stevenson's *Pulvis et Umbra* there is a sentence with 332 words—no less. Neither man would have thought of using such style at the height of his fame and intellectual maturity.

Henry James was among the three or four most imaginative novelists of his generation. But he prided himself upon "fine writing," and never condescended to cultivate the habit of forming easy sentences. Consequently, his books sold poorly and are seldom read.

Many writers with established reputations seem to take pride in being hard to follow. Since difficult language is often associated with specialized learning, some persons are so foolish as to regard muddy style as a sign of profundity. Schopenhauer pointed out that his fellow Germans have a habit of breaking their principal sentences into bits, then shoving other sentences into the cracks. To him, this was a reflection of hidden egotism. "If it is an impertinent thing to interrupt another person when he is speaking," said he, "it is no less impertinent to interrupt oneself."

Traditionally, ministers are especially prone to parade their learning by adoption of a difficult style. Adjectives, adverbs, and modifying clauses are stuffed into sentences without regard for the listener's task of translation. It is significant that in *Love's Labour Lost* it is Sir Nathaniel the curate, and not a member of another occupational group, who says: "I praise God for you, sir: your reasons at dinner have been sharp and sententious: pleasant without scurrility, witty without affection, audacious without impudency, learned without opinion, and strange without heresy."

If that sounds like impious mockery of the wordy parson, consider the Rev. Sydney Smith's blast at the style of the great Dr. Parr. There are numbers of learned men, Smith intimated,

of whom Dr. Parr might be happy to say, that they have profundity without obscurity—perspicuity without prolixity—ornament without glare—terseness without bareness—penetration without subtlety—comprehensiveness without digression—and a great number of other things without a great number of other things.[d]

Pompous diction has been so strongly associated with the pulpit that professional pride may urge one toward long sentences. Legend has it that Jeremy Taylor deliberately preached over the heads of his congregation once a year—in order to keep his listeners from forgetting that he knew more than they!

That story may be apocryphal. But the tendency toward conscious use of pompous diction was strong enough to attract the venom of Thorstein Veblen. He dipped his pen in gall, then wrote:

It is of moment to know with some precision what is the degree of archaism conventionally required in speaking on any given topic. Usage differs appreciably from the pulpit to the marketplace. . . . A discriminate avoidance of neologisms is honorific, not only because it argues that time has been wasted in acquiring the obsolescent habit of speech, but also as showing that the speaker has from infancy associated with persons who have been familiar with the obsolescent idiom. . . .

The diction proper to the sanctuary and to the priestly office
[d](226).

should also carry little if any suggestion of everyday life, and should not draw upon the vocabulary of modern trade or industry.[e]

It is beside the point that Veblen convicts himself by his own indictment. What matters is his relevant jibe that the pulpit tends to foster obscure and pedantic style. Ernest Weekley charges that "in a cultured center like Boston, even the owls say, 'to whit, to whom' "; in an upper-class church, the preacher is tempted to exert every effort to be as stuffy as he thinks he is expected to be.

(2) *Short words* are as important as short sentences. In general, the preacher should never use a five-syllable word when he can possibly substitute a word of one or two syllables. There is experimental evidence that material presented orally is more difficult to comprehend than the same material presented visually.[f] This may be due to the fact that the speech situation does not permit the listener to go back and retrace his steps, as the reader can.

It is no accident that such passages as The Lord's Prayer, The Twenty-Third Psalm, and the Gettysburg Address contain many one-syllable words. Ease of understanding, and not beauty of thought alone, contributes to the place which a passage wins in the hearts of men.

Spurgeon told his students that "the costermonger cannot learn the language of the college." That was obvious; no one would dispute it. But many preachers dispute—in practice if not in theory—the conclusion drawn by the evangelist. Granting that market place and college are poles apart, Spurgeon threw down the challenge: "Let the college learn the language of the costermonger!"

Long, technical words are costly. They provide ready-made opportunities not only for lack of understanding, but

[e] (227), 398ff.
[f] (228).

also for positive misunderstanding. There is a tale to the effect that young Benjamin Franklin had a taste for high-flying words, and once confronted his mother with the statement: "Mother, I have imbibed an acephalus molluscous." Frightened out of her wits, the good woman promptly forced him to take a huge dose of an emetic. Recovering from the effects of the potent medicine, the boy protested that he had eaten nothing but an ordinary oyster. Angry at having been deceived, his mother gave him a sound thrashing. So Ben made a resolution that he'd never again use big words where little ones would do.

Josh Billings has a famous "affurism" that might have been coined for the pulpit. "Young man," he warned, "when you have tew search Webster's Dickshinnary tew find words big enuff tew convey yure meaning yu kan make up yure mind that yu don't mean mutch."

Short words, combined into brief sentences, yield maximum efficiency in public address. Like Tennyson's scholar, the preacher should "wear his weight of learning lightly as a flower."

(3) *Informal, personal style* contributes greatly to ease of understanding. Flesch has found indisputable evidence that material high in content of "personal words" is low in difficulty. Names and personal pronouns are like low spots in the wall that must be crossed in communication; even the handicapped listener can crawl over at these points.

Nineteenth-century oratory permitted no usage more informal than the "editorial we." It was considered improper to address the listener as "you," or to refer to one's self as "I." A stiff, third-person style was one of the trademarks of the conventional preacher. Rule-book grammar was regarded as a must.

Modern analysis of language has exploded the myth of

inviolate rules. "Correct" speech is nothing but speech that employs those forms which are considered "correct" in a particular era. Part of the task of grammarians and dictionary makers is to reflect usage as well as attempt to mold and crystallize it.

Vigorous speech has a healthy regard for contemporary customs, but refuses to adopt stilted and awkward conventions. When a person has something he wishes to communicate forcefully, he is likely to rise above the pettiness of copy-book conventions. Contractions and slang terms are used if they are effective in conveying ideas. Occasionally, a writer with established reputation dares to write as his contemporaries speak. Thus, early in *The Path to Rome*, Hilaire Belloc warns that he will not inhibit his self-expression by stiff rules. He promises that if the occasion arises, he will not hesitate to "split his infinitives from helm to saddle."

Sir Winston Churchill, no mean craftsman by any standard, insists that the user of language—and not language itself —be master. One of his famous wartime speeches is said to have been given the red pencil by an alert secretary. Finding a sentence ending with a preposition, the formalist pounced on it with sadistic glee, and marked it for revision. Crossing out the proposed change, the prime minster scribbled: "This is the kind of arrant pedantry up with which I will not put!"

There is, of course, no virtue in eccentric speech. Ignorance of conventional usage, or disdain for it, does not guarantee intelligible style. Neither does frequent use of personal pronouns, contractions, and informal words ensure that a sermon will be easy to understand.

Both "personal words" and conversational style are marks of earnest communication. When one has something vital to say, he does not retreat into the most obscure language of which he is capable. Rather, he seeks to express himself in the most direct fashion possible. He does not hesitate to use the same word twice in a sentence, to inject his own personality into the message, to split an occasional infinitive, or even to chop his thoughts into clauses that are not true sentences.

Personal matter is understandable not only because it tends to be simple, but also because it has intrinsic interest. Both the speaker and the listener are more interested in what has happened to the speaker, than in moral exhortation of the essay type. When attention is waning, any member of any audience will be stimulated by a communication unit which begins: "You will be interested in an experience I once had . . ."

Emerson records an instance of hearing a preacher who tempted him never to go back to church. Snow was falling outside the building—a silent but vivid reminder that life never can be static. Said the philosopher:

The snowstorm was real, the preacher merely spectral; and the eye felt the sad contrast in looking at him, and then, out of the window behind him, into the beautiful meteor of the snow. He had lived in vain. He had no one word intimating that he had laughed or wept, was married or in love; had been commanded, or cheated, or chagrined. If he had ever lived and acted, we were none the wiser for it. The capital secret of his profession—namely, to convert life into truth—he had not learned. Not one fact in all his experience had he yet imported into his doctrine. This man had ploughed and planted, and talked, and bought and sold, he had read books, he had eaten and drunken, his head aches, his heart throbs, he smiles and suffers; yet was there not a surmise, not a hint, in all the discourse *that he had ever lived at all.*

Warm, personal address frequently captures the benefits of short words and sentences without effort. Speaking fervently and naturally about a matter that is close to one's heart, a preacher is likely to adopt a relatively easy style.

MOOD AND TEMPO

Deliberate variety in sentence structure is like the background music in a movie—it creates moods without forcing itself into the attention field of the listener.

Brief sentences carry punch. A sense of action is aroused. Tension may be created; ideas are hammered home. Rapid movement is implied.

Long, leisurely sentences tend to enhance passivity, so that the listener feels there is neither urgency nor hurry. He drifts with the swirling current of the speaker's words, floating rather than swimming, basking in the delightfulness of the present rather than struggling toward some distant goal.

Tempo is greatly affected by sentence type, as well as by length. Exclamations give an intensity that cannot be gained by declarative sentences alone. Questions introduce qualitative elements that have strong attention value through contrast with exposition and description.

Occasional use of a terse and striking statement helps hold attention as well as rivet an argument in place. Jesus' speech included many splendid examples of the paradox—a form that is vivid, but very difficult to phrase. A much easier form is the witticism—a short sentence which is a self-contained unit of speech. No explanations are necessary; the single sentence carries clear meaning. Frequently there is a deliberate play upon sharply contrasting elements:

"Our Gospel is not the survival of the fit; but the revival of the unfit."—Charles Silvester Horne

"No man can be said to support the Church; the Church supports the man."—J. H. Leckie

"It is dangerous for a man to have a little bit of money; it is tragic for a little bit of money to have a man."

"Death is for man, not man for death."—G. B.
Foster

"We named our daughters Charity, but they were
not always charitable; we named them Peace, but
they were often warlike."—Arthur J. Moore

"I wish I could be as sure of anything as Macaulay is of everything!"—Thackeray

Note that the antithetical sentence frequently rests upon
using a word in two slightly different senses. In the example
from Leckie, "support" means one thing in the first clause,
another in the second. There is a similar play upon "to have"
in the anonymous witticism. By experimenting with key words
in a particular sermon, the preacher can usually devise one
or more antithetical statements—pertinent, compelling, and
vivid. Supplementing one's original sentences with suitable
epigrams and proverbs from printed sources, the very language of the sermon takes on sparkle and zest. Numerous
source books are listed in Chapter VI.

Words are as varied as sentences. Some are thin and
brittle, full of sharp-pointed sounds: *tinkle, rattle, titter*.
Others are vowel-loaded, broad, and majestic: *thunder, sonor-
ous, honorable*. Some break off abruptly with a final conso-
nant: *snap, jump, hit*. Others drift leisurely to a soft end:
murmur, gracefully, conventional. There are words with suitable qualities to suggest any desired mood or tempo.

One of the most delightful products of word-wizardry is
Poe's *The Bells*; in various stanzas he makes the reader
actually hear different types of bells:

> Hear the sledges with the bells,
>   Silver bells!
> What a world of merriment their melody foretells!
> How they tinkle, tinkle, tinkle,
>   In the icy air of night

While the stars that oversprinkle
All the Heavens seem to twinkle
    With a crystalline delight . . .

Then the contrast of the following stanza:

> Hear the mellow wedding bells,
>   Golden bells!
> What a world of happiness their harmony foretells
> Through the balmy air of night
> How they ring out their delight!
> From the molten golden notes,
>   And all in tune
> What a liquid ditty floats
> To the turtle-dove that listens while she gloats
>   On the moon!

Obviously, the preacher cannot match the poet in time spent per line of composition. That is both impossible by virtue of the volume of the preacher's output, and unnecessary in the light of its nature. Only occasionally is there a spot in the sermon where deliberate creation of mood is desirable. But when such an occasion arises—as it does at least once in nearly every sermon—there is no substitute for style. It may be said of the sermon as Dekker said of honesty: "She goes upon lame feet unless there be music in her."

At this point the preacher can well reread the gospels with emphasis upon the style of Jesus. His speech was not only simple and direct; he was a master of words. Gilbert K. Chesterton described his speech as *gigantesque*; Ernest C. Colwell points out that his very words "have the rugged fibre of the cypress tree and the jagged edge of the crosscut saw."[g]

Mastery of style is more a matter of absorption than learning rules. One can know how to use all the architect's instruments, yet be incapable of laying out a cathedral. Fluent,

[g] (229), 11.

powerful speech does not stem from memorizing books of grammar. It comes from forceful ideas conveyed in words and sentences that help produce desired effects. Conscious striving for particular elements of style, coupled with wide reading and analysis, will yield finer results than any amount of time spent poring over books of rules.

Jack London learned to write by painstaking analysis and imitation of Kipling. Thomas Wolfe literally absorbed style from Walt Whitman. Stevenson frankly and bluntly admitted that he developed skill by imitating Wordsworth, Lamb, Defoe, Hazlitt, Hawthorne, and Sir Thomas Browne.

Henry Ward Beecher gained literary power by living with the classics—especially the works of Shakespeare and Milton. Instead of beginning to coast after being made pastor of Plymouth Church, he intensified his efforts. With a library of 15,000 volumes, he constantly read for style and vocabulary. As a result, he gained a fluency that has seldom been matched. Questioned on the subject, he declared: "When I am well started, I don't need to hunt for words! They come in crowds, getting in one another's way, and each one saying, 'Take me! Take me!' "[h]

To develop your own style read many types of literature, noting such matters as: sentence length, sentence type, average word length, use of modifiers and clauses, creation of mood and tempo. Some fruitful sources outside the Bible are the works of Shakespeare, Poe, Milton, and Carlyle. Study the literary style of the great poetry of the Old Testament, and browse through volumes of modern lyrics. Make careful analysis of sermons written by ancient apologists as well as those by such modern masters of style as Charles E. Jefferson, Charles Reynolds Brown, and Peter Marshall. Dip into such diverse streams as the books of Conrad, Kipling, Mark

[h](230), 22.

Twain, Maupassant, Steinbeck, Swift, Defoe, Whitman, Damon Runyan, Emerson, Flaubert, and T. S. Eliot.

And this is heresy—but so be it! Read less sermons and more feature articles in mass-circulation magazines. Study an occasional issue of a "confession" magazine in order to see how the writers achieve the strongly personal touch. Analyze stories in first-class mystery magazines, and find what techniques contribute to building up suspense. Underline strategic paragraphs in good fiction of all types, observing the extent and manner in which conflict is used to hold reader interest.

In short, study all types of literature that attract large numbers of readers. Try to find out why the material is read, and how you may use similar style in writing sermons.

CONCRETE VERSUS ABSTRACT

Early in your analysis of literature you will discover that good material tends to be concrete, rather than abstract. A typical Victorian essay can be taken as the secular literary form most nearly related to the usual sermon, and most removed from the vitality demanded by the modern reader and listener. Like theological and philosophical works, essays tend to focus upon the general and the abstract; everyday life tends to focus largely upon the particular and the specific.

There are two especially effective ways to bring concrete elements into the sermon: (1) use of specific rather than general words; (2) liberal use of illustrations which employ names, dates, and other factual elements.

(1) *Specific words* help bring the sensory organism of the listener into action. References to exact things rather than to general classes appeal to memories of things seen, heard, tasted, smelled, and touched.

No image is produced by saying, "Thomas went down

the road"—*went* and *road* are general to the point of being vague and fuzzy. Listeners see both action and surroundings in such statements as: "Thomas ambled down the path"; "Thomas swaggered down the boulevard"; "Thomas darted down the turnpike"; or "Thomas marched down the avenue." Though no two of these specific statements produce the same image, each gives the listener something to see.

"House" is a vague word; it can designate almost any abode, so it has no sharp, vivid meaning. More clearly defined word-pictures are drawn by precise labels such as *bungalow, lean-to, tenement, castle, shanty, cabin, duplex, cubby-hole.* It is the exceptional listener who hears anything at the bare mention of music playing. But almost every listener will hear something when the speaker describes the ecstatic stabbing of trumpet notes, the eerie wail of muted wood-winds, or the brassy blare of a trombone.

Concrete style involves not only specific words, but also use of enough details to create a specific rather than a general situation. No precise focus is involved in saying, "He listened to the night sounds." Added details will take the audience to a particular scene:

"He strained to catch the faint lapping of waves against the side of the ketch, the occasional 'plump' of a salmon in the distance"; or,

"He cocked his head, tense until he identified the faint scraping as made by a limb pulsating in the wind. Somewhere in the empty blackness of the adjoining room, a wood borer was eating his way into a timber."

It is at the point of specific versus abstract words that the work of Rudolph Flesch is open to some question. His formulas for measuring readability rest upon counting the average number of syllables in a piece of writing. But a city-bred child who stares blankly at the mention of an axe may twinkle with understanding at a reference to an airplane. One word falls within his experience, and the other does not.

Nor does mere use of short words guarantee sufficient concreteness to convey precise meaning. Many brief words are broad to the point of ambiguity: *love, duty, right, justice,* and *truth* are a few examples. Stuart Chase points out that "one does not understand a story in Russian just because it is written in words of one syllable."[1] Specific, limited words which come within the experience of the listener are easy to understand, even if relatively long. Vague, ambiguous words which apply to a wide range of possible experiences are easy to misunderstand, even if very short.

Since the vocabulary of religion is heavy with words which have no precise referents, it becomes all the more necessary that the preacher use as many specific and descriptive terms as possible.

Just as the specific is to be sought, so the empty phrase is to be avoided. Many communication symbols have been so overused that they have become purely conventional and therefore meaningless. They occupy space on a page or time in an address, but convey neither information nor emotion. Thus, a speaker may devote seven words to the phrase, "as you may or may not know . . ." Not only does he fill a brief space with sound that signifies nothing; he has given the listener an opportunity to shift his mental gears and turn to a stimulus more compelling than the cliché. Examples are easily multiplied.

Though speaker and audience know quite well that the former has prepared an allusion that he has every intention of making, he may fill the air with meaningless noises such as: "If you will permit me, I should like to say . . ."; "One or two of you may have heard me tell this anecdote, and I

[1] (9), 142.

hope you will forgive me for repeating it . . ."; "Without objection, I propose to develop this topic in greater detail . . ." Though the preacher knows quite well where his text is found, and the listener knows that he knows, time may be wasted on a statement such as: "The text is found, as I believe you will discover upon looking it up, in . . ."

Along with hollow phrases, the preacher should discard as many weak words as possible. "The" is probably more badly abused than any other English word. Time without end, it is used when it adds nothing to the communication. This practice is especially marked in connection with the beginning of sentences. Amateur writers often produce whole paragraphs in which every sentence limps to a start with *The . . . The . . . The.* Not only does this produce monotony; it weakens the passage by reducing actual details of communication. Given only one hundred words in which to express an idea, it is disgraceful to waste opportunities with six or eight "the's" that say nothing.

Mere rejection of vague, ambiguous, and meaningless communication symbols is not enough, of course. Concrete style grows out of deliberate emphasis upon specific nouns, verbs, and modifiers. Mark Twain points out that "the difference between the right word and almost the right word is the difference between lightning and the lightning bug."

No matter how large one's vocabulary, there are times when mere exercise of memory will not produce the term that exactly meets a need. Hazlitt recognized the problem and advised the writer to wait: "Is it strange that among twenty thousand words in the English language, the one of all others that he most needs should have escaped him? There are more things in nature than there are words in the English language, and he must not expect to lay rash hands on them all at once."[1]

[1] (231), 25.

But the modern preacher-writer has resources not known to the essayist. A number of very fine reference books have been developed for the specific purpose of supplying words when needed.

Noble thoughts and exalted ideas are like gold nuggets and raw diamonds—valuable, but crude and imperfect instruments of exchange. One would find it almost impossible to give value received for a glass of milk by chipping a fragment from a ten-carat diamond. But when that diamond is converted into tokens of copper, silver, and paper, it becomes an easy matter to buy articles of every description. Words are the currency of communication; until a treasure of thought is transformed into five- and ten-cent words—with an occasional greenback—commerce is impossible.

Word books are the banks of verbal communication: inexhaustible riches have been placed on deposit to your account. In order to benefit from these assets, you have only to withdraw a few words at a time and place them in circulation. Consistent use of some of the volumes listed below will gradually build your vocabulary to the point that you will need to consult the books only in special cases.

A good word book is a tool, not a panacea. Ownership, or even use of several volumes does not guarantee development of good style. These books are designed to give help in emergencies; they are worth owning even if used only occasionally. Automobile mechanics must own and know how to use such special tools as those necessary for grinding valves. Though a particular shop may have a valve-grinding job only once a month, it is essential to have the proper tools. When needed, they are essential; no substitutes will do their work. That is the rôle played by special word books; even if used only a few times a year, a volume can be very valuable. Titles listed below are English word books.

Roget's International Thesaurus, the best-known work in the field, is a standard reference book. Words are grouped by categories, permitting one to find terms that are both closely and loosely related to particular topics.

Roget's International Thesaurus in Dictionary Form is virtually a book of synonyms. It is somewhat easier to use than the regular thesaurus, but is not a substitute for it. Words are arranged alphabetically, rather than in major groups of categories. When one merely wants a synonym for a known word this volume gives faster service than the regular thesaurus.

Webster's Dictionary of Synonyms, unlike most word lists, distinguishes shades of differences between related words. It is also especially valuable in listing analogous words, antonyms, and contrasted words.

Hartrampf's Vocabularies is a book of synonyms arranged on different principles of classification from Roget. Hence the two volumes are complementary, rather than mutually exclusive.

Sholl's Humanitome is still another book of synonyms, more highly specialized than either Roget or Hartrampf. Developed for use by writers, it deals exclusively with description and delineation of human appearance, character, and relationships. It is especially suggestive in descriptive terms which deal with clothing, occupations, the body, and action.

The Word Finder, compiled by J. I. Rodale, was also developed for use by writers. Unlike the thesaurus, it does not specialize in offering substitute words. Rather, it helps provide additional ideas by which to embellish and enlarge upon particular thoughts.

(2) *Concrete illustrations* contribute greatly to the flesh-and-bone quality of a sermon. An exhortation without illustrations is likely to be almost entirely abstract—a faintly visible ghost that is fit for nothing but haunting ruined cathedrals.

Since illustrations are treated at length in Chapter VIII, detailed analysis is limited to that chapter. Here it is necessary only to insist that the illustration be specific. For example, a joke which employs the "he said . . . she said" form is ab-

stract. No definite persons are pictured, no specific situations
are created. Anecdotes are far more valuable, for they involve
the use of such definite words as names and descriptions of
persons and places. Listeners are given something tangible,
whose impact is proportional to its density, or degree of concreteness in content.

FIGURES OF SPEECH

Skillful and extensive use of figures of speech is a major
factor in vivid style. Almost without exception, the literary
gems of the world—religious as well as secular—contain a
heavy proportion of figurative language. David compares God
with a Palestinian shepherd in the first line of Psalm 23; in the
last line he depicts heaven as being like the house of a benev-
olent patriarch. Jesus bases The Lord's Prayer upon the resemblance between God's attitude toward men and a father's
attitude toward his children. Thick books have been written
about the figures of speech employed by such literary giants
as Dante, Browning, Shakespeare, Meredith, Chrysostom,
Milton, Goethe, Byron, George Eliot, Hardy, and their fellows.

Figures of speech may be divided into two major groups;
one has to do with sounds and the other with resemblances.

Alliteration is the most widely used figure of speech
which exploits the sounds of words. Based primarily upon
initial letters, it gains its effect by repetition. Such masters as
Tennyson, Shakespeare, Gray, and Milton made extensive
use of "apt alliteration's artful aid."

Harmony is the chief, but not the only, effect that may
be gained from alliteration. Pope produces an atmosphere
of breathlessness by his noted line: "Up the high hill he
heaved the huge round stone." Skillful use of the initial *h*
leaves the reader panting as though from physical effort.

Unfortunately, the sheer simplicity of selecting syllables

starting with similar sounds sometimes tempts the stylist to sin. Crude and extensive use of alliteration—as in the last sentence—calls attention to itself. It defeats its own purpose by serving as an ornament rather than a communication device. An occasional good piece of alliteration is better than a great deal of third-rate material.

Alliteration is probably the most effective figure of speech for use in sermon titles. By its boldness it attracts attention; by its repetition it thrusts a sound deep into the listener's mind and makes the phrase memorable. Many noted preachers have developed great skill at this point.

Onomatopoeia, second member of the class which exploits sounds, rests upon imitation. Modern philologists term words of this type "echoic speech." That is, the names of many sounds express the sounds themselves: *hiss, murmur, splash, purr, patter, crackle*, and numerous other words have this quality. Onomatopoeia is especially valuable in creating atmosphere or mood, because in addition to symbolic meaning, the sounds convey a direct appeal to the sensory apparatus of the listener.

Figures of resemblance are more varied and also more important than figures which rest upon sounds. All figures in this class grow out of express or implied comparisons. Hence, each may be said to be a special variation of metaphor or a derivative therefrom. A detailed discussion of the rôle of metaphor in communication is included in Chapter VIII.

Metaphor, which is the most important of all figures of speech, is usually defined as a comparison in which verbal connectives are omitted. *Simile* is the same figure with the verbal connectives included.

Metaphor is involved in the statement, "Bismarck ruled Germany with an iron hand." Simile is found in the sentence, "Bismarck ruled Germany with a hand like iron." For practical purposes, the distinctions are purely formal; both simile and metaphor involve statements of unqualified resemblance.

Suggestions for forming original metaphors are given in the following chapter. In addition, much valuable material may be found in the one reference book in the field, *Wilstach's Dictionary of Similes.*

Allegory is prolonged and extended metaphor. Usually taking the form of a story, characters and actions of the allegory symbolize persons and situations that are implied but not designated. *Pilgrim's Progress,* a detailed metaphor comparing the Christian life with a journey, is the most famous allegory in the English language.

Allegory is especially valuable when one wishes to avoid a frontal attack upon a controversial subject. Devising an imaginary situation which bears close resemblance to a real one, the preacher can make his point by implication. Brief allegories also help make conventional ideas vivid.

Fables rest upon comparisons between humans and animals. Characteristics of men are attributed to beasts, and wise or witty conclusions are drawn. A favorite literary form for many centuries, the fable is presently found chiefly in children's literature. Some notable modern fables for adults have been produced by humorists and satirists. Whether originally slanted toward youngsters or their elders, the fable is an effective type of illustration. It is so flexible in nature that if a printed version cannot be found to fit a particular need, one can always devise an original one.

Parables, unlike allegories and fables, usually stress one important point of resemblance. There is no attempt to provide a one-to-one correspondence between the parts of the parable and some other situation. Attempts to read symbolic meaning into every detail of Jesus' parables represents a distortion, if not a perversion of interpretative method. Parables do not

pretend to offer such completeness. They are more like char-
coal sketches than oil paintings. At most, two or three significant qualities or features are emphasized and magnified.

Many "preacher stories" of doubtful authenticity can be
made useful by transforming them into parabolic form. An
anecdote which has incredible aspects can be reworked into
a parable which clearly emphasizes a particular point. Take,
for example, the utterly fantastic temperance illustration about
a householder and his pet rattlesnake (Chapter VIII). Offered
as sober fact, such a story insults the intelligence of the listener unless it can be documented. But it becomes useful when
made into a parable such as:

"Alcohol is like a poisonous reptile. When a father brings
it into his home, it is as though he should take a rattlesnake
for a pet. Harmless enough in infancy, the reptile grows daily
more dangerous. Eventually it will strike some member of the
family—perhaps Johnny or Sally. Grieving as he sits by the
bedside of the stricken youngster, the father repents too late.
He never should have brought the beast into his home."

Personification, a favorite device of preachers as well as
poets, rests upon treating things and creatures as though they
had human qualities. "Towering over the village, the mountain
frowned grimly and occasionally growled a threat." By treating the volcano as though it were a person, it is made to seem
actively aggressive; a dynamic is introduced that would be
impossible in more prosaic style. Personification of abstract
qualities, such as hope and evil, helps create vividness and
sense of conflict.

Hyperbole is nothing more than exaggeration that is extreme, but not ludicrous. A point of resemblance is inflated to
such an extent that contrast becomes obvious. Skillfully used,
hyperbole has qualities of grandeur. Macaulay called it "the
boldest figure in rhetoric."

Jesus once told a doubter that God has numbered the very hairs of the head, that not a sparrow falls to the ground without His knowledge. Taken literally, this might tempt a cynic to declare that God hasn't much to do if He keeps a chart of every head and marks off each hair as it drops out. Taken as hyperbole, that statement becomes a breath-taking metaphor which inspires a leap of the imagination so stupendous that God's concern for His children is seen in majestic perspective.

Irony is a more or less intense form of satire. It conveys information or emotion by saying the opposite of what is actually meant. "Brutus is an honorable man" was readily understood by all who heard it. Repeated at strategic intervals, the phrase became a call to action, convincing the crowd that "Brutus is a dishonorable man—a scoundrel—a wretch."

SPECIAL CHARACTERISTICS OF ORAL STYLE

Most of the preceding discussion applies to both written and oral communication. Both the written and the spoken word must be understood in order to be effective; mood and tempo may be varied at will in both media. Concrete words are essential in writing as well as in speaking, and figures of speech add zest to both forms of communication.

In spite of the many resemblances, however, oral style cannot be equated with written. There are important differences which, if ignored, tend to drain much of the vitality from public speech. Conversely, material couched in good oral style seldom proves effective in print.

These differences have been recognized for many centuries. "It should be observed," Aristotle told his students, "that each kind of rhetoric has its own appropriate style. The style of written prose is not that of oratory. Both the written and the spoken style must be known."

History has verified the Stagirite's conclusion. Macaulay

wrote well, spoke poorly. So he calmly admitted, "Nobody can think it strange that a great writer should fail as a speaker." Spurgeon spoke well, wrote clumsily. So he anticipated the jibes of critics by his frank recognition, "Nothing that I say in public is fit to be printed as I say it."

Like most critics of his century, Hazlitt gave all the laurels to written communication:

> The most dashing orator I ever heard is the flattest writer I ever read. In speaking, he was like a volcano vomiting out lava; in writing . . . nothing but the dry cinders, the hard shell remains. The tongues of flame, with which . . . he used to illuminate his subject, and almost scorched up the panting air, do not appear painted on the margin of his works.[k]

Spoken communication tends to be inferior in print, the essayist concluded, because it lacks

> the orator's vehemence of gesture, the loudness of his voice, the speaking eye, the conscious attitude, the inexplicable dumb show and noise—all "those brave sublunary things that made his raptures clear"—are no longer there, and without these he is nothing;—his "fire and air" turn to puddle and ditch-water, and the god of eloquence and of our idolatry sinks into a common mortal, or an image of lead, with a few labels, nicknames, and party watchwords stuck in his mouth.[l]

That indictment stings. It is typical of most analysis prior to the twentieth century. Literary critics are more likely to be good writers than effective speakers, so it was inevitable that they should disparage oral style as compared with written. They judged the spoken word by the canons of printed literature. This was a grave error. Any attempt to define the merits or demerits of one form in terms of the other is like estimating the worth of men in units based upon analysis of women. They form similar but separate groups, and neither is properly evaluated in terms of the other.

What Hazlitt failed to recognize is that much of the world's noblest literature is fundamentally unsuited for oral delivery. Though the left shoe does not fit the right foot, neither does the right shoe fit the left foot. With the exception of a handful of great dramas and a few volumes of exalted lyric poetry, it may be taken as a working rule that good oral material will not be outstanding in print and that distinguished written material will be weak when delivered orally.

Failure to recognize that speech and writing constitute two distinct media has produced a great deal of abominable oral communication, modeled upon written classics. It has even affected the handling of certain bodies of literature that are notable in style as well as content. W. H. D. Rouse complains that "translators habitually make Cicero and Demosthenes say things which no speaker would have said, because they would not pass over to the audience. They write in a library, and their sentences would not pass muster on the platform."[m]

Most translators of the Scriptures have committed the same sin. Though the Authorized Version of the Bible is one of the monumental literary achievements of the English-speaking world, few portions of it are suitable for oral use. That is one of the chief reasons for the fact that the Scripture Reading may be the low spot of a worship service in terms of communication and attention value. Various attempts have been made to meet this problem, among which the most notable was the production of a Bible especially designed for public reading.

Speech is actually a far more versatile medium than writing. Tones, force, pitch, and gesture extend the power of the spoken word. It is comparatively easy for a speaker using

[m] (224), 60.

gestures as well as words, to describe a circular staircase to a person who has never seen one; but to communicate approximately the same meaning the writer must resort to a complex and lengthy dissertation.

On the other hand, the writer has a distinct advantage in the fact that each reader can proceed at whatever pace may suit his capacity. Suppose three hundred men, women, and children are gathered in a sanctuary some Sunday morning. There is great diversity in intellectual ability, self-discipline, and personal wants. Let each of the group have a copy of the same printed sermon—say, 3,000 words in length. A few readers will finish it in ten minutes or less, and the majority in fifteen to twenty-five minutes. But there will be some who have not reached "In the third place . . ." by the time others get bored and go home.

As a result of differences among listeners, the preacher must proceed slowly enough and simply enough to take the bulk of his audience along with him. At the same time, he must give his message enough verve and substance to keep the interested attention of those listeners who are capable of proceeding rapidly. His appeal to the eyes of listeners may be adapted not only to their likes and dislikes, but also to the size of the audience. Adolf Hitler, frequently quoted in these pages, recognized that "the pathos and gesture which the great room, holding a thousand people, demands," becomes extreme or even ludicrous before a small audience.[n]

Straightforward development is far more important in oral than written communication. Parenthetical statements and interpolations throw the listener off the track. Having no opportunity to go back and re-establish a broken connection, he may become confused or altogether lost when the thread of understanding is snapped. Since any word or sentence may

[n] (232), 703.

have extreme potency because of its relation to a particular set of wants, it is easy for the listener to bolt off at a tangent.

Listeners are like metal blocks scattered about the surface of a revolving disc. Centrifugal force tends to throw the blocks off the disc, but an electromagnet at the center will hold them in place. Turn off the current only an instant; with the swirling force of the disc no longer neutralized, blocks will fly out of the experimental field. Just so, a single break in the magnetic power of the speaker's persuasion may cost him one or more listeners.

Brief, simple sentences are highly desirable. This quality should not be carried too far; if developed to an extreme point there is danger of producing a choppy style. In general, however, it is easier to make one's sentences too long and involved than too brief and simple.

Careful use of silence is related to both factors mentioned above. Writers have a number of devices to indicate breaks and transitions in the development of an idea: the period, comma, colon, semi-colon, and dash are the most important ones. All these symbols were developed as substitutes for pauses and emphases in oral communication.

Committed to writing, speech tends to become stiff and formal. Strict rules are developed, and grammarians attempt to reduce communication to mechanical manipulation of fixed symbols. Though the rules are developed for written communication, they are transferred to oral, with the result that public speech begins to march like a stiff-jointed puppet rather than to saunter with natural ease.

This process has taken place not once, but many times. Like the rise and fall of empires, Western civilization has seen many periods of shifting back and forth between spoken style and written. Invention of printing gave new force and dignity to the latter, with the result that for a period of many generations critics attempted to establish written style as the standard and spoken as a crude and imperfect derivative. What radio and television will eventually do to the written word is anyone's guess!

As indicated above, an attempt to employ written style in public address is like trying to play checkers on a back-gammon board. Differences in the two media are funda-mental, and cannot be reconciled.

Silence—supplemented by gesture and changes in tone and force—has to serve as comma, period, question mark, exclamation point, colon, dash, and every other punctuation device. Failure to use silence produces oral communication that is like an ancient Hebrew scroll—plenty of ideas, but all crowded together, rolling on and on with majestic and in-comprehensible unconcern. Ralph G. Nichols suggests that silence may well be considered "the most important of all aural symbols."[°] In making deliberate experiments with si-lence it is important to remember that an interval of stillness tends to seem much longer to a speaker than to a listener.

Visual and oral transitions are to speech as modifiers and special punctuation marks are to writing. Conversations are expressed quite differently in the two media. This point of contrast is extremely important, and is one of the most dis-tinctive criteria by which to judge a piece of communication as "written" or "oral" in style.

A writer who wishes to indicate mood and action in a conversation must resort to words; a speaker must express both in his voice and body. Take an anecdote about Lincoln; in writing, it might be necessary to say: "Lincoln was dis-gusted. He turned to his opponent and drawled, 'Freedom is mighty precious to those who don't have it!' "

Required to convey the same information in a sermon,

°(233), 84.

the speaker will use only half as many words as the writer. It is essential to convey Lincoln's actual statement in words. But the president's disgust and his drawl should be indicated by manner and emphasis. Thus the actual words used in written and spoken conversation will vary widely in conveying precisely the same information and emotion.

All such transitional phrases as, "Then he objected . . ."; "There was a pause, and she admitted . . ."; "Smiling with sudden understanding, he commented . . ." belong in written but not in oral communication. Unable to express his meaning in any other way, the writer is forced to use a great many words that are superfluous in the speech situation. In written style, words are used to designate and distinguish the various persons whose speech is reported; in spoken style, tone and manner distinguish between persons in a dialogue, and the connectives are not needed.

There is one special difficulty the speaker faces. Unlike the writer, he cannot use quotation marks to indicate material that is not his own. It is awkward to say, "Quote . . . unquote"; silence and gesture are the most effective substitutes for quotation marks. Unless they are employed effectively, the listener will be unable to determine when a quotation begins or ends. Few long quotations are suitable for oral use in their exact length and language; that is why it is easy to lose listeners when reading lengthy extracts from even outstanding written works. One of the chief weaknesses resulting from use of a manuscript is the tendency to speak in a style unsuited for oral communication; this is also likely to be quite marked in the case of a sermon written out in full, then memorized.

Skill in development of oral style comes largely from practice. In order to gain a vivid understanding of the problems involved and the methods by which they may be met, it is helpful to read aloud. Children's stories are particularly good; take printed versions and experiment to see how many words may be omitted when read aloud. Deliberately cultivate skill in conveying moods, transitions, and qualities with the voice and hands, as well as with words.

CONCLUSIONS

Every speaker and writer acquires a style, whether he consciously strives for it or not. Style is actually a part of the total communication process, for ideas cannot be entirely separated from the vehicles by which they are conveyed.

Ease of understanding is the first requisite for good style. Short words and brief sentences are the most obvious features of "listenability." Informal style is also important.

Mood and tempo may be created by careful choice of words and variety in sentence structure. Specific words and concrete illustrations help to convey powerful stimuli and to hold listener attention. To secure desired effects from words, it is often necessary to consult word books—a list of which is included above.

Figures of speech add tone and color to both oral and written communication. Many figurative expressions can be devised to suit the needs of particular sermons; written resource material also provides much good matter.

Oral style has special characteristics of its own, and cannot be equated with written. Contrary to Victorian sentiment, the spoken word is not inferior in quality to the written. Rather, it serves special purposes and employs special techniques. Of these, the most important are: straightforward development, simple and direct construction, careful use of silence, and employment of visual-auditory transitional devices rather than verbal connectives and modifiers.

Chapter VI

SOURCES OF MATERIAL

ONE OF BISHOP WARREN A. CANDLER'S FAVORITE STORIES
had to do with an undertaker who was also a local preacher
in the M. E. Church, South. There was a serious shortage
of preachers one year, and the undertaker was appointed
supply pastor of a country circuit. He stuck it out for eight
weeks—long enough to make his circuit twice—then returned
to his old trade.

"This business of preaching isn't what it might seem,"
he explained ruefully. "It'd be all right if folks would be
satisfied with just one or two good sermons. But do you think
they are? No, sir, they're got to hear a new sermon every
month!"

Great productivity is expected of the preacher. If he is
pastor of only one church he must prepare from one hundred
to one hundred and fifty messages a year. Should his sermons
average only 3,000 words in length, his literary productivity
totals one-third to one-half million words a year. Few professional writers, devoting full time to their craft, maintain
a greater output than that.

Granted that the average church member does not demand that his preacher's messages be comparable to magazine articles in literary quality, that one may take full advantage of special emphases in the church year, that it is frequently legitimate to revise old sermons and use them again after going to a new parish, nevertheless, any except the most slovenly preaching requires a tremendous supply of both sermon ideas and illustrative materials. Preaching of high quality depends to a large degree upon developing adequate sources of supply.

ADVANCE PLANNING

Many sermon writers spread their material too thin, not because there is not enough available but because they have not developed efficient methods of using what they actually find. For this purpose the most important single practice is long-range planning. Instead of writing sermons from week to week, it is advisable to select subjects weeks or months in advance. Working always, say, four to six months ahead of his actual preaching schedule, one has sixteen to twenty-four weeks in which to find material.

Schopenhauer advised that one should write "the way an architect builds, who first drafts his plan and designs every detail." That theory is fine enough for the writer of fiction or the man who produces a small amount of non-fiction without having to meet a definite schedule. But the opposite method is likely to prove more satisfactory to the preacher: select a subject, gather as much material as possible, then let the material guide the treatment.

When a person is constantly aware of numerous subjects he expects to use in the future, it is amazing how much material he finds without looking for it. Relevant ideas and illustrations turn up in the most unlikely places and at the most improbable times. This process of discovery is like casually kicking up nuggets in one's ordinary walking rather than digging in the rocks hours a day in search of the same gold.

There is a strong tradition to the effect that *Life With Father* was written in seventeen days—but the authors had been gathering material for more than two years. Kipling frequently kept a short story "in the works" for as long as three to five years. Stevenson produced his best work when he let his ideas mature slowly. "I find that I must let things take their time," he confided to Sidney Colvin in 1874.

Beecher always wrote both his sermons on Sunday: one after breakfast and the other after lunch. Spurgeon was somewhat more cautious—though he wrote his evening sermon on Sunday afternoon, he usually prepared the morning message on Saturday night! For both these extraordinary men, however, the actual process of writing the sermon was almost incidental. Each usually worked with a subject for months before he was ready to use it. Simultaneously gathering material for many different messages, no idea was pulled out of the "seed bed" until its creator felt it to be mature and ripe.

Hazlitt advises the writer, no matter what his medium, to take things leisurely:

He may have caught a glimpse of a simile, and it may have vanished again: let him be on the watch for it, as the idle boy watches for the lurking place of the adder. He can wait. He is not satisfied with a reason he has offered for something: let him wait until he finds a better reason. There is some word, some phrase, some idiom that expresses a particular idea better than any other, but he cannot for the life of him recollect it: let him wait till he does.[a]

This procedure is sound in more than one respect.

First, it is highly efficient because *it utilizes the principle*

[a] (231), 25.

of change of pace. There seems to be no question whatever that variety in one's work leads to greater output. This applies to both physical and mental work.

"In most cases," concludes a psychological analyst, "boredom develops within the first half hour of work. . . . Output on a heterogeneous task tends to increase and output on a homogeneous task to decrease."[b] If one works, say, ten hours on a sermon—a relatively short time to devote to a literary unit of three to four thousand words—he will actually get more done in twenty periods of half an hour than in two periods of five hours.

Again, long-range planning *makes it possible to get good use from small units of time* that would otherwise be wasted. Given ten minutes before a caller is due, one can hardly profit from attempting to write the outline of next Sunday's sermon. But that brief period can be effectively used in copying an illustration from your notebook, devising an effective analogy by which to clarify a point, or jotting down a few questions that should be considered in writing the outline of a future sermon.

There is no point in complaining about lack of time. Everyone has exactly the same amount—twenty-four hours a day. It is difference in use, not quantity, that affects results accomplished. Many persons who guard their hours are careless with their minutes; a major aspect of efficiency is the habit of using small bits of time rather than wasting them.

Finally, *the process of slow ripening reduces pressure.* A preacher who writes his sermons only from Sunday to Sunday is under constant strain. He is like a workman without a contract, employed only one day at a time. He never knows what to expect tomorrow, and a stomach upset on Saturday night would prove disastrous. Working leisurely

[b](217), 80; cf. (204), 2.

for months, one can bring his sermon to gradual completion. He is under no strain, for a day or even a week of delay will not be a source of major concern. Actual writing of a sermon for delivery is an easy matter; selecting a folder that has grown fat from many small contributions, one does not have to search for material. His only task is to arrange what he has already gathered.

IDEAS AND ILLUSTRATIONS FROM PERSONAL EXPERIENCE

One bright Spring morning, a weatherbeaten Scot was riding beside the driver of a stage. "John," he demanded, "why did you hit your off leader with the whip just now?"

"I cracked him because of that white stone yonder," explained the coachman. "He's a nervous animal, and used to shy away every time we passed this spot. So I sting him a little to get his mind off the stone, and he never notices it any more."

Jotting down a brief memorandum about the incident, the passenger expanded the idea some months later. That is how Thomas Chalmers came to write his famous sermon, "The Expulsive Power of a New Affection."

Preaching material stems from two aspects of personal experience: deliberate search for the extraordinary and the unusual, plus imaginative analysis of ordinary, everyday life.

Travel is the most widely used method of finding unusual experiences. In extent, it may vary from a trip around the world to merely stepping outside one's daily routine. Many a preacher has visited Europe and the Holy Land in search of sermon fodder. Like Chalmers, Beecher used to ask permission to ride with the pilot of a boat or driver of a stage rather than with the passengers. Talmadge prowled through the red-light districts of New York in order to gather material for sermons on vice.

In general, one tends to be more alert for potential material in unusual than in ordinary situations. Thus, Leeming points out that "the man or woman who travels by the 8:00 train after riding on the 8:15 can find a new world."[e] Precisely because a thing is part of one's everyday experience he is likely to overlook it.

There are two dangers associated with every attempt to seek ideas and illustrations in unusual experiences.

First, it is easy for a casual observer to make gross errors in his interpretations of unfamiliar occupations, ideas, cultures, or viewpoints. There is a stock joke that travelers who spend a day in England or Russia feel much more competent to write books on the country than do persons who have spent years there.

Second, and far more important, material drawn from an area of experience that is a-typical for both the preacher and his listeners is likely to be low in vitality. It would seem that a visit to the circus would yield dozens of good ideas; this is a field far apart from ordinary life, and full of color. With rare exceptions, however, such trips are likely to be barren. Circus life is so far removed from ordinary life that nearly all of it is strange. There are not enough points of similarity to provide a basis for effective metaphor.

This condition is even more marked in the case of foreign travel. All that one sees is new and to some degree unusual; overwhelmed by a barrage of newness, the ordinary traveler is unable to bring order into chaos. He cannot synthesize the great mass of new experiences with his total set of memories, wants, and understanding. So he returns home with relatively few vivid and usable recollections.

Even these are likely to be of doubtful value in preaching. Unless the travel illustration deals with some matter

[e](234), 84.

that touches the first- or second-hand experience of the listener, no effective metaphor is formed. An allusion that is fresh and striking may fall flat because it does not enable the listener to begin on familiar ground. At best, he is a spectator and not a participant in the scene or incident described.

This means that, contrary to popular opinion, typical foreign travel is one of the poorest sources of preaching material. In order to be usable, the strange must not be too strange. It must be linked with the known by at least a narrow causeway. If cut off by an ocean, it requires extensive bridge-building that defeats its own purpose. In general, the preacher will find more good material by spending a day in some part of his own community that he has never explored than by spending a day in Jerusalem or Paris.

Imaginative analysis of ordinary life is the form of experience that pays greatest dividends in terms of preaching material.

Preaching is not entirely separable from other forms of literary creativity; in a very real respect every preacher is a feature writer. And, warns a veteran teacher of journalism, "If you can't see a feature article at home, you won't see it at the South Pole or in Tibet."[d]

Great experiences grow, not out of finding unusual adventures, but from taking unusual insight to the commonplace activities of life. It is no accident that much of the world's great imaginative literature has been built about the dramas of relatively ordinary people facing typical problems. One thinks immediately of Ibsen, Dickens, and Dostoevski. Arnold Bennett found high adventure in the lives of old ladies; Lewis Carroll looked at the world through the eyes of an imaginative mathematician and found glory in a rabbit

[d](235), 119.

hole; Chekhov made peasants immortal. Nor is it any accident that many of the world's most noted paintings depict
ordinary folk. Kings and rulers are of course found in the
great galleries—but most of the best-known and best-loved
canvasses in the world have caught subjects such as proud
fisherman, a pensive child, or a work-worn farmer.

"What is adventure?" demands Gilbert K. Chesterton.
"Not necessarily a thrilling escape from death, a holdup on
a dark road at midnight. There are others."

> The newsboy, for instance, who runs after you when you have over-
> paid him a penny; the lark by the roadside on a spring morning; the
> hilltop when life seems suddenly fresh and worth while again; the
> fireside and a good friend when the blizzard howls about; the limping
> dog, the sobbing child, the merry quip, the chance acquaintance.
> These and a thousand other bits of living are all adventures, and those
> who meet them with the adventurer's heart will catch the extra
> pungency of their flavor till the day of their death.[e]

With the deepest of reverence, the preacher cannot but
recognize that such a "flair for adventure" was among the
prominent marks of the Saviour. His immortal parables
came, not from visits to great and strange cities of the old
world, but from the everyday lives of ordinary men, women,
and children.

Imaginative insight marks the work of all great writers.
Third-rate hacks tend to grind out limping lines which deal
with the extraordinary, the colossal, the magnificent. Masters
write about roses, larks, and oaks; tears, marriage, and
death. To a man of tender and sensitive imagination a tiny
flower in a crannied wall was a messenger from God; to
another

> A primrose by a river's brim
> A yellow primrose was to him
> And it was nothing more.

*(236).

Gilbert Murray holds that "the great difference, intellectually speaking, between one man and another is simply the number of things they can see in a given cubic yard of earth."[f] George Bernard Shaw, with his usual refreshing objectivity, once declared that "few people think more than two or three times a year." Then he added: "I have made an international reputation by thinking once or twice a week."[g]

Fabre found heroism and tragedy in a spider's web. Archimedes pushed science forward from his bathtub. Before he left Sweden for his first field trip, Linnaeus had discovered plant life to be as exotic as grand opera. Kant traveled more than ten miles from Konigsberg only a few times in his entire life. Shakespeare's perambulations in search of material were limited to a tiny strip on a little island. Hogarth found all the ideas he could use in walking the streets of his own city, and the incomparable Raphael never felt moved to leave Italy in search of subjects.

Preaching material is everywhere. In order to find and use it only two things are necessary: seeing eyes and a nimble imagination. Foreign travel, like domestic jaunts, becomes tremendously fruitful when analyzed continually with imagination and insight.

Like writers and artists, you should cultivate the habit of frequently looking at the ordinary aspects of life through the eyes of a stranger. Attempt to discover what would be interesting and significant to a visitor from Mars. Analyze the explanations that would have to be made to such a guest, and try to see what ordinary activities would be thrilling, absurd, and mysterious.

Always carry a notebook or index cards and jot down ideas and descriptions as they are noted. Memory is fleeting,

[f] Cited in (28), 82.
[g] (237).

and the human will is capricious. Stimuli that help provoke an unusual flash of insight may not be repeated. Unless the idea is preserved in at least rough form it may be lost forever. There have been few if any artists in the use of words, pigments, musical notes, clay or stone, who have felt that they could function efficiently without some sort of scrapbook or notebook. Fleeting impressions, brief moods, and trivial encounters have been expanded into many a literary and artistic masterpiece. Arnold Bennett was so wedded to his practice of observing and jotting down that he even made notes at his mother's funeral. Among other things, he noted that after a rain some bricks dry before others.

Once having "discovered" commonplace or even trivial aspects of life, it is necessary to find applications in order to use them. His literary legacy is too immense to make the search, but if one should check, he would probably find that somewhere Arnold Bennett made use of his observation that bricks dry at an uneven rate.

For preaching purposes an observation does not become a source of material until an application is found. Just as Whistler might sketch in his notebook the droop of an ostrich feather in a dowager's hat, without having in mind a definite use for that aspect of dress, so a preacher might note that it is unpleasant to pick up garbage after a neighbor's dog has knocked over the can. Sooner or later the artist is likely to need to know how an ostrich feather droops; eventually the preacher may want to illustrate unpleasant necessity by reference to dog and garbage.

Given a large supply of observations, plus the challenge of numerous sermon topics constantly in one's thinking, the most commonplace notations are likely to assume sudden relevance. Because they grow out of ordinary experience, they prove extremely effective vehicles for the transfer of ideas and images.

For example, many a husband has had the experience of becoming angry with his wife and stalking out of the house—to walk around the block or go to the office in order to "cool off." That sort of thing happens every day in every community, and it is a rare marriage that has not been marked by at least one incident of the sort. A vivid description of the mingled shame and hope felt by the now-penitent husband as he returns home can become a metaphor by which to help spiritually insensitive listeners grasp the ecstasy of forgiveness for sin.

Observations that are likely to prove fruitful concern such matters as:

> . . . driving in a 10-mile zone with a car that will not throttle down under 20.
>
> . . . rushing over to speak to an old friend in a crowd, tapping him on the shoulder—and being confronted by a stranger.
>
> . . . learning to ride a bicycle—one minute you can't; the next minute you can.
>
> . . . leaving home for a trip, and fifty miles out of town beginning to wonder whether you turned off the oven.
>
> The feeling that follows when you call a wrong number in the middle of the night.
>
> . . . reaching home, loaded down with bundles, and fumbling for the keyhole in the dark.
>
> . . . watching a trolley head for the barn, without a single passenger aboard.
>
> . . . biting the end of a straw, and then trying to suck your soda.
>
> . . . driving up to a place where you want to stop, and finding a sign: "No Parking at Any Time."
>
> . . . hurrying to the station, only to find that your train has just left.

. . . trying to water the lawn when your hose is short
   and the pressure is low.

With your wife away on a visit, piling up dishes in
   the kitchen sink—until the day comes that dishes
   must be washed.

. . . driving down a one-way street in the wrong
   direction.

. . . watching a woman's feet as she talks over the
   telephone.

. . . racing to answer the telephone, and having the
   other party hang up just as you reach your end
   of the line.

Such observations are not often susceptible of lengthy treatment. Clovis Chappell, preaching on the importance of an attitude of trust, uses less than one hundred words to compare worry with his own fear at hearing strange noises when sleeping alone in an isolated house.[h] But the importance of such an allusion is not measured by the space it occupies. By vivid and imaginative use of an almost universal experience, Chappell takes his listeners across a bridge of metaphor. His sermon is not only more understandable and more enjoyable; it is also more compelling because he has made skillful use of insight into everyday life.

This approach, which requires little time and no skills that may not be acquired by anyone, will help fill one's sermon reservoir with ideas and illustrations that meet all the criteria of first-rate units of communication.

HOMILETICAL MATERIALS FROM PRINTED SOURCES

Special publications for preachers are significant chiefly in terms of bulk. Whether volumes of sermons, cyclopedia of ideas and outlines, or compilations of illustrations, preacher-

[h] (238).

slanted publications can at best provide second-hand stimuli. At worst, they offer trite material couched in the literary style of a bygone era.

As early as the eighth century there was limited circulation of preaching aids. Four centuries later the sermon writer could choose from many types of books. In addition to commentaries, there were volumes of occasional sermons, compilations of texts, and great exegetical tomes. Industrious collectors gathered impressive numbers of fables, holy legends, and miscellaneous illustrations. Many a parish library included such anthologies as *The Book of Sparkling Points*, *The Garden of Delight*, and *The Flower of the Apostles*,[1] Even bestiaries enjoyed wide pulpit use.

Volumes of general speech material give the modern preacher valuable resources not available to his medieval predecessor. In general, the anthology intended for sale to secular speakers and writers contains fresher material than that published primarily for preachers. No such collection, whether secular or religious in nature, contains altogether usable material. Indeed, the typical volume in this field includes perhaps ten per cent fresh, stimulating ideas or illustrations. Much of the rest that is new is insipid; most of that which is not insipid has been worked to death.

There is one exception to that general statement. Within recent years a number of very fine anthologies of quotations, proverbs, and epigrams have appeared. So vast is the scope of the material that much of it is necessarily fresh for almost any reader or listener.

Several collections of speech material are listed below. Those in print at publication date of this volume are marked (*). Others can be found at second-hand booksellers or shops specializing in religious material. A list of such shops is also

[1] (239), 148.

included, since you will get little benefit from volumes of speech material without purchasing your personal copies.

Books of General and Religious Speech Material

1. Preacher-slanted anthologies:

*Hallock, G. B. F., *2500 Best Modern Illustrations.*
 Hallock, G. B. F., *5000 Best Modern Illustrations.*
*Knight, Walter B., *3000 Illustrations for Christian Service.*
*Webb, Aquilla, *1001 Illustrations for Pulpit and Platform.*
*Webb, Aquilla, *1000 New Illustrations.*
*Stidger, William L., *There Are Sermons in Stories.*
*Stidger, William L., *More Sermons in Stories.*
*Stidger, William L., *Sermon Nuggets in Stories.*
*Stidger, William L., *Sermon Stories of Faith and Hope.*

2. Collections of general speech material and humor:

*Cerf, Bennett, *Try and Stop Me.*
*Cerf, Bennett, *Laughing Stock.*
*Cerf, Bennett, *Anything for a Laugh.*
*Cerf, Bennett, *Shake Well Before Using.*
*Cerf, Bennett, *Bedside Book of Famous American Stories.*
*Cerf, Bennett, *Bedside Book of Famous British Stories.*
*Copeland, Lewis & Faye, *10,000 Jokes, Toasts & Stories.*
*Copeland, Lewis, *The World's Best Jokes.*
*Droke, Maxwell, *Anthology of Anecdotes.*
*Droke, Maxwell, *Speaker's Treasury of Anecdotes.*
*Esar, Evan, *Esar's Joke Dictionary.*
*Ford, Ed., et. al., *Can You Top This?*
 Fuller, Edmund, *Thesaurus of Anecdotes.*
*Goodman, Jack & Albert Rice, *I Wish I'd Said That!*
 Johnson, J. H., et. al., *The Laughter Library.*
*Komroff, Manuel, ed., *The Great Fables of All Nations.*
*Lawson, J. Gilchrist, *The World's Best Humorous Anecdotes.*
*Lupton, Martha, ed., *Speaker's Desk Book.*
 Lupton, Martha, ed., *Treasury of Modern Humor.*
 Meier, Frederick, ed., *The Joke Teller's Joke Book.*
 Meiers, Mildred & Jack Knapp, *Thesaurus of Humor.*

Mendelsohn, S. Felix, *Let Laughter Ring*.
*Mendelsohn, S. Felix, *Merry Heart*.
Moulton, S. Powers, *2500 Jokes*.
*Allen, Edward F., *Modern Humor for Effective Speaking*.
*Botkin, B. A., *Treasury of American Folklore*.
*Botkin, B. A., *Treasury of New England Folklore*.
*Botkin, B. A., *Treasury of Western Folklore*.
*Botkin, B. A., *Treasury of Southern Folklore*.

3. *Quotations, proverbs, and epigrams:*

Benham, William G., *Benham's Book of Quotations, Proverbs and
    Household Words*.
*Bierce, Ambrose, *The Devil's Dictionary*.
*Champion, Selwyn G., *Racial Proverbs*.
Dalbiac, Philip, *Dictionary of Quotations* (English)
*Davidoff, Henry, *A World Treasury of Proverbs*.
Edwards, Tryon, *The New Dictionary of Thoughts*.
*Forbes, B. C., *Scrapbook of Thoughts*.
*Fuller, Edmund, *Thesaurus of Epigrams*.
*Gilbert, Mark, *Wisdom of the Ages*.
Lawson, J. Gilchrist, *The World's Best Epigrams*.
Lawson, J. Gilchrist, *The World's Best Proverbs and Maxims*.
*Lockridge, Norman, *World's Wit and Wisdom*.
*Mencken, H. L., *A New Dictionary of Quotations*.
*Roberts, Kate L., ed., *Hoyt's New Cyclopedia of Practical Quotations*.
*Stevenson, Burton, *The Home Book of Proverbs*.
*Stevenson, Burton, *The Home Book of Quotations*.
Oxford Dictionary of Quotations.
*Prochnow, Herbert V., *Public Speaker's Treasure Chest*.

4. *Brief factual material, primarily off-trail in nature:*

Bombaugh, C. C., *Facts and Fancies for the Curious*.
Brewer, E. C., *Dictionary of Phrase and Fable*.
Brewer, E. C., *The Historic Note Book*.
Brewer, E. C., *Encyclopedia of Literature*.
*Ackermann, A. S. E., *Popular Fallacies*.
*Forbes, B. C., *101 Unusual Experiences*.
Guild, Leo, *You Bet Your Life!*

*Guild, Leo, *What Are The Odds?*
Holt, Alfred H., *Phrase Origins.*
O'Hara, Neal, *Thoughts While Shaving.*
Knowlson, T. Sharper, *The Origin of Popular Superstitions and Customs.*
*Mitchell, Albert, *Here's the Answer.*
Radford, Edwin, *Unusual Words and How They Came About.*
*Ripley, Robert, *Believe It Or Not.*
*Ripley, Robert, *Second Believe It Or Not*
Shankle, George E., *American Nicknames.*
Stewart, George R., *Names on the Land.*
*Shipley, Joseph T., *Dictionary of Word Origins.*
*Shipley, Joseph T., *Encyclopedia of Literature.*
*Stimpson, George, *Information Roundup.*
*Stimpson, George, *A Book About American History.*
*Stimpson, George, *A Book About American Politics.*
*Stimpson, George, *A Book About A Thousand Things.*
*Stimpson, George, *A Book About the Bible.*
Stimpson, George, *Uncommon Knowledge.*
Stimpson, George, *Things Worth Knowing.*
Stimpson, George, *Popular Questions Answered.*
Walsh, William S., *Handy Book of Curious Information.*
*Walsh, William S., *Handy Book of Literary Curiosities.*
*Walsh, William S., *Curiosities of Popular Customs.*
World Almanac, all volumes.

Hundreds of booklets, on almost every conceivable subject, are available free or at nominal cost from the U. S. Govt. Printing Office. For information and lists address Supt. of Documents, U. S. Govt. Printing Office, Washington.

5. *Collections of short biographies:*

Though not published primarily as speech material, volumes of brief biographical studies are extremely valuable. In general, the short biography gives a much higher per cent of human interest material than the full-length study. Writing primarily for the casual reader rather than for the student of history, the author of the short biography must make heavy use of the unusual and interesting aspects of his subject. In many instances, a twenty-page treatment will yield more speech material than the full-length biography—partly because condensation makes it easier to note suitable material.

The following list is suggestive rather than exhaustive:

Barry, Philip B., *Twenty Human Monsters.*
Blei, Franz, *Fascinating Women.*
Bolitho, William, *Twelve Against the Gods.*
*Bolitho, William, *As God Made Them.*
Bradford, Gamaliel, *Confederate Portraits.*
Bradford, Gamaliel, *Daughters of Eve.*
Bradford, Gamaliel, *Damaged Souls.*
*Bradford, Gamaliel, *Portraits of Women.*
Bradford, Gamaliel, *The Quick and the Dead.*
Bradford, Gamaliel, *Saints and Sinners.*
Brown, Charles Reynolds, *They Were Giants.*
Carnegie, Dale, *Biographical Roundup.*
Carnegie, Dale, *Five Minute Biographies.*
Carnegie, Dale, *Little Known Facts About Well Known People.*
*de Kruif, Paul, *Hunger Fighters.*
*de Kruif, Paul, *Men Against Death.*
*de Kruif, Paul, *Microbe Hunters.*
Dibble, R. F., *Strenuous Americans.*
Finger, Charles J., *Romantic Rascals.*
Forbes, B. C., *Automotive Giants of America.*
*Forbes, B. C., *Little Bits About Big Men.*
*Forbes, B. C., *Life Stories of Fifty American Business Leaders.*
Forbes, B. C., *Men Who Are Making America.*
Forbes, B. C., *Men Who Are Making the West.*
*Hagedorn, Hermann, *Americans: A Book of Lives.*
*Jaffe, Bernard, *Crucibles.*
*Jaffe, Bernard, *Men of Science in America.*
James, Marquis, *They Had Their Hour.*
*Josephson, Matthew, *President Makers.*
*Josephson, Matthew, *The Robber Barons.*
Kobbe, Gustav, *The Loves of Great Composers.*
Marks, Edward B., *They All Had Glamour.*
*Prochnow, Herbert V., *Great Stories from Great Lives.*
*Shaw, Charles G., *The Low Down.*

*Thomas, Dana, *Crusaders for God.*
*Thomas, Henry and Dana Lee, *Living Biographies of Famous Men.*
* *Living Biographies of Famous Novelists.*
* *Living Biographies of Famous Women.*
* *Living Biographies of Great Composers.*
* *Living Biographies of Great Philosophers.*
* *Living Biographies of Religious Leaders.*

Thomas, Henry and Dana Lee, *Living Biographies of Great Poets.*
Living Biographies of Famous Rulers.
Living Biographies of Great Scientists.
Living Biographies of Famous Americans.
Living Biographies of American Statesmen.

Wallace, Archer, *Blazing New Trails.*
*Wallace, Archer, *In Spite of All.*
Wallace, Archer, *Stories of Grit.*
Wallace, Archer, *More Stories of Grit.*
Wright, Richardson, *Forgotten Ladies.*

DEALERS IN SECOND-HAND BOOKS

Abrahams Magazine Service, 56 East 13th Street, New York 3
Alicat Book Shop, 287 S. Broadway, Yonkers 5, N. Y.
Allen, William H., 2031 Walnut Street, Philadelphia 3, Pa.
Argosy Book Stores, 114 East 59th St., New York 23
Baker Book House, 1019 Wealthy St., S.E., Grand Rapids 6, Mich.
Barnes & Noble, Inc., 105 Fifth Avenue, New York 3
Blackwell, B. H., Ltd., 48-51 Broad St., Oxford, England
Blessing Book Stores, Inc., 81 W. Van Buren St., Chicago 5, Ill.
Bouma's Boekhuis, Groningen, Holland

Brill, E. J., Oude Rijn 33a, Leiden, Holland

Brimmer, Ormie R., 757 W. Atlanta, Altandena, Cal.

Calder, Albert, G.P.O. Box 463, New York 1

Cellar Book Shop, Box 58, Wyandanch, New York

Connecticut Book Finders, P. O. Box 271, West Hartford, Conn.

Corner Book Shop, 102 Fourth Avenue, New York 3

Daniel, John, 1240 East Fourth St., Bethlehem, Pa.

Dauber and Pine Bookshops, Inc., 66 Fifth Avenue, New York 11

Delachaux & Niestle, S.A., Neuchetal, Switzerland

Dimler, Fred J., 303 Fourth Avenue, New York 10

Duschnes, Philip C., 66 East 56th St., New York 22

Erga Foreign Books, 70 Ware St., Cambridge 38, Mass.

Evans, H. H., 1157 Sutter, San Francisco 9, Cal.

Verry Fisher & Co., 6 East 23rd St., N. Y. 10

Fordham Book Co., 1827 White Plains Road, New York 60

W. & G. Foyle, Ltd., 119-125 Charing Cross Road, London, WC2, England

William George's Sons, Ltd., 89 Park Street, Bristol 1, England

Galloway & Porter, Ltd., University Booksellers, Cambridge, England

B. C. Goodpasture, 932 Caldwell Lane, Nashville 4, Tenn.

John Grant Booksellers, Ltd., 31 George IV Bridge, Edinburgh, Scotland

Green Book Shop, 110 Fourth Avenue, New York 3

W. Heffner & Sons, Ltd., Cambridge, England

W. J. Henneman, 4707 North Western Avenue, Chicago 25, Ill.

B. Herder Book Co., 15-17 South Broadway, St. Louis 2, Mo.

International Art and Science Book Co., 192 Broadway, New York 7

A. M. Kelley, Inc., 31 E. 10th Street, New York 3

M. Kershner Book Shop, 1825 White Plains Road, New York 60

Jay Kieffer, Conestoga Book Service, Rahway, N. J.

H. P. Kraus, 16 East 46th St., New York 17

Edgar Krebs, 1958 Lincoln Avenue, Chicago 14, Ill.

L. Krupp, 799 Broadway, New York 3

J. Krutina, 45 York Street, Broadstairs, Kent, England

S. R. Kurtz, Box 2022, Middle City Station, Philadelphia 3, Pa.

The Lamp Press, Old Town, Slapham, London, SW4, England

Lincoln Book Shoppe, 907 Westminster St., Providence, R. I.

Lindmark's New and Antiquarian Booksellers, Poughkeepsie, N. Y.

Lawyer, David A., Plains, Montana

Arthur Lowell, 5920 Ridge Avenue, Chicago 26, Ill.

David Low Booksellers, Ltd., 17 Cecil Court, Charing Cross Road, London WC2

Eric Malden, Gardner Road, Southwold, Suffolk, England

L. F. Manfredi, 3633 Market St., San Francisco 14, California

Midwest Book Co., Marietta, Ohio

Kenneth Mummery, 9 St. Winifred's Road, Bournemouth, England

National Bibliophile Service, 321 Fifth Avenue, New York 16

National Library Service, 55 East 11th St., New York 3

Ohio Book Store, 544 Main St., Cincinnati 2, Ohio

Old Settler Book Shop, Walpole, New Hampshire

P. S. and Ione Perkins, P. O. Box 167, Pasadena, Cal.

Plaks Book Service, 669 Ralph Avenue, Brooklyn 12, New York

Potter, Carl, 4404 Frazier, Fort Worth 10, Texas

Louis Schucman, 77 Fourth Avenue, New York City

Schulte's Book Store, Inc., 80 Fourth Avenue at 10th St., New York 3

Sharan's Magazines, 111 West 17th Street, New York

William Sloane Assoc., 119 West 57th St., New York 19

Ralph Lee Smith, Cheyney, Pa.

Henry Sotheran Ltd., 2-5 Sackville St., Piccadilly, London W1, England

Southern Library Service, 421 S. Seguin Avenue, New Braunfels, Texas

D. R. Spaight, 837 Dumaine St., New Orleans, La.

B. F. Stevens & Brown, Ltd., New Ruskin House, 28-30 Little Russell St., WC1, London England

Strand Book Shop, 81 Fourth Avenue, New York 3

James Thin, 54-56 South Bridge St., Edinburgh, Scotland

C. C. Thomas, 301-27 E. Lawrence, Springfield, Illinois

J. Thornton & Sons, 11 Broad St., Oxford, England

Charles W. Traylen, 87 North Street, Guildford, Surrey, England

University Book Reserve, 12 Hewins St., Dorchester 21, Mass.

Veith, Paul, Lucy, La.

G. W. Walford, 186 Upper St., London N1, England

Edward L. Weiss, 475 Sixth Avenue, New York 11

Sigmund Weiss, 1910 Arthur Avenue, New York 57

Frederick Welty, 4917 Walnut St., Philadelphia, Pa.

Maxwell Whiteman, 4674 N. Syndenham St., Philadelphia 40, Pa.
Alfred Wilson, 155 Victoria St., London SW1, England
A. D. Woodhouse, Ltd., 19 Bristol St., Birmingham 5, England

THE PREACHER'S GENERAL READING

Every housewife sometimes finds herself short of food.
In such emergencies it may be necessary to serve the next
day's breakfast buns for supper. At best, this is a makeshift
measure. If the family is to eat the next morning someone
will have to go to the store before breakfast.

Something of the same desperation is involved in reading one week in order to be able to preach the following
Sunday. When such a condition prevails, one's inventory is
too low. For the sake of efficiency and peace of mind one's
larder should be so well stocked that he can always select
from a number of alternatives—and never be forced to strip
his shelves bare in order to serve a particular meal.

But pastoral and administrative duties are heavy and
growing. No man should work all the time; some play is
necessary. How can a man possibly look after a parish, play
two or three rounds of golf a week—under par, of course—
take in all the social activities of the community, and do
enough reading to continually put more into his preaching
reservoir than he draws from it?

The answer is: few men can do it.

For many ministers, if not most, the solution lies in a
redistribution of values. One must discover play values in
some activity that is closely related to his major ends if he
is to obtain maximum effectiveness. Claude G. Bowers, the
biographer-diplomat, explained his literary activity in this
fashion: "During seventeen years as Ambassador in Spain
and Chile I have found time to write by avoiding bridge and
golf."[j] What Bowers really meant was, not that he wrote

[j] Cited in (161), 148.

biographies in order to avoid ordinary amusements, but that he fell so passionately in love with writing that he lost all desire to play bridge or golf.

"A career is something you would pay others to let you do if they didn't pay you," says Margaret Mead, of the American Museum of Natural History. Such a view has dominated the lives of many noted persons, working in fields as diverse as music, literature, and science. Mozart admitted that "writing music is my one and only passion and joy." Edison solemnly planned more than one vacation, only to cancel his reservations and run back to his beloved laboratory. Steinmetz followed a similar pattern. "To succeed," he says, "is to make a living at work which interests you. . . . The wise man learns to live. The shrewd man learns to make money. But the man who has learned to live is the happier of the two. Because his work interests him it is not work at all."

Much of the preacher's personal development depends upon learning to enjoy those activities that might sometimes be regarded as work. It is attitude, not activity, that divides work and play. Hunting, fishing, and golf require much greater physical effort than many types of work. Model planes or railroads, chess, or a stamp collection can demand more ingenuity and patience than many a white-collar job. No matter what the nature or demands of an activity, if one enjoys it with zest and abandon, it yields all the benefits of a purely recreational pastime.

In the case of the minister it is doubly imperative that he fall in love with a functional hobby. He is engaged in serious business. Nothing less than his very best is expected of him. A veteran preacher, writing to a young friend, put it like this:

No soldier on service gets entangled in civilian pursuits, since his aim is to satisfy the one who enlisted him. An athlete is not crowned unless he competes according to the rules. It is the hardworking farmer who ought to have the first share of the crops (II Tim. 2:4-6).

Bluntly, the preacher must work. Of all men, he should be the last to have any reason to "kill time." What an abominable phrase that is! "What would be the use of immortality," Emerson demands, "to a person who cannot use well a half hour?"

Chatting with Lord Northcliffe at a fashionable dinner, a society matron gushed: "It's perfectly wonderful how everyone is raving about that man Thackeray. Just to think, he hadn't been heard of a fortnight ago. Why, he awoke one morning and found himself famous."

"Madam," growled Lord Northcliffe, "on the morning that Thackeray woke up and found himself famous, he had been writing eight hours a day for fifteen years. The man who wakes up and finds himself famous, my dear lady, hasn't been asleep."

Michael Angelo frequently slept in his clothes in order to get back to his work without loss of time; often he took a block of marble to his bedroom so that he might get up and work on it during periods of sleeplessness. John James Audubon apologized for some trifling bit of carelessness in his famous drawing of mockingbirds attacked by a snake. He made that sketch in Louisiana, he explained, and the heat was so intense that he had to stop work after only sixteen hours. Sir Walter Scott, goaded on by determination to clear his good name, wrote the Waverly novels at the rate of a volume a month. Examples might be cited from every field of endeavor. Almost without exception, men in every type of religious and secular pursuit have won success at the price of prodigious work.

Call the roll of the truly great evangelistic preachers—
men who have influenced not merely a year or a generation,
but centuries of religious thought. Virtually to a man, they
have been scholars as well as saints. Men like Moses, Isaiah,
and St. Paul were ahead of their generation intellectually as
well as spiritually. Every great reformation in religion has involved mental as well as devotional stimuli. Easy living and
slipshod study did not produce Savonarola, Luther, Calvin,
Huss, Knox, Wesley, or any other man worthy to stand in their
ranks.

Variety and abundance of sermon material are gained
through extensive as well as intensive reading and study.
Ministers need to dip into many different fields of thought
rather than limit reading to material that is in or close to
religion. In addition to books, mass-circulation magazines
are important and valuable. In some quarters there is a
tendency to sneer at such publications as *Reader's Digest.*
Never forget that this magazine, and numerous others of
smaller circulation, win readers through sheer interest-value
of contents. Any article or story that is read by millions of
persons can have at least suggestion value for the preacher.
Major pocket-size magazines are particularly rich in short
features, condensed biographies, and other potential speech
material.

Always read with pencil in hand, marking personal
volumes and making notes from borrowed ones. Such notes
should indicate source, for convenience and accuracy in
future use.

Out-of-print books may be secured from two sources:
second-hand book stores (listed above), and lending libraries.
Many communities have inadequate library service or none
at all. In such cases it is usually possible to borrow by mail.
Some libraries of state universities lend to any citizen in the

state. In addition, there are a number of special collections offering material for religious workers. Some of these are listed below, with size of collection in 1950 indicated.

MAJOR LIBRARIES WHICH LEND BY MAIL

Andover-Harvard Theological Library, Cambridge, Mass.   200,000 vols.

Asbury Theological Seminary, Wilmore, Ky.   27,000 vols.

Augustana Theological Seminary Library, Rock Island, Ill.   30,000 vols.

Austin Presbyterian Seminary Library, Austin, Texas.   22,000 vols.

Berkeley Baptist Seminary Library, Berkeley 4, Cal.   22,250 vols.

Calvin Theological Seminary Library, Grand Rapids 6, Mich.   36,-000 vols.

Chicago Lutheran Theological Seminary, Maywood, Ill.   17,500 vols.

Hammond Library, Chicago Theological Seminary, 5757 University Avenue, Chicago, Ill.   56,750 vols.

Church Divinity School of the Pacific, Berkeley 9, Cal.   22,000 vols.

Pritzlaff Memorial Library, Concordia Seminary, St. Louis 5, Mo.   70,000 vols.

Congregational Library, 14 Beacon St., Boston 8, Mass.   150,000 vols.

Crozer Theological Seminary Library, Chester, Pa.   70,000 vols.

Dallas Theological Seminary Library, Dallas 4, Texas.   23,000 vols.

Drew University Library, Madison, N. J.   200,000 vols.

Eastern Baptist Theological Seminary Library, Lancaster Avenue, Philadelphia 31, Pa.   28,750 vols.

Episcopal Theological Seminary Library, Cambridge 38, Mass.   42,500 vols.

Evangelical and Reformed Theological Seminary Library, Lancaster, Pa.   34,000 vols.

Garrett Biblical Institute Library, Evanston, Ill.   172,500 vols.

General Theological Library, 53 Mt. Vernon St., Boston 8, Mass.   45,000 vols.

General Theological Seminary Library, Chelsea Square, New York City.   112,000 vols.

Gettysburg Theological Seminary Library, Gettysburg, Pa.   58,000 vols.

Gordon College of Theology and Missions Library, 30 Evans Way, Boston 15, Mass.   28,000 vols.

Howard University School of Religion Library, Washington 1, D. C.   50,000 vols.

Caven Library, Knox College, Toronto 5, Ontario, Canada.   40,500 vols.

Louisville Presbyterian Theological Seminary Library, Louisville 2, Ky.   32,500 vols.

Lutheran Theological Seminary Library, 7301 Germantown Avenue, Philadelphia 19, Pa.   52,500 vols.

Virginia Library, McCormick Theological Seminary, 2330 N. Halsted St., Chicago, 14, Ill.   97,000 vols. (circulation limited to denomination)

Missionary Research Library, Broadway at 120 St., New York 27.   85,000 vols.

Moravian College Library, Bethlehem, Pa.   38,000 vols.

New Orleans Baptist Theological Seminary Library, New Orleans, La.   30,000 vols.

Northern Baptist Theological Seminary Library, 3040 W. Washington Blvd., Chicago 12, Ill.   41,500 vols.

Pacific School of Religion Library, Berkeley 9, Cal.   35,750 vols.

Philadelphia Divinity School Library, 4205 Spruce St., Philadelphia 4, Pa.   46,750 vols.

Phillips University Library, Enid, Oklahoma.   51,500 vols.

Pittsburgh Xenia Theological Seminary Library, Pittsburg 12, Pa.   39,000 vols.

Princeton Theological Seminary Library, Princeton, N. J.   224,000 vols.

Queen's University Library, Kingston, Ontario, Canada.   219,000 vols.

San Francisco Theological Seminary Library, San Anselmo, Cal.   39,000 vols.

Seabury-Western Theological Seminary Library, Evanston, Ill.   27,-000 vols. (alumni only).

Mary Couts Burnett Library, Texas Christian University, Fort Worth, Texas.   162,750 vols.

Union Theological Seminary Library, Richmond 27, Va.   50,000 vols.

Virginia Union University Library, Richmond 20, Va.   30,000 vols.

Wartburg Theological Seminary Library, Dubuque, Iowa   30,000 vols.

Western Theological Seminary Library, Holland, Mich.   23,000 vols.

Western Theological Seminary Library, 731 Ridge Avenue, Pittsburg 18, Pa.   53,000 vols.

Wittenberg College Library, Springfield, Ohio.   84,250 vols.

Special collections for mail circulation:

Circulating Library, Duke Divinity School, Durham, N. C.   2,700 vols.

Circulating Library, Emory University School of Theology, Emory University, Georgia.   1,500 vols.

Circulating Library, Perkins School of Theology, Southern Methodist University, Dallas, Texas.   1,700 vols.

Circulating Library, Southern Baptist Theological Seminary, Louisville 6, Ky.   1,000 vols.

Keesler Circulating Library, Vanderbilt School of Religion, Vanderbilt University, Nashville, Tenn.   6,500 vols.

Zion Research Library, 120 Seaver Street, Brookline 46, Mass.   13,000 vols.

(All figures concerning size of collections are as of 1950. Most institutions in the above list will lend to any accredited religious worker. For exact regulations inquire for literature from libraries in which you are interested. Most institutions require borrower to pay postage both ways; a number pay postage one way; Asbury, General Theological Library (Boston) and Zion Research pay postage both ways.)

A PERSONAL FILING SYSTEM

Material that you yourself discover, whether in personal experience or reading, is nearly always vastly superior to the bulk of that printed in books for preachers or speakers. In order to keep your material in usable, accessible form, you need an efficient filing system.

Notebooks and scrapbooks are useful; they are much

better than nothing. But material kept in such form can be classified according to only one subject. Use of a cross-index filing system permits the listing of an item under as many subjects as may be pertinent; thus the effective use-value of filed and indexed material may be three or four times as great as the same material in scrapbooks.

Any system that works is a good one. Here is how to set up one type of workable system:

Use relatively small sheets of paper. Five by eight inches is a good size—big enough to hold almost any ordinary clipping, and small enough to be easily handled. Since this is a standard size, commercial filing equipment may be bought. Trays made of apple boxes or plywood are just as good and much less expensive.

Number sheets consecutively, in the upper right-hand corner. Then mount clippings or copy quotations—placing only one on a sheet. For pasting, use rubber cement; it does not cause the paper to curl, and clippings may be pulled off without tearing.

After accumulating, say, fifty or one hundred pieces of material, you can begin preparing your index. Use a separate index card for each subject; copy the number of a particular piece of material (as mounted for filing) on the index card dealing with each appropriate subject. For example, piece #48 may be a biographical anecdote. It may deal with patience, courage, and ingenuity. So #48 should be indicated on the index cards for "patience," "courage," and "ingenuity."

Your filing system will be strengthened by extending the index to cover books in your preaching library. Using a code or numbering system to designate titles, material in collections and anthologies can be indexed on the same cards with clippings and quotations. This both extends the quantity of material on given subjects, and makes your books more useful. Material that cannot be found when wanted might as well be nonexistent.

Small investments of time over a period of years will produce a set of files with thousands of pieces of homiletical material—quickly available by topic. Even an hour or two of work a week will yield more material than can possibly be used in current sermons. As a result, you will gradually build up enough material to be highly selective in your use of it—seldom being forced to use weak or inappropriate material simply because you can't find anything better.

CONCLUSIONS

Ideas and illustrative materials are so abundant that no man need ever lack all he can use. Imaginative insight into both commonplace and unusual experiences will yield great quantities of useful material. This source should be supplemented by wide general reading. An efficient filing system should be prepared, incorporating both personal notes and special books of preaching and speech material.

All these procedures are of maximum usefulness when one plans his sermons weeks or months in advance, working slowly and leisurely in order to take advantage of small units of time, change of working pace, and the peace of mind that results from working without pressure.

No matter what the location of one's parish, he can find adventures in everyday life. Moreover, the world's great books are as close to him as his mail box, and small monthly purchases of second-hand books will soon produce a worthy personal library.

Chapter VII

FORM AND ORDER IN
THE SKELETON OF THE SERMON

ONLY EXPERTS AND SPECIALISTS GET EXCITED OVER FINDING
"a diamond in the rough," no matter how huge it may be.
Ordinary folk will not even recognize such a stone as a price-
less gem. But when the rough diamond is cut by an artist, it
gains such beauty that all who examine it become speechless
with awe.

A sermon is like a diamond. No matter how fine the raw
gem, it requires skillful workmanship—imparting form and
order—before its inherent power can be realized. And just
as there is no standard pattern by which to cut major gems,
so there is no "best" outline by which to shape a sermon.
Each is a problem in itself. Beecher's first series of Yale
Lectures included a strong word of caution against "the
sterile, conventional, regulation plans that are laid down in
books, and are frequently taught in seminaries. There is no
proper plan."[a]

Note, however, that Beecher decries only the attempt
to organize material according to a standard and conventional

[a] (210), 218.

150

plan; he does not question plans as such. With his word of warning ringing in our ears, we may well listen to Spurgeon as he points out the result of plan-less preaching:

It is possible to heap up a vast mass of good things all in a muddle. Ever since the day I was sent to shop with a basket, and purchased a pound of tea, a quarter-of-a-pound of mustard, and three pounds of rice, and on my way home saw a pack of hounds and felt it necessary to follow them over hedge and ditch (as I always did when I was a boy), and found when I reached home that all the goods were amalgamated—tea, mustard, and rice—into one awful mess, I have understood the necessity of packing up my subjects in good stout parcels, bound round with the thread of my discourse; and this makes me keep to firstly, secondly, thirdly, however unfashionable that method may now be. People will not drink your mustardy tea, nor will they enjoy muddled up sermons, in which you cannot tell head from tail, because they have neither.[b]

There are, then, two untenable positions concerning the form and order of a sermon. One holds that every message must be trimmed and pushed into a standard form, like chickens prepared for canning. At the opposite extreme it is held that no preparation is necessary: just whack off a piece of chicken big enough to fill a can, and stuff it in—feet, feathers, and all. Great piles of left-over pieces will accumulate; these may then be thrown into other cans, helter-skelter.

Between these extremes there is a middle position: insistence upon the necessity of a pattern, but development of an individual pattern for each sermon—so shaped that one makes maximum use of the available materials.

PRELIMINARY ANALYSIS OF THE SERMON SUBJECT

Having made tentative selection of a subject, to be used weeks or months in the future, one can immediately begin

[b] (202), I, 211.

gathering relevant material. As the folder begins to grow thicker, it is helpful to make a preliminary analysis of the proposed subject.

It is essential that the basic proposition be examined to see whether or not it can be presented with intellectual honesty. Many sermons are aimed largely at strengthening or reactivating ideas already held by listeners. There may be little or no intention to communicate information or to present new facts. This condition is partly due to the fact that the person who does not give nominal assent to the postulates of Christianity is not likely to listen to a sermon.

That this condition prevails is no credit to the vitality of the modern Church. It means that Christianity is not touching the vast numbers of educated and intelligent persons who are indifferent or hostile to our basic propositions. There is little incentive for the honest doubter to listen to sermons; his problems are not likely to be touched.

No matter what the character of his audience, however, the preacher should at least be aware of the difference between "propositions of fact" and "propositions of policy." He dare not proceed on the assumption that every listener will give automatic assent to all the beliefs of the preacher. There must be a dash of logic in the sermon, as well as a measure of emotional appeal. "If people do not believe what you are saying," holds a contemporary analyst, "it makes no difference how effectively you say it. If you are a great artist, for the moment, your hearers may be carried away by your skill, but on second thought they desert you."[c] This problem is made more acute by the character of our age. W. Norwood Brigance warns:

To people influenced by the spirit of scientific inquiry, the speaker is less of an oracle than formerly and more of a plain man talking, for

[c] (240), 579.

the public has climbed onto the platform with him. He must rely less on prestige and eloquence, and more on pertinent and impelling facts.[d]

Preachers tend to be righteously indignant in condemning the hasty generalizations of scientists such as Darwin and Freud. Such caution is right and proper—but it must be observed by the Christian preacher as well as by the opponents whom he condemns.

Many a generally accepted scientific theory is actually based on limited evidence. Data secured within a given experimental field are used to form general laws—purporting to apply to conditions outside the field of test. Such a process of "going beyond established points" is termed *extrapolation*.

There is a great deal of "pulpit extrapolation" which consists of hasty pronouncements and precarious conclusions based upon limited and selected data. It is a fallacy ever to refer to "all scientists" or "the higher critics"; to "the parents," "modern youth," "the Russians," or "the Roman Catholics." These are descriptive labels, no more. No one has studied all members of any large class with such care that he can make statements which apply to every individual in the class.

It was said of Pope that he mistook a coterie for mankind; honesty forbids that the preacher trade on insubstantial abstractions made general.

Negative extropolation, which provides the semblance of truth, is particularly prevalent in certain types of evangelistic preaching. There is a kind of cheap applause to be won by smashing indictments directed against flaming youth, greedy capitalists, selfish labor leaders, landlords, tenants, urban folk, or any other class not heavily represented in a particular audience. Condemnation of vices not actually prevalent in a

[d](241), 73.

particular congregation makes the hearer feel smug and superior. "I do not do this terrible thing the preacher talks about," the listener tells himself. "Therefore, I am a good man."

Nor is there the slightest justification for that form of extrapolation which consists of drawing false historical parallels based upon a few selected resemblances and ignoring many major differences in the cultures compared. Modern America is frequently and loudly charged with being precisely like Israel under Solomon, Rome at the apex of her glory, France before the Revolution, Egypt holding the Hebrews in bondage, the Greek states before their collapse, England before Cromwell, and Italy under the Borgias. Far the most popular of these comparisons is with Rome.

Actually, there are no exact historical parallels. Some hearers applaud with fiendish fervor when America is shown to have a few features that bear more or less resemblance to evils that helped send Rome toppling. What the extrapolationist fails to say here is that for every feature in common there are many totally unlike in the two civilizations.

Contemporary America differs from ancient Rome in her systems of education, communication, and transportation, in agricultural methods and policies, in religious organization and manufacturing methods, in political theory and national organization—as well as in dominant world views, which in America are empirical and in Rome were authoritarian. Any comparison which rests upon a few selected elements and ignores a vast complexity of others is metaphor, not analogy. Unchecked, it can degenerate into pulpit pounding of the worst sort.

This example illustrates the urgency of the search for intellectual honesty. It also points to some specific steps in preliminary analysis of a sermon subject.

As early as 1928 Fosdick insisted that the sermon should

be "a co-operative dialogue" rather than a dogmatic monologue. This means that the preacher "must see clearly and
state fairly what other persons are thinking on the matter
in hand," rather than present only his own views. "He
may often make this so explicit as to begin paragraphs with
such phrases as, 'But some of you will say,' or 'Let us consider a few questions that inevitably arise,' or 'Some of you
have had experiences that seem to contradict what we are
saying'."[e]

In order to answer the listener's questions, doubts, and
objections, they must have been considered in the course of
preparing the sermon. Here are several helpful procedures:

(1) Reduce the entire sermon to a question and an
answer.

(2) Analyze your proposed subject and determine: (a)
To what degree is this subject controversial? Do listeners take
the conclusions for granted, or is there genuine conflict involved? (b) To what extent are you, the preacher, genuinely
interested in the subject? Do you propose to use it in order to
communicate vital conclusions, or merely in order to meet
the obligation of preaching on a particular Sunday? (c) Is
the subject defined so clearly that it can be adequately treated
in the time available?

(3) Simplify the central statement as much as possible,
bringing it to a sharp focus and phrasing it in everyday
language.

(4) List possible objections to the way in which you
have answered the main question.

(5) Outline a brief argument for a conclusion exactly
opposite to that which you present.

(6) Make a diagram or chart of your line of thought.
(Suggestions are given below.)

(7) Reach a clear idea of the nature of the problem

[e](242).

with which your sermon deals. (a) Is it a problem of truth, or a problem of policy? (b) Is it a restricted problem, of such nature that it must be answered either "yes" or "no"? Or is it unrestricted in nature—susceptible of being answered in a variety of ways?

(8) List the propositions used in the sermon, for which you advance no proof and treat as automatically accepted by your listeners. This may include such elements as, for example: the existence of a personal God, the divinity and humanity of Jesus, the nature of future states of reward and punishment. Careful observance of this principle of scrutiny will, incidentally, help you to clarify your own thinking on basic issues.

(9) List the primary wants of the listener which will be touched by your proposed treatment. In your appeal for acceptance of your proposition, do you offer satisfaction of desires for such ends as recognition, power, happiness . . . or do you appeal primarily to the listener's sense of duty?

(10) List specific ways in which your sermon will tell the listener *how* as well as *what*. That is, determine the extent to which you offer guidance to persons genuinely concerned, and eager to accept the solution you propose—but not knowing how to reach it in their own lives. There has been entirely too much preaching of the type which tells the listener what he should do, but offers him no plan by which to achieve the desired end.

VIGOROUS FORMS OF THE OUTLINE

There are many sermon types: expository, topical, biographical, textual, life situation, parabolic, symphonic. . . . Regardless of its type, the sermon is made up of introduction, body, and conclusion. Special functions are performed by the introduction and the conclusion; hence they are treated in separate sections of this chapter.

Sermon material may be divided into three major types: (1) communication units which pose questions; (2) units which serve connective, transitional, logical, and explanatory rôles; and (3) communication units which challenge to action or decision. These may be represented, respectively, by ?, →, and !. Using these symbols, the movement of any sermon may be reduced to a diagram.

Within the broad framework of introduction-body-conclusion there is room for a great deal of variety. One may take a general principle and apply it to particular problems; or he may cite a number of specific cases and draw a conclusion from them. He may contrast two alternatives and drive for acceptance of one; or he may pose a problem and plead for action on the single conclusion that he regards as possible.

Since the time of Demosthenes it has been generally agreed that the body of the address—no matter what its type—should be arranged in climax order. That is, there should be a building up of interest and power by presenting the weakest argument first and the strongest last, with intermediate material providing gradual transition.

At least two notable preachers have proved that the climax order is not so integral a factor as has been supposed. Brooks ignored the law of climax, and Fosdick actually made a habit of placing the intellectual peak of his sermon near the beginning. Harold Sonberg, making an objective study of the problem, found strong evidence that the traditional pattern is less effective than that of using one's best argument first and letting the others follow.[f] Lund reached a similar conclusion from an independent study, finding that the listener is most likely to be convinced when the most startling or challenging point is presented first.[g] (These studies

[f] (243).
[g] (244).

did not attempt to measure position-value of illustrations with emotional impact.)

These findings support other evidence that the traditional emphasis upon "sermon outline" is somewhat artificial. One may have a precise and orderly outline, yet produce a dreary sermon. One may violate some of the usual principles of outline, yet produce a vivid and dynamic message.

Hence this volume makes no attempt to suggest any particular type of outline that is likely to be effective under all conditions. Rather, our emphasis will be upon careful personal analysis of each sermon—with a view of always rearranging one's initial plan in order to make it as strong as possible in the light of material actually available for use.

Using the symbols indicated above, a typical Thanksgiving sermon is likely to look like (a) $\rightarrow\rightarrow\rightarrow\rightarrow\rightarrow\rightarrow\rightarrow$ or (b) $\rightarrow\rightarrow\rightarrow\rightarrow\rightarrow\rightarrow\rightarrow\rightarrow\rightarrow$! . An extremely emotional evangelistic sermon, calling for personal surrender at the altar, may look like this: (c) ! ! ! ! ! ! ! .

It is readily apparent that (a) moves smoothly toward a single objective, having neither alternatives nor emotional climax. It is also obvious that (a) is completely lacking in conflict. There are no major questions involved, and the listener is never in doubt as to the speaker's conclusion. It is simply a question of how much time and speech will intervene before that conclusion is reached.

Sermon (b) is the same type, modified only by addition of an element of challenge in the conclusion. Sermon (c) has plenty of emotional impact, but does not proceed smoothly toward a goal. There are a number of relatively disconnected communication units, each urging decision but none supported by logical explanation.

Brief attention to diagrams will unearth major difficulties in some familiar sermon types. Take, for example, almost any typical sermon preached on the text, "They let out four anchors from the stern, and prayed for day to come" (Acts 27:29). Development of this text usually comes to focus upon the four anchors. There is no logical necessity for the choice of any particular "anchors," so the outline of this sermon might be:

I. Introduction: statement of background of text.
II. Body: our need for anchors.
   A. Faith.
   B. Courage.
   C. Christian fellowship.
   D. Divine encouragement.
III. Conclusion: challenge to listener to "cast out four anchors" and find personal security.

Such an outline violates tradition at only one point: four, rather than three main divisions are included in the body of the sermon. Weakness of the sermon skeleton is not apparent in the outline; reduced to diagram form, however, however, the sermon looks like this:

$$\text{Courage}$$
$$\uparrow$$
$$\uparrow$$
$$\text{Faith} \leftarrow \leftarrow \ ! \ \rightarrow \rightarrow \text{Christian Fellowship}$$
$$\downarrow$$
$$\downarrow$$
$$\text{Divine Encouragement}$$

Beginning with a challenge (!), the sermon proceeds in four directions, then concludes with repetition of the initial challenge. There is no coherence in the challenge, no logic in the order of the points, no necessity for any particular set of points, no suspense or uncertainty in the development.

Many familiar texts lend themselves to "four anchor" treatment. Simply list any group of selected qualities, treat

them briefly in whatever order happens to occur to you, and
repeat the text in the conclusion—you have a sermon, of
sorts. It is clear that the spread of such a sermon is too great;
there is no powerful impact at any point.

A hunter who wishes to kill an elephant uses a rifle, not
a blunderbuss. All his power is concentrated in a single bullet, so that the thick bone of the target is pierced—while shot
from a blunderbuss would only sting the animal's tough
hide.

Using the same four-anchor text, a far more vigorous
development may be arranged. Here are the major elements
in the Biblical passage: (1) personal danger—the storm;
(2) strong efforts to help selves—casting out anchors; (3)
appeal to God—prayer for day and light. Thus we have the
following potential material:

> *Suspense*—what will happen in the storm?
> *Challenge*—the necessity of some action.
> *Specific action:*
>   Self-help—throwing out anchors;
>   Appeal for divine aid—praying for day.
> *Victory*—riding out the storm.
> *Concluding challenge*—challenge to listener to ride
>   out personal storms by doing his own best and
>   turning to God for aid.

These elements may be combined in a number of ways,
one of which is:

I. Introduction: emphasis upon frequency of
    storms in life.
II. Body: *question*—What can be done?
    A. Make strenuous efforts (throw out an-
        chors).
    B. Throw self upon God for help.

III. Conclusion: achievement of success; challenge
     to use same procedure in personal problems.

Reduced to diagram form, this sermon becomes:

$$! \rightarrow ? \begin{array}{c} \rightarrow \rightarrow \\ \rightarrow \rightarrow \end{array} !$$

Another familiar type, often termed the "jewel" sermon, presents several facets of a single truth. Like the "four
anchor" skeleton, it may begin and end on a single note of
challenge. But instead of spreading, the various ideas of the
sermon converge on a single goal, thus:

$$\begin{array}{c} \downarrow \\ \rightarrow \rightarrow \; ! \; \leftarrow \leftarrow \\ \uparrow \end{array}$$

In debating the respective merits of "four-anchor" and "jewel"
preaching, the two types may be compared with tent stakes.
In the former case, one takes four stakes and gives each a
single blow. In the latter, one takes a single stake and gives
it many blows. It is beyond dispute that the latter will sink
deeper and be much harder to pull out than the former.

Chapter X includes a detailed discussion of conflict in
the sermon. A message may drive toward a single goal, may
present two strong alternatives, or offer a combination of
weak and strong alternatives. Any combination of units (? , !
and →) may be fitted into any of these conflict patterns.

In general, the diagram of a strong sermon will include
all three types of communication units, blended so as to be
coherent and smooth. Any sermon that consists exclusively
of one type unit should be questioned.

Some weak forms are:

→ → → → → → → →   (One look indicates
the lack of vitality; this is almost certain to be very
dull.)

? ? ? ? ? ? ? ?   (Strong in conflict, but
weak in logical support and lacking in positive
challenge.)

! ! ! ! ! ! ! !   (Full of challenge, but
lacking logical support and conflict.)

Some strong forms are:

? → → → → → → → !   (Catching listener-in-
terest through conflict, then moving through logical
steps to challenging conclusion.)

→ → → → →
?   → → → → → !   (This sermon presents two
→ → → → →   strong and contrasted alternatives, so is especially high in conflict. It may
be varied by making one or the other alternative
much stronger than the other, and by introducing
an element of challenge in the climax.)

Regardless of the shape of the skeleton selected for a
particular message, it is essential that sufficient flesh be available. As a general rule, it will prove helpful to gather
enough material for a forty minute sermon, then cut it to
twenty-five minutes. Attention, interest, suspense, and conflict may be greatly augmented by suitable illustrations; see
Chapters VIII-XI.

EMPHASIS

All methods of giving emphasis in oral address may be
divided into three categories. Though only one of these is

connected with the order of the sermon, the entire matter is treated at this point.

Arrangement of the outline can produce two types of emphasis. Of these, position is obvious. Especially if it has intrinsic vividness, material has considerable emphasis value when included in the first or last paragraph of a spoken message.

Deliberate use of repetition is a far more powerful device. Since ancient times, it has been recognized that frequent use of a phrase or an idea causes the listener to remember it. Vivid examples may be found in several of the great speeches in Shakespeare's major plays. Poe made superlative use of repetition in "The Raven" and Whitman employed the same device in "It Sit and Look Out" as well as "Song at Sunset." Franklin D. Roosevelt was so impressed by the latter two poems that he studied them for style, and himself became a master of repetitive devices.[h] Charles James Fox, one of the outstanding political orators of his century, bluntly admitted that in debate he considered it just as effective to "dish out the same reason in ten different forms" as to offer ten different reasons.

Johann Friedrich Herbart's famous "five rules for effective teaching" actually reduce to three: preparation, presentation, and recapitulation. That is, the great analyst held it necessary that the speaker prepare the mind of the listener, enlarge upon that preparation, then summarize the message and drive it home. That is nothing more than a sophisticated version of the old formula: "Tell 'em what you are going to say; say it; tell 'em what you've said."

Several extensive studies have been made; of these, the most helpful was guided by Arthur Jersild. On the basis of exhaustive tests, he concluded that repetition is the most ef-

[h] (245), 222.

fective single method of securing emphasis. It is highly significant that he found power of repetition greatest when the various presentations are separated by other items of discourse. And quantitative tests indicated that optimum emphasis comes from three repetitions; whereas the value of additional repetitions decreases rapidly with frequency.[1] Thus, six repetitions would have little more emphasis value than three; in the case of as many as nine repetitions, the last would add no emphasis and might prove boring.

Emphasis from content is largely a matter of style. An extremely vivid illustration tends to stand out above the surrounding context. This is one reason a good illustration must be pertinent; strong emphasis that is not directly related to the central theme may actually weaken the total impact of the sermon.

Vivid sentences are always more emphatic than commonplace ones. An epigram or paradox gains impact power from its very form; interrogative and exclamatory sentences nearly always exert greater force than simple declarative sentences.

Emphasis in delivery is comparatively easy to achieve, and produces rather high test results. Shouting and banging on the pulpit does not, however, produce so great emphasis as simply directing the listener's attention to a forthcoming statement. "This is central in the sermon," or "It is important that you get this . . ." is probably the most effective single verbal mode of emphasis. Reaction to humor or emotional elements may be greatly increased by giving the listener notice that he should be alert for forthcoming humor, pathos, hope, joy, or other elements.

Variation in the speed of speech and pitch of the voice are also valuable; in general, such variation brings emphasis chiefly when the change is in the direction of greater speed

[1] (246), 620.

and higher pitch. Slow speech in a low tone tends to detract from rather than supplement emphasis.

Any attempt to formulate a precise rule for good introductions is defeated in advance; the rôle of the introduction necessarily varies with the nature of the speech occasion. Given a well-organized and expectant audience, the introduction may do nothing more than state the line of development which will follow. But when confronted by apathetic listeners the speaker may need to secure attention in his introduction; given positively hostile listeners, the introduction may function as a means of gaining good will.

Guided by the needs of the particular occasion, the skillful speaker can use one of several types of introductions.

(1) *A startling statement* tends to jolt listeners out of their lethargy and attract their vital attenion. A famous example is that of the sermon whose first sentence was, "God is in the garbage can." Instead of adopting a conventional approach to God's omnipresence, the writer of that introduction deliberately set out to shock his listeners.

This example, while illustrating the possibilities, also reveals some potential dangers. If too far off the beaten path, a startling statement may win attention—but also arouse antagonism or false expectations. Should such an introduction suggest an emphasis that is not followed, it is an attempt to cheat the listener—to gain his attention by a piece of gaudy trickery. It is like the ruse of the preacher who attracted a large audience by his promise to exhibit something that never had been seen before, and never would be seen again. By way of making good his word, he shelled a peanut and ate it. Such cheap methods are not only open to question on ethical grounds; they are likely to antagonize the listener at the beginning of the sermon.

So the startling statement is valuable only if it is an honest introduction to the real topic of the speaker, and not so phrased that it offends the sensibilities of the listener.

(2) *Introductory anecdotes* are high in attention value. An indifferent audience may be awakened by an appeal to emotion or humor; a hostile audience may be softened by a hearty laugh at the speaker or the group he represents.

Like the startling statement, the introductory anecdote should be pertinent to the theme. Modern preachers rarely confront an audience of such nature that there is justification for telling a string of unrelated humorous stories. Provided that it is pertinent, the anecdote may be used to introduce almost any type of sermon. Before World War I, Fosdick was very influential in fostering the use of such introductions, which have since become widely popular.

(3) *A Biblical text* is among the most important traditional types of introduction. Such an introduction may be very effective—provided that it actually introduces. There is an increasing tendency to write topical sermons, then find some remotely related text and drag it in by the hair of its head. Use of such a text may be a springboard for the ensuing development of the topic, or it may be nothing more than a courteous bow to custom.

Familiarity with Scripture tends to reduce its attention value; hence, with rare exceptions, other types of introductions are more effective in winning attention. That is probably why Fosdick pioneered in the practice of reading his text after having won the interest of his listeners.

(4) *A direct question* is always a powerful form of address. Especially if it touches upon the "wish and strife life" of the listener does it tend to reach out and grasp his atten-

tion. As a sermon introduction the question has the additional value of indicating the major lines of the discussion.

(5) *Summary statements* may serve as introductions, especially in situations where the listeners are already giving strong attention. Such an introduction serves the additional value of affording an opportunity to gain emphasis through distributed repetitions.

(5) *Descriptive statements* may form an effective introduction, especially in biographical and historical sermons. Such an introduction should make strong use of concrete and vivid words, painting a picture that the listener can actually see or creating a mood that he cannot escape feeling.

Splendid examples of such introductions may be found in some of the stories of Edgar Allan Poe. There is no reason why the preacher should permit the writer of fiction to be a more skillful craftsman than he; many Biblical heroes lived under conditions that lend themselves admirably to vivid descriptive introductions.

No matter what its type, the lead should serve to win attention and to indicate the direction of the sermon. Poor introductions are usually dull, irrelevant, or both.

Perhaps the most common example of the introduction that is both dull and remote from the subject is the prolonged apology. No matter what its nature—whether the speaker has a sore throat, did not sleep well the night before, has lost his notes, or feels generally inadequate to meet the demands of the occasion—his apology is likely to be uninteresting and impertinent. It neither wins attention nor suggests the direction the speaker will take in the body of the message. Furthermore, it adds insult to injury by suggesting to the listener that he is expected to give his attention to a man who seriously doubts that he should be speaking.

In general, any type of introduction is valuable provided that it is interesting, pertinent, and relatively brief.

FUNCTIONS AND TYPES OF CONCLUSIONS

Two major purposes may be served by the conclusion: summary of the argument and challenge to specific application. Types are considerably less varied than in the case of the introduction.

(1) *A vivid anecdote* tends to help the sermon close on a note of high attention and interest. Such a conclusion is especially effective if the anecdote is directly related to the theme of the sermon, and is strong in emotional power. An irrelevant or loosely related conclusion may weaken the sermon rather than strengthen it.

(2) *Summary statements* have high value in terms of emphasis, but tend to be less vivid than anecdotes. A recapitulation should be quite brief, not attempting to strengthen the preceding argument but merely lifting out its major points. An epigram or paradox may frequently be used to achieve a clear-cut end.

(3) *A challenge to action* may serve as an effective conclusion to any sermon that gives the listener an opportunity actually to do something. Such a challenge gains effectiveness, not from logic, but from emotional power.

All the emphasis should be directed upon what to do rather than why. Argument is futile at this point; if the listener is not already convinced, he will not be won by fresh appeals to reason. But if he has accepted the preacher's conclusion, he may need a strong challenge in order to find incentive to act.

It is highly important that the conclusion, no matter what its type, be actually used to conclude. There is a common psychological phenomenon termed "talking past the point." This seems to grow out of a vague and undefined desire to press the argument, sensing that listeners are not yet convinced. After reaching and passing his conclusion, the speaker may rehash his entire sermon—usually presenting it in relatively monotonous and ineffective fashion. In extreme forms this practice produces most ninety-minute sermons—which are likely to be thirty-minute sermons repeated three times.

In order to avoid talking past the point, a specific conclusion should be prepared. Many speakers find it helpful to frame the actual wording of the last three or four sentences. These sentences have strong position value, and should be fresh and vigorous in style.

Like the punch line of sparkling humor, the conclusion gains force through exploitation of explosive qualities. Cutting off clean, with material of high quality, the speaker leaves the listener feeling "ready for more" rather than bored to inattention.

CONCLUSIONS

There are no standard patterns into which every sermon should fit; development of a particular idea must be shaped both by its nature and the type and extent of material available. However, a plan of some sort is essential.

It is important that the sermon subject be thoroughly analyzed, to determine whether or not it may be developed with intellectual honesty. Logic is to the sermon as a slip is to smart feminine attire—it isn't intended to show, but if it isn't there at all, people are sure to notice.

Given a sound idea and logical development, one should be certain that every message has a vigorous outline—including not only elements of exposition, but also conflict and emotional challenge. Weaknesses that are not apparent from examination of an outline become clear when sermons are reduced to diagram form.

Introductions and conclusions are of several types, and may play various special rôles; hence these sections of the sermon should receive special attention.

It is possible to make an analysis of any sermon, measuring the strength of the outline with approximate accuracy. Here is a scale that has been tested with student speakers; best results are secured when the preacher scores his own sermon before delivery, then has at least two listeners score it in the actual preaching situation.

SCALE FOR MEASURING SERMON OUTLINE

Test Factor	Strong	Medium	Weak	Absent
1. How sharp is the focus of the basic question?	30	20	10	−20
2. With what degree of clearness is a plan of action presented?	30	20	10	−10
3. How strong is the relation of the sermon to basic wants of listeners?	30	20	10	−30
4. What is the degree of intellectual honesty and logical clarity?	20	15	10	−10
5. Are transitional elements smooth?	15	10	5	−10
6. How much variety is there in type of communication units (?, !,→)?	30	20	10	−20
7. What degree of vividness is there in the introduction?	10	5	0	− 5
8. What degree of relevance is there in the introduction?	10	5	0	−10
9. What degree of vividness is there in the conclusion?	15	10	5	−10
10. What degree of relevance is there in the conclusion?	10	5	0	−10

A sermon scoring 120 or under needs to be reworked and strengthened; 125-150 indicates a good outline; 155 or more, excellent.

Chapter VIII

THE ILLUSTRATION: PUTTING FLESH ON THE BONES

IT IS A COMMONPLACE THAT MOST MASTERS OF PUBLIC address have been adept in the use of illustrative materials. Men so diverse as Chrysostom and Conwell, Spurgeon, Guthrie, Lincoln, Bryan, and Fosdick have been alike in their regard for the illustration as an integral component of speech. In the case of Beecher a careful analysis yielded the conclusion that "the one outstanding characteristic of his sermons is their wealth of illustrations. No other instrument of persuasion did he cultivate so painstakingly."[a]

An illustration may be serious or humorous, long or short. It may take the form of prose or verse; it may appeal primarily to the ears or chiefly to the eyes of the listener. There are only two qualities which remain constant, and are found in every illustration, no matter what its type, form, length, or application.

First, the illustration is a self-contained unit of communication. It has definite boundary lines—a beginning and an end. If removed from the surrounding context, its application may not be apparent, but it remains intelligible in its

[a] (247), 57; cf. (230), 22.

own right. That is to say, the illustration is a *Gestalt* of communication. There is a meaning of the whole that is more than the sum of meaning attached to the parts. An anecdote about John Wesley's blunders in Georgia cannot be completely dissected into words or even sentences. There are subtle overtones which are missing when mere parts are treated, but which become prominent when the illustration is regarded as a unit, a whole.

Second, every illustration serves a connective rôle. A strong element of comparison is involved, and the illustration is actually—in function if not in form—a more or less extended metaphor. This matter is so fundamental that it must be treated at some length.

METAPHOR AS A UNIT OF INSTRUCTION AND PERSUASION

Early in the construction of a house the plumbing contractor delivers a load of equipment. In terms of bulk, lengths of lead pipe are the most important pieces of material. Linked together, they will conduct water most of the distance it will have to travel in the new home. But such long, straight pieces are useless without elbows, T-joints, and unions. It is not the function of an elbow to convey water a great distance. Rather, it serves merely to change the course of the flowing water, to send it where it could not otherwise go.

That is the major rôle of metaphor. It diverts thought into new directions, making possible the formation of links between the known and unknown, the old and the new.

All learning and all discovery proceed by leaps of the mind; through recognition of similar and dissimilar, new experience is related to old and incorported into a system of knowledge. Take, for example, any simple class concept, such as "dog." Use of the same word to name a fox terrier and a St. Bernard involves an implied simile. Fox terriers are like St. Bernards in some respects; this condition of likeness is recognized by calling members of both groups by the same name.

Isaac Goldberg points out that name formation is always based upon linking the unfamiliar with the familiar.[b] *Broadcasting* of news and entertainment gets its name from the fact that radio waves are scattered in all directions, like the grain *broadcast* by a farmer when sowing his crop. Since radio is somewhat like a telephone system without wires, in the early days of the industry the man on the street insisted upon using a name that linked the strange new device with a familiar old one. Scorning *radio,* which had no link with the known, nonprofessionals termed the new device, "wireless telephony."

In the same fashion the automobile was widely known as the "horseless carriage." And though nothing comparable to telegraph lines is involved, comparison with the earlier form of communication produced the name *television.* This process has been going on for centuries. When Greeks became acquainted with a big cat that seemed to have qualities of both the lion and the tiger, they froze metaphor into name by calling the animal *leopard* (lion-tiger).

Bain concludes that "in every subject implying thought, . . . the power of identifying like things, through distance and disguise, is the main element of intellectual force."[c] Ribot challenges "anyone to produce a solitary example of invention wrought out in abstract. . . . Human nature does not allow such a miracle."[d] Joshua Gregory concludes that "the mind inevitably interprets the less understood by what is known or previously assumed—it does, and must, think by analogy."[e] And logician James E. Creighton affirms that "to explain is just to show that some fact or group of facts is re-

---

[b](248), 72.
[c](249), 341.
[d](182), 32.
[e](250), 264.

lated in an orderly way to some other fact or group with which we are acquainted."[t]

In order to clarify the meaning of these formal statements it is necessary to resort to metaphor!

Learning is like building a bridge. Every bridge is built with a single goal: to connect points which are separated by an obstacle. Actual building of the bridge is a slow process. Some firm point of departure is established, and using this as a base the construction pushes forward.

Likewise, mental growth consists in throwing out girders from the base of present knowledge. A child understands the meaning of "pear" by comparing it with the familiar "apple." An adult comprehends the significance of an instrument of atomic destruction only by comparing it with familiar T.N.T. and calling it a "bomb." A theologian, wrestling with the concept of atonement, is forced to use metaphorical language and describe the human race as "washed in the blood of the Lamb." Thus he links the abstruse idea of divine propitiation with a familiar ceremony of ritualistic sacrifice. An astronomer, confounded by radio waves which originate from unseen masses of matter in outer space, coins the paradoxical term, "invisible star." Thus he links the little understood "cloud of matter" with the familiar idea, *star*.

Effective preaching demands the use of devices that will help the listener form or use new links. Analysis of a specific example will (as always) make this principle clear—not by explanation, but by illustration. Take the following anecdote:

All the boys and girls of Wesley Sunday School were eager to help raise money for the building program. Tommy, the organist's son, was trying to save all his nickels; but it was a difficult job.

One night as he was saying his prayers, his mother heard him pleading earnestly:

[t](251), 309.

"Lord, please help me save my money for the church—and don't let the ice cream man come down this street!"

This story can serve as a bridge, persuading the listener to move from a position that he readily accepts to one that is a step in advance. Reduced to a diagram, that anecdote looks like this:

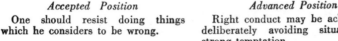

Accepted Position	*Advanced Position*
One should resist doing things which he considers to be wrong.	Right conduct may be achieved by deliberately avoiding situations of strong temptation.

Instead of attempting to jump from A to B—across a gap that may prove too wide for some individuals—the listener can leisurely and pleasantly make his way across the bridge of metaphor.

It is highly significant that metaphors abound in the gospels; Benjamin W. Robinson has counted 164 examples in the synoptics alone.[g] Extended metaphors, or illustrations, are chiefly in the form of parables. It is impossible to know whether or not the recorded sayings of Jesus are typical in their per cent of parabolic content. Some scholars believe the very large place which the parable plays in the gospel record is due to the fact that stories are more memorable than other forms of discourse. This much is certain: even the disciples noticed and were puzzled by Jesus' heavy reliance upon illustrations. On at least one occasion they inquired why He spoke in parables (Matt. 13:10).

Schopenhauer has a famous bit of advice to the effect that one should think like a philosopher, but speak like the

[g] (252), 114.

man in the street. Literal achievement of such a goal is impossible. Technical ideas are not susceptible to treatment in the language of casual conversation. One cannot explain marriage to a three-year-old. But abstract principles can frequently be made clear through a story, when every other form of explanation fails.

Jesus seldom gave a detailed dissertation on the meaning of a complex idea. He simply told stories about everyday life, then emphasized points of similarity between the familiar incident and the strange idea. Such treatment makes it possible to use emotional attachments much more effectively than in purely didactic speech. Hence the illustration serves to persuade as well as to instruct.

Part of the power of metaphor grows out of the fact that some degree of distortion is involved. No two things or situations are actually identical. Emphasis upon points of similarity involves treating points of difference as irrelevant for the particular comparison that is being made. To call a young woman a "budding rose" is to center upon a few selected points of likeness while ignoring many points of difference.

Consequently, no illustration conveys truth in every detail. When one attempts to find symbolic meaning in words or phrases that are not germane to the central point of the comparison, he quickly runs into problems. That is to say, there is not a one-to-one correspondence between the parts of the two entities compared. Beauty of a young woman may be like beauty of a rose, and dewdrops on a blossom may be compared with tender tears of love. But a rose has no parts whose functions are comparable to the hands, ears, eyes, or feet of a young woman.

Only the direct analogy attempts to establish one-to-one correspondence between parts. Such illustrative forms as the

anecdote and the parable usually focus upon a single aspect
of resemblance; at most a very few qualities may be compared. Though some ancient scholars attempted to find symbolic meaning in every word of every parable in the gospels, most modern interpreters agree that such a process
impoverishes rather than enriches the contribution of the illustrative parable.

Within limits, however, the illustration which distorts
reality by focus upon selected parts of an entity becomes one
of the most powerful units of communication. Just as a painter
produces a faithful portrait by selective distortion, rather
than by making a mechanical copy of his subject, so the
speaker makes truth vivid by using illustrations that over-
emphasize the relationship which he wishes to make clear.

Georges Seurat, founder of a school of impressionistic
art, once criticized Van Gogh for failure to copy nature exactly. Van Gogh replied:

> Tell Seurat that I should despair if my figures were correct.
> . . . Tell him that I think Michaelangelo's figures magnificent, even
> though the legs are certainly too long and the hips and pelvis bones
> a little too broad. . . . Tell him that it is my most fervent desire to
> know how one can achieve such deviations from reality, such inac-
> curacies and such transfigurations . . . Well, yes, if you like, they
> are lies; but they are more valuable than the real values.[h]

Wilbur M. Urban, who cites that statement with approval,
illustrates the point with a quotation from T. S. Eliot's
"Morning at the Window":

> I am aware of the damp souls of the housemaids
> Sprouting despondently at area gates.

Housemaids do not have damp souls. Neither do their
souls—wet or dry—sprout like corn. "Yet," concludes Urban,
"it is by precisely such deviations from the real that certain

[h](253), 23.

aspects of reality, otherwise inexpressible, are actually expressed."[1]

"A man who is anxious to speak wisely and also eloquently should strive," urges St. Augustine, "that he may be listened to with understanding, pleasure, and persuasion . . ." No other single communication form contributes so effectively to this triad of purposes as does the illustration. It is a speech tool that, properly used, has neither substitute nor equal.

CRITERIA OF THE "GOOD" ILLUSTRATION

All value judgments tend to be relative, based on subjective and functional standards. A "good" illustration is not an illustration that meets an inflexible standard, but one which serves the purpose for which it is intended. Following Augustine, three major purposes of speech may be distinguished:

(1) To interest the listener.
(2) To instruct the listener.
(3) To persuade the listener to action.

A particular illustration may serve a simple or complex purpose. It may have no function other than that of catching the listener's interested attention; it may be designed primarily to persuade the listener to act upon a principle that he already accepts. In general, however, the most effective illustrations will have all three qualities—interest will be linked with instruction and persuasion.

For working purposes a somewhat more precise analysis is necessary. There are at least six criteria by which an illustration may be judged.

(1) *Every illustration must be understandable.* We have already noted that effective metaphor proceeds from the known to the unknown. If the illustration rests upon a base outside

[1] (254), 473f.

the experience of any listener, it is impossible for that listener to walk over the bridge erected by the preacher. Each listener stands upon an island of experience; if he is to use the bridge its base must rest upon his own island. In the diagram below, Listener X can profit from Illustration (b) but not from Illustration (a):

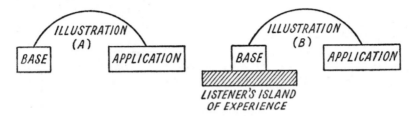

A listener's "island of experience" is itself composed of two major parts. There is an area of firm, well-drained land. This is the area of actual, physical experience. Around that center there is a strip of marsh, shallow near the shore but growing deeper and deeper in the distance. This marsh is the area of vicarious experience. In it are all the experiences gained at second- or third-hand. Accounts of others, books, pictures, and other media of communication give substance to the marsh.

Obviously, an "illustration bridge" that rests upon the central area of personal experience is more useful than one whose base is rapidly sinking in the ooze of a listener's third-hand experience.

Suppose you wish to illustrate a point by reference to the Holland Tunnel. Your bridge of metaphor will be offered to three types of listeners: (a) those who have no understanding whatever of the point of departure; (b) those who have read about the tunnel and who have seen pictures of it; (c) those who have actually been through the tunnel.

Persons in class (a) are untouched by the illustration;

their islands are separated from the base of the bridge by an expanse of water. Persons in class (b) can reach the base, but in order to do so, they must wade through a strip of swamp. Persons in class (c) can reach the bridge from the firm, dry land of personal experience:

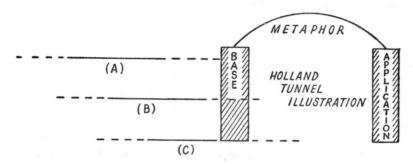

As with the listener, so with the preacher. He, too, lives upon an island of personal experience surrounded by marsh lands of second-hand knowledge. Without exception, his most effective illustrations begin within the area of his own first-hand experience. Material known only through reading or reports of others cannot afford the solid foundation necessary for building a cantilever bridge across some chasm of thought.

These four aspects of experience are made clear in the diagram below. Circle P-1 represents the actual, first-hand experience of the preacher, and Circle P-2 his total experience —including reading, imagination, and other sources. Circle L-1 represents the personal experience of the listener, and L-2 his total experience. Shaded areas indicate common ground.

If the listener is to understand an illustration, it must begin somewhere within L-2; its base must rest either upon his personal island or the surrounding marsh land. If the preacher is to give vitality to an illustration, it must originate within P-2. He cannot illustrate with material that is completely outside his own experience. An illustration that begins in the heavily shaded area—personal experience of both preacher and listener—is more understandable and vital than any other type of illustration. Second in value are those illustrations that begin in the lightly shaded areas.

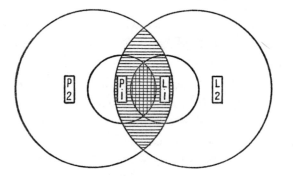

The number of listeners touched by an illustration varies directly with the frequency in which the starting point, or base, is found in ordinary experience. When a preacher quotes Hegel, he will reach perhaps one per cent of his listeners—those who have read Hegel. But when a preacher draws an analogy from an experience of holding a baby he may touch ninety-nine per cent of his audience—all who have ever held a baby or seen others do so.

If a speaker wishes to illustrate the insidious power of greed he will find numerous obscure stories in grand opera. But he will be wiser to describe a preacher eating a chicken dinner—pointing out that the preacher usually selects a breast, occasionally a back, and never a neck.

A description of the awe felt when standing on top of the R.C.A. building is not nearly so powerful as an appeal to so commonplace an experience as watching a calf take its first tottering steps. Many illustrations based upon travel or out-of-the-ordinary experiences actually tend to set the

preacher apart from his listeners. Thus, a reference to a painting seen on one's last trip to Italy touches only casually—if
at all—the experience of the listener. But when the preacher
describes sensations felt when forced to wade through mud
he creates a sympathetic bond with every listener who has
ever been caught in mire.

Jesus' illustrations are drawn exclusively from everyday
experience. He built bridges on bases erected in the kitchen,
market place, sheep cote, and banquet hall. From an early
study of the New Testament, Beecher concluded that "the
apostles were successful in their preaching because they began
with the experience of the audience and addressed their re-
marks to the wants of the audience."[j] That the young preacher
was profoundly influenced is without question; he, too, "got
sermons from shops and streets, ferries and factories; studied
life more than books."[k]

Here is an example of the type of illustrations that
proved effective in the first centuries of Christianity:

> When a man fills an ample number of jars with good wine,
> and among these jars there are a few half-empty, he does not pay
> attention to the full ones when he comes to his wine jugs, because
> he knows that they are full. But he is concerned lest the empty ones
> have turned sour, because empty jars quickly turn sour, and the
> wine's good taste is lost.[l]

It doesn't take an intellectual giant to apply that illustration
to the task of the Christian shepherd. Had the author selected
an obscure incident in Persian history, his illustration would
have been more scholarly but far less effective. Chrysostom
used metaphors from athletics—boxing, wrestling, and other
forms of physical competition; they are so frequent in his

[j] (255).
[k] (256), 360.
[l] *The Shepherd of Hermas*, Mandate V, 3.

sermons that one of his commentators could only term the number "extraordinary."[m]

Spurgeon and Beecher gained much of their power from ability to interpret the commonplace; so did Lincoln and Franklin D. Roosevelt. It is indicative of Roosevelt's approach that he reached the nation through "fireside chats" rather than through formal addresses. A student of his public speech reports that the president's style was obviously and avowedly influenced by the homespun fiction of Mark Twain. Like the novelist, Roosevelt was committed to the principle: "How welcome is the familiar to our ears—if sensitively used."[n]

(2) *A good illustration is pertinent.* Since the chief function of the illustration is to ease an intellectual or emotional transition for the listener, an irrelevant metaphor may actually detract from the sermon. Occasionally an illustration may be used for interest value alone, when the preacher wishes to gain attention in difficult circumstances. Such situations are rare, and even when they prevail do not justify extensive use of such material as a string of unrelated jokes.

This is perhaps the chief point of weakness in use of the illustration. When one discovers a story that has nearly everything in the way of interest-value and emotional impact, there is a temptation to split next Sunday's sermon down the middle, spread the story between the pieces, and nail them back together. As a rule, it is dangerous to use a story or anecdote that requires explanation. Unless a piece of material actually *illustrates* it does not deserve to be called an illustration.

J. H. Jowett has put the matter in unsurpassed form:

A lamp should do its own work. I have seen illustrations that were like pretty drawing-room lamps, calling attention to themselves.

m (257).
n (245), 224.

A real preacher's illustrations are like street lamps, scarcely noticed, but throwing floods of light upon the road. Ornamental lamps will be of little or no use to you: honest street-lamps will serve your purpose at every turning.[o]

(3) *A good illustration must be fresh.* Even St. Paul, whose letters do not abound in major illustrations, insisted that "speech always be gracious, seasoned with salt" (Col. 4:6). "Give them manna fresh from the skies," insisted Spurgeon to his students; "not the same thing over and over again, in the same form *ad nauseam*, like workhouse bread cut into the same shape all the year round."[p]

Laboratory tests support Spurgeon's plea: "From stock anecdotes may both ourselves and our hearers be mercifully delivered."[q] Jokes told an audience of college students, then repeated after an interval of six months, fell nearly 33 per cent in funniness rating.[r] This reduction in impact grew out of a single repetition. One palls at the thought of the astronomical figures required to express the loss in power when an illustration has been heard, off and on at irregular intervals, from the lips of one preacher after another.

Nearly all the illustrations found in standard expository works and in anthologies compiled for sale to preachers are worthless in the existing form. So are stories read in major magazines, heard over radio or television, or told at meetings of civic clubs. No matter how fresh one of these gems may seem when discovered by the preacher, there will be some listener who knows it by heart—if, indeed, half the audience do not begin to groan inwardly when they recognize the faltering footsteps of a senile anecdote.

Three factors contribute to the element of freshness.

[o](258), 140.
[p](202), I, 211.
[q](202), I, 221.
[r](259), 407.

First, vitality in spoken style can give life to an illustration, no matter how well-worn it may be. Such treatment, however, is seldom worth the cost in effort. It is like spending $1,250 to repair an old car when the rattletrap could be turned in on a new model at a cost of only $900. No matter how many new parts are added to a jalopy, you still have an old car.

Second, one may give a new twist to an old story. Provided that the fresh application is valid and revealing, such treatment may be extremely effective. Some students of humor hold that listeners actually prefer situations so familiar that everyone knows just when to laugh. Careful adaptation of old material is known to professional humorists as "making a switch." Preachers can use this technique with as much success as popular entertainers.

Finally, an illustration may have intrinsic freshness. This is of course the highest form of novelty, and usually is found only in the case of material derived from the speaker's personal experience. Much good material is not available for use; anything gained in counseling, and anything that might injure even one listener, must be carefully edited if not omitted.

An illustration that cannot be judged fresh by one or more standards is at best a questionable asset to a sermon.

(4) *A good illustration must be convincing.* Unless the listener accepts the validity of the comparison involved in the illustration, he does not cross the preacher's bridge of thought. Two elements reduce the power of an illustration to convince: errors in fact, and statements that offend the common sense of the listener.

Errors in fact grow out of borrowed illustrations more often than first-hand experiences. Given a published anecdote, derived from a field unfamiliar to the preacher, it is very easy to base a comparison upon gross error. For example, a widely-sold book of sermon illustrations contains a story about the planting of "mummy wheat." According to it, archeologists once found a few grains of wheat in an Egyptian tomb. They planted it, and were rewarded by six or eight stalks of grain quite different from modern varieties.

This seems to be a powerful illustration of salvation—breaking through the husk of sin like the germ of wheat lying dormant for 3,000 years, the soul attains a thrilling new life! Accepting that story without questioning its accuracy, I once used it in a sermon to a group of farmers. After the service, some of them—graduates of the state college of agriculture—called me aside and gave me the facts concerning the maximum life of untreated wheat germ. My palpably false illustration had not only served no good purpose; it had effectively prevented these listeners from accepting those elements of the sermon that were accurate and valid.

Not only is it dangerous to use published illustrations without a careful check; one should also be accurate in his historical, biographical, literary and scientific allusions. This is most obvious in the case of Scripture references; numerous persons will note and be momentarily or permanently distracted by a mistake in an illustration drawn from the Bible. But nearly every congregation will include listeners who notice other types of errors.

An occasional minor inaccuracy is not likely to be fatal to persuasion of the listener. But when errors accumulate, they tend to neutralize the positive effect of a message.

There is a legend in Atlanta concerning an evangelist who was once invited to go out to the railroad shops and address several thousand workmen in a special service. He made a hasty and superficial attempt to master railroad lingo, then went out and preached about "Catching the Heaven-

bound Limited." As the congregation dispersed, a big machinist muttered the sentiments of the whole crowd: "There
are two things that preacher doesn't know anything about—
railroads and religion!"

Not only should the preacher stay within areas in which
he is reasonably well informed, and even there check any
questionable statements; he should avoid the made-up
"preacher story" like the plague. Nearly every "encyclopedia
of illustrations" includes stories, all shiny with pretty-pretty
moral applications, that do not make even a cool nod to
probability.

There is a well-worn temperance illustration, cited in
Chapter V, which tells of a man who brought a rattlesnake
into his home as a pet. Months passed, and the fellow grew
more and more fond of the snake. One day, however, it became angry and bit the man's small daughter. She died, of
course, on the way to the hospital!

Actually, a rare individual might be foolish enough to
make a pet of a rattlesnake without having his venom removed—but the idea places a terrific strain on the listener's
credulity.

Here is the skeleton of a story that made the rounds
late in 1952: Chinese communists accuse an American missionary of treason. Without giving him a trial, they sentence
him to have his hands cut off. Through the whole grim business, the Christian keeps his composure. In fact, his poise so
infuriates the communist leader that after cutting off the missionary's hands he announces that the foreigner must be de-
capitated as well. Lying with his head on the block, bleeding
to death from severed wrists, the missionary says: "Communist, if you ever get to America, tell my son to come and
take my place in China!" Then he dies like a hero.

That can be handled in such fashion that it is an ex-

tremely moving story. But the critical listener is not satisfied. How did the story get to America? It may be taken
for granted that the communists did not spread it; nothing
in the account indicates that there were Christian witnesses
to the execution. Without explanatory details giving sources,
such a story sounds suspiciously like a new and supercharged
model in the famous old line of preacher stories.

Two cautions should be observed. First, check statements of fact; if possible, secure verification from well-known
authorities. Second, give the source of factual illustrations
that cannot be checked. If an illustration is found in print
without source references and separated from explanatory
context, it should be viewed with suspicion and used with extreme caution. Many militant Christian groups are guilty of
printing and circulating tracts which include "factual" illustrations that are patently made-up stories not even having
a speaking acquaintance with real life.

Every illustration, argument, and proposition should be
scrutinized in the light of the reaction it might produce when
heard by a skeptical listener. For example, a well-known
contemporary speaker, addressing great audiences in many
parts of the nation, customarily offers to pray for his listeners—by name and in terms of requested petitions—daily for
an indefinite (unspecified) period. Reflection shows only three
possible results of such an offer: (a) the speaker gets little
or no response; (b) he gets a large response, but cannot be
faithful in keeping his promise because of the tremendous
amount of time involved; (c) he is a charlatan, making the
offer for no other purpose than to parade his own piety. No
matter which of these should be believed by the listener, the
speaker's influence is weakened or destroyed.

Stories which strain the credulity of the listener, or are
of doubtful authenticity, need not necessarily be discarded.
It is always possible to use a made-up or doubtful story by

treating it as a parable or fable. Frank statements in such cases will strengthen the authority of those illustrations that are actually authentic.

One other type of pulpit dishonesty should be scrupulously avoided: the temptation to tell a second-hand story as a personal experience. It is true that the approach, "It happened to me. . . ," tends to create greater interest value. But leaving aside the moral problem, it is a matter of some importance that one conviction of dishonesty brands a preacher as a liar. A story gleaned from some version of *Homiletical Gems*, and retailed as a personal experience, is quite likely to be recognized. After all, other preachers own that book, too. That very story may have been used with this congregation a few months or years before.

Dishonest use of stories is like sipping alcohol; there may not appear to be much danger in strict moderation—but it is far safer never to cultivate a taste for the heady stuff.

(5) *A good illustration must be commensurate with the theme.* Trivial ideas may be illustrated by commonplace allusions. But a great idea requires a majestic illustration—else the idea is weakened by the company it keeps.

Legend has it that an American traveler once bought a necklace in a Parisian pawnshop. He paid only a small amount for it, but when the piece was cleaned, it was found to be genuine jade—bearing an inscription proving that Napoleon once gave it to Josephine. Now, the permanence of that inscription can be cited as an illustration of the enduring nature of God's image in mankind. But the illustration is not so lofty as the idea it would illuminate. In the same way it weakens a sermon to compare God's judgment with the tenacity of the Canadian Mounted Police. It is far more appropriate to show that God's judgment is as inevitable and majestic as the returning of the tide.

Any illustration that cheapens the argument, or tends to

divert the listener's mind into less exalted channels, should be avoided.

(6) *A good illustration must have interest value.* Unless the listener's attention is held, he will not be persuaded to take the mental and/or spiritual leap which the preacher proposes. An insipid anecdote is like lukewarm coffee—not fit to drink, but filling the cup so effectively that there is no room to pour in enough to make it hot.

Much of the discussion in the chapters on "Attention" and "Style" is pertinent at this point. In addition, it is impossible to place too much emphasis on the significance of sympathetic projection into the actual atmosphere of an illustrative story. To tell a story effectively, the speaker must enter the situation in his imagination.

According to early Methodist tradition, Lord Chesterfield sometimes sat in Lady Huntingdon's pew when Whitefield was preaching. On one occasion the evangelist illustrated a point by describing a blind beggar's progress along a winding road. Soon the traveler was deserted by his little dog, and forced to tap his way along the side of a sheer cliff. Stumbling, he dropped his stick. He stopped to pick it up, leaned over the edge of the precipice, and began swaying. "Great God," cried Chesterfield, "he's gone!"

That sort of interruption is the highest tribute a listener can pay a speaker. As a rule, the preacher is afraid that he will be accused of acting. So he speaks casually about the stoning of Stephen and makes Nathan's visit to David as commonplace as a trip to the corner store.

CONCLUSIONS

Contrary to some schools of thought, the illustration is not merely ornamental in nature. It is a special type of communication unit—an extended metaphor—whose function is to convey information as well as stir emotion. No phase of the preacher's art is more important than the mastery of illustrative techniques; persuasive power is very closely related to skillful use of comparisons by which bridges are built between the known and the unknown, the accepted and the questioned.

Illustrations are self-contained units, with definite boundary lines. So clear are the essential criteria of good illustrations that it is possible to measure material with some accuracy. Using the following scale of values, you can determine the approximate usefulness of any illustration. Note, however, that the total score of a particular piece of material is not a constant, but a variable. The context surrounding an illustration and the audience hearing it affect the ratings of almost all criteria. Hence, it is necessary to score a piece in connection with each message in which it is used and each congregation to which it is presented.

SCALE FOR MEASURING THE ILLUSTRATION:

Criterion	Very high	High	Low	Absent
1. Degree of intelligibility	25	20	10	−20
2. Degree of pertinence	25	15	10	−15
3. Degree of freshness	25	15	10	−10
4. Degree of credibility	25	15	10	−10
5. Degree of commensurabil- ity with theme	25	15	10	−15
6. Degree of interest value	25	20	10	−20

An illustration with total score of 60 or less may be regarded as of poor quality; good, average illustrations will score 65-95; a total of 100 or more indicates high-quality material for use on a particular occasion.

Chapter IX

HUMOR IN THE PULPIT

WITH CHARACTERISTIC ABRUPTNESS, WILLIAM L. STIDGER declares, "God knows that we preachers need a touch of humor."[a] Phrased in such fashion, his emphasis has undercurrents that come close to profanity. But this chapter seeks to support the conclusion that it is an affront to the God whom we serve to neglect skillful use of humor in our preaching.

A few preachers are criticized—chiefly by other preachers—for relying too heavily on humor. There have been few great speakers or writers, lay or clerical, who have scorned its use. By its use one can produce effects that can be secured in no other way. Yet the preacher who handles humor effectively is a rarity; large numbers of his colleagues either avoid it altogether or present it with extreme ineptness.

PSYCHOLOGY OF HUMOR

Since the time of Aristotle humor has received considerable attention from analysts. However, laboratory investigations were not initiated until the second decade of the present century. Since that time there has been a large volume of

[a] (260), 77.

literature growing out of special studies. Numerous theories of humor have been advanced. While there are many controversial aspects of the problem, there is a growing consensus on certain fundamental matters. At least four rather clearly defined principles may be discerned.

(1) *Disparagement* is a basis for much humor. Albert Rapp, whose approach is based largely upon an attempt to trace humor from primitive origins, holds that "laughter is a fundamental human reaction to *any* mishap," subject only to the check of sympathetic pain.[b] He supports that contention by citing the almost universal tendency to laugh at accidents and brutality. Any weakness, says he, can be a target for jibes. For example, among the Greeks "a favorite humorous epithet for an old man was 'tombstone,' and for an old lady, 'raisin,' or other dried fruit."[c]

As early as 450 B. C., Sophocles held that "the pleasantest laugh is at the expense of our enemies." Five centuries later, Quintilian echoed that verdict, adding: "Sayings designed to raise a laugh are generally untrue and never complimentary. Laughter is never far removed from derision."

Stephen Leacock would reduce primitive humor to "the sense of personal triumph over one's enemies, the sense of delight in seeing something—anything—demolished or knocked out of shape."[d] Certainly, these elements contribute to much slapstick comedy and to comic books.

On the basis of psychological study of modern race-disparagement jokes a group of scientists concluded that any "unaffiliated object" in a disparaging situation can give rise to laughter.[e] Virtually the same conclusion is voiced by a professional gag-writer, who analyzes his own work by saying:

[b] (261), 39.
[c] (261), 37.
[d] (262), 24.
[e] (263), 344.

"Any laugh-getting enterprise . . . is based upon one trick—
the building up of an emotion, and the acceptable release of
that emotion. . . . I suspect that emotion is plain, old-fashioned
hostility."[f]

(2) *Superiority* on the part of the laugher is a major
element in many types of humor. It is closely related to disparagement, and perhaps inseparable from it except in theory.

Thomas Hobbes seems to have been first to offer a clear
theory of superiority as the basis of much humor. He developed that idea in both *Human Nature* and the *Leviathan*;
numerous thinkers have subsequently accepted his conclusions:

> Laughter is nothing but sudden glory arising from some sudden
> conception of some eminency in ourselves, by comparison with the
> infirmity of others, or with our own formerly. . . . That laughter
> consisteth in wit, or as they call it, in jest, experience confuteth, for
> men laugh at mischances and indecencies wherein there lieth no
> wit nor jest at all.[g]

Rapp points out that "in the *Iliad*, where we find humorous
laughter in its simplest form, it is always the person who
stands in the superior relationship who laughs."[h] Baruch
Spinoza flatly declared that "a man hates what he laughs at."
And an experimental psychologist uses slightly different
language to express the same idea. We laugh, says Carpenter,
"because occasions of laughter permit us to recognize and
glory in our own good sense."[i]

This theory gives a plausible explanation of laughter
that ranges from guffaws over the physical buffets suffered by
a clown to titters which result from a pun. Both situations
cause the laugher to feel his superiority.

[f] (264), 12.
[g] (265).
[h] (261), 61.
[i] (266), 253.

(3) *Release from suppression* appears to be a third source of humor. It has been mentioned by T. G. Andrews[j] and J. C. Gregory,[k] as well as by Rapp, who holds that "any joke can be made funnier by giving it added suppressive content, by having it tap an impulse which has been restrained."[l]

According to this view, when authority is flouted, laughter is always possible. No other theory accounts for the manner in which persons of diverse cultural background laugh at stories which violate social standards. Among present-day Americans and Europeans a joke which taps sexual repressions is likely to be far more explosive than one whose humor depends upon seeing diverse, but innocent, meaning in a pun.

Charlie Chaplin once told a reporter that he believed the highest function of humor to be "public confessional." He declared that the humor in his own pictures was based upon his "doing what people would like to do, but dare not—as slapping a dowager."[m]

Laughter is especially loud where some sort of authority is made to look ridiculous. For example, take the following story:

A well-known Methodist bishop, starting out on a speaking tour, delivered his initial address to the men's club of a large church. He told several fresh, sparkling anecdotes. But because he wished to repeat them at other meetings, he requested reporters not to include any of them in their accounts.

A cub reporter turned in a glowing report of the occasion. He gave a concise summary of the address, then concluded: "The bishop also told a number of good stories that cannot be published."

While there are overtones of suggestiveness in that anecdote, the chief laugh-getter is the manner in which a person of authority is made to look ridiculous. Total laughter in re-

[j](267), 223.
[k](266), 250.
[l](261), 110.
[m](268), 68.

sponse to this story is likely to be greatest when the audience is made up of preachers who have more or less tendency to kick against the pricks of episcopal authority.

(4) *Incongruity* is a fourth major source of humor. Analysts from Aristotle to Schopenhauer have agreed on this point, if no other. Says the German: "The cause of laughter is simply the sudden perception of the incongruity between a concept and the real object."

Modern psychological studies tend to support such a view. Stephen Leacock puts it like this: "The perception of incongruity is the primal source of laughter, but where ends are standardized as in social life, we have the permanent conditions of laughter, since any departure from social standards is incongruous."[n]

Importance of this factor is indicated by analysis of humor in music. Experimental studies show that music alone —without title or program—can express humor. Sudden contrast, or incongruity, has been isolated as "the most frequent intrinsic source."[o]

Anything radically "out of character" is a potential source of laughter. Examples are: a minister in clerical garb riding a motor scooter, saucy lines on a tombstone, a freshman cap on the bust of the founder of a university, a motorist getting the better of a law-enforcement officer.

FUNCTIONS OF PULPIT HUMOR

At the beginning of this discussion, it is necessary to keep in mind the fact that any element of speech has value only in a functional sense. If, for example, the purpose of a particular occasion is to create a mood of passivity—as in prayerful self-examination—humor may be actually harmful. In general, however, the preaching situation involves a goal

[n](262), 253; cf. (205), 215.
[o](269), 566.

which is related to active moods. Given such a goal, humor can serve several purposes.

Entertainment of the listener is frequently considered beneath the dignity of the pulpit. People should come to church, it is argued, for the good of their souls. It should not be necessary to offer bait in the form of entertaining and interesting sermons.

Granted that the minister must not degenerate into a clown or showman, that the primary purpose of preaching is not entertainment, but regeneration of the listener, that it is possible to amuse an audience without moving even one listener toward a better life; granted all this, nevertheless, there remain some very important considerations.

No preacher can use his pulpit to lift the lives of persons who do not choose to bring themselves within sound of his voice. There are no laws to compel church attendance. Neither is social pressure a significant force in the average contemporary community. A few persons attend church because of pure love of God. Others listen to the preacher Sunday after Sunday because they have a strong sense of duty or have formed a habit of church attendance. Rarely are individuals suddenly impelled to begin attending church services because they are seeking answers to problems.

But the average respectable citizen has no more than good-natured tolerance for sermons. Unless he is definitely *attracted* to the house of worship, he will go fishing, look at television, sleep, arrange a round of golf, or take the family on a trip in preference to even a spasmodic round of sermon-tasting.

Nothing in the history of preaching indicates that sinners are converted by dull sermons only. Perhaps, after all, it is wholesome and right that the listener should enjoy at least some elements of a sermon.

It must also be remembered that the preacher has an

obligation to children and youth. Youngsters who are full of the joy of life cannot be expected to listen eagerly to a somber and spiritless dissertation on some abstruse aspect of Christian apologetics. Organization of a "children's church" may be a disguised and sugar-coated admission that the typical sermon cannot hold the attention of today's uninhibited youngster. Preaching, to a degree greater than any other public speech situation, should be family-centered. This necessarily involves deliberate use of elements that will appeal to younger members of the family.

Jesus did not consider it beneath His dignity to give His listeners an occasional hearty chuckle. He built incongruous, laughter-provoking statements upon the idea of lighting a lamp and placing it in an absurd place—"under a bushel, or under a bed" (Mark 4:21; Luke 11:33; Luke 8:16). He told a delightful story about the stupidity of a group of young women who went to an all-night party without sufficient oil for their lamps. In that day only a fool would do such a thing. Yet the improvident girls had the cheek to ask their friends: "Give us some of your oil, for our lamps are going out" (Matt. 25:3-8).

Much of Jesus' incidental humor is overlooked by readers who view the ancient speech-situations reported in the gospels through modern eyes.

It is hard to escape the conviction that herdsmen and farmers broke into chuckles at the sudden incongruity in the query: "What did you go out into the wilderness to behold? A reed shaken by the wind? Why then did you go out? To see a man clothed in soft raiment?" (Matt. 11:7; cf. Luke 7:24-25).

Again, there is a story of a rich man who was a hard master. One of his servants, discharged for incompetence, makes a comment that must have provoked a roar of laughter from Jesus' hearers: "What shall I do, since my master is taking away the stewardship from me? I am not strong enough to dig, and I am ashamed to beg" (Luke 16:1-3).

Polarization of the audience is strengthened every time listeners join in any demonstration of amusement. Given an extremely heterogeneous and unorganized congregation, the preacher may well devote several minutes to humor of such type that he gains the undivided attention of his listeners. Many a sermon is like a load of hay that must be stacked for winter; by using a small portion of it as a cover, the bulk of the material is preserved in desirable form.

Such initial humor should be tailored not only to attract and polarize attention, but also to create a bond between speaker and listener. This is best accomplished by making the speaker the butt of his own humor. Should one adopt the opposite course, making himself the hero of his anecdotes, he creates a definite barrier to effective communication.

This fact, which seems rather strange at first look, is actually an outgrowth of psychological bases of laughter. Nearly all forms of laughter flatter the ego of the laugher. Children and adults alike scream at the antics of a circus clown because his fumbling, stumbling, and stupid mishaps enhance the superiority-feeling of the laugher. A gale of laughter results when the clown walks off the back of an elephant and tumbles in the sawdust. Basic meaning behind resulting guffaws is: "Look how stupid that fellow is! I am much more intelligent. I would not make so foolish a mistake!"

Physical setting of the preaching situation tends to create a psychological gulf between speaker and listener. Elevated in such fashion that the listener must look up to him, the speaker also represents an honored group in society. Furthermore, he is the official representative of the religious institution. For the moment at least, he is the epitome of authority.

Many listeners tend to be intimidated, to occupy subordinate rôles in the conversation group. In order to create a strong "we" feeling, the preacher must bridge the gap and come down to the level of the listener. No device accomplishes this so quickly and effectively as humor directed at the preacher himself.

Emotional conditioning results from careful use of humor. Any overt reaction on the part of the listener breaks down his reserve. This applies not only to repetitions of similar stimuli, but also to quite diverse stimuli. Thus, a person who has laughed heartily is sympathetic to suggestions tending to produce indignation, tears, or physical action such as responding to an evangelistic invitation.

Hearty laughter actually has physical as well as mental effects. Large supplies of oxygen are inhaled. Major organs receive a sort of "natural massage." Tension disappears, and is succeeded by a general feeling of well-being.

Humor is a special vehicle of communication, a variety within the class, "illustrations." It can convey meaning that is difficult or impossible to express through any other medium.

Ernest Harms holds that "there is no doubt that there are imaginary or pictorial factors in humor that cannot . . . be expressed in any other way."[p] Take the following case, in which a down-trodden widow was victor over a pompous civic official. Full of incongruity and leading to a feeling of satisfaction on the part of all victims of the social system, humorous overtones convey subtle meaning that could be expressed in no other form:

"In a certain city there was a judge who neither feared God nor regarded man; and there was a widow in that city who kept com-

[p](270), 355.

ing to him and saying, 'Vindicate me against my adversary.' For a while he refused; but afterward he said to himself, 'Though I neither fear God nor regard man, yet because this widow bothers me, I will vindicate her, or she will wear me out by her continual coming.' " (Luke 18:2-5).

Satire, irony, and more direct forms of humor can frequently make it easy for the listener to grasp an emphasis. Even if capable of being expressed in coldly prosaic dress, the stolid form of the idea would not gain ready entrance into the listener's mind. Especially where a vivid metaphor is involved the humorous unit of speech stands upon its own feet, quite apart from the entertainment value involved.

Humor, finally, is a major instrument of social control. Mark Twain put it like this: "Humor must not professedly teach, and it must not professedly preach, but it must do both if it would live forever."[q]

A person who is the butt of open laughter is likely to burn with rage. To be ridiculed in front of a crowd is an experience that may have far more lasting effects than physical punishment.

"There are few who would not rather be hated than laughed at," points out Sydney Smith.[r] Some primitive societies actually employ laughter as a method of punishment for those who violate the mores.[s] K. M. Wilson notes that "all humorous situations are disagreeable if taken seriously,"[t] and Harold Hoffding regards humor as a sort of "fundamental propensity"—a force of far greater significance than is generally recognized.[u] In another context he points out that "the mere possibility of employing laughter as a weapon shows that it involves the idea of power."

[q](271), 37.
[r](272), Lecture II.
[s](273), 710; note 1.
[t](274).
[u](275).

Analyzing humor directed against the heads of modern totalitarian states, Obrdlik concludes that it

is a social phenomenon the importance of which, under certain circumstances, may be tremendous. It originates in the process of social interaction and bears marks of the particular group by which it was created and accepted. . . . The specificity of the gallows-humor type lies in that it is always intentional in the very real sense of the word. Not humor-for-humor, but humor with a definite purpose—that is, to ridicule, with irony, invectives, and sarcasm, in order to become a means of an effective social control.[v]

Known to sociologists as "gallows humor," the joke directed against the dictator flourishes in every tyrannical state. Many oppressed persons "even dare to collect the jokes as philatelists collect stamps."[w] Skillfully used, humor becomes an important instrument of social control. Many a movement has been literally laughed into oblivion.

Though the fact is not generally recognized, Jesus was extremely adept in such use of humor. Two factors make it difficult for modern readers to appreciate the full sweep of the Saviour's power with this weapon. First, we tend to read Scripture in a solemn mood, looking for emphases quite contrary to humor. Second, it is difficult for us to grasp the full impact of incongruity which rests upon first-century conditions, no longer prevailing in society.

In order to fully understand some of Jesus' statements we must adopt—in imagination—the ideas and attitudes that were characteristic of his actual listeners. These people were, in general, members of a low social and economic class, groaning under the oppression of legalistic religion applied with a greedy and tyrannical civil authority.

A few persons have seen the following passage as a great joke—a rich piece of satire:

[v] (273), 716.
[w] (273), 715.

"Woe to you, scribes and Pharisees, hypocrites! for you tithe mint and dill and cummin, and have neglected the weightier matters of the law, justice and mercy and faith; . . . You blind guides, straining out a gnat and swallowing a camel!" (Matt. 23:23-24; cf. Luke 11:42).

Remember that this was addressed to persons who probably did not tithe their gold—and who certainly considered it ridiculous to tithe garden herbs. Camels and gnats were very much a part of their everyday life, and the superb incongruity of straining out the insect and swallowing the beast of burden would bring a hearty laugh—enhanced by release of suppressed animosity toward the tyrannical priestly class.

Jesus scoffed at professional religionists for disfiguring their faces (Matt. 6:16), strutting about in pompous attire (Matt 23:5-7, Mark 12:38, Luke 20:45-7), and wiping the outside of their dishes while leaving the inside dirty (Matt. 23:26, Luke 11:37).

He jeered at them for acting like children, sulking at their playmates (Matt. 11:16-19); He accused them of having trumpets blown in order to attract attention to their acts of charity (Matt. 6:2-4). And He mocked the prayer of a hard-hearted oppressor of the poor who poured the oil of adulation over his own bowed head (Luke 18:10-11).

Swinging the cudgel of humor, Jesus attacked wealth and the wealthy. He declared that "it is easier for a camel to go through the eye of a needle than for a rich man to enter the kingdom of God" (Matt. 19:23-24; cf. Mark 10:25, Luke 18:25). Prosaic scholars with a background of 20th-century western culture have made far-fetched attempts to whittle that statement down to "sensible" proportions. Any such tampering destroys the incongruity which made the contrast laughable to those who actually heard it from the lips of the Master.

Modern preaching would be greatly strengthened by wider use of laughter as a persuasive device. Many an attitude or movement that resists frontal attack could be weakened—even conquered—by laughter.

DANGERS IN USE OF HUMOR

Since listeners are usually frank and sometimes boisterous in their approval of pulpit humor, the preacher may be tempted to place his chief emphasis upon entertainment. Instead of using humor as a tool with which to attract and shape listeners for his basic message, he may degenerate into a semi-professional funny man.

In general, what is regarded as overuse of humor is actually wrong use. Humorous material is dragged by the arm and made to stand in the breach of a sermon, whether supporting its conclusions or not. Anecdotes and situations are selected, not on the basis of their ability to illuminate a point, but solely upon the assumption that they will get a laugh. When a preacher adopts such a policy, his effectiveness is greatly reduced.

Far more common than this extreme position is a milder form of the same disease. Though humor is used with restraint, the speaker develops little skill in treating it as a basic sermon material. If the humorous portions of his message were deleted, the listener's understanding and acceptance of the main proposition would be unaffected. Such treatment grows out of the attitude that all humor is made of the same stuff. It is thought to be like water, having like nature in every case and adapting itself to the shape of its container. Actually, humor is more like ice than water. Every piece has definite shape.

A bit of humor is not wet concrete to be carelessly poured into a sermon to fill space between the joints. Rather it is like a small stone—just as important and just as inflexible as the great chunks of granite that make up the bulk of the structure. A humorous anecdote, though no larger than a man's fist, cannot be inserted just anywhere in any wall. It has utility only when it fits the space in which it is placed. Failure to observe this fundamental rule of building is the chief sin in use of pulpit humor.

But there is a second danger. Laughter that grows out of disparagement, and at the same time fosters feelings of superiority, may be strongly anti-Christian in its effects. There are sadistic, vindictive elements in many forms of humor. For example, Russell Maloney notes that the night after American forces announced the dropping of the first atomic bomb on Japan "there was not a comedy program (on radio or television) that didn't have its A-bomb joke."[x]

William L. Stidger says of a fictional friend, mouthpiece for many of his humorous stories: "Conrad has no racial prejudice, but he enjoys racial humor."[y] Psychological studies indicate that such a judgment is sheer nonsense—wishful thinking adorned with a halo.

"Laughter," points out Kimball Young, "socializes those who laugh together, but not as a rule the laugher and the laughee."[z] Murry found laboratory evidence, in terms of measurable emotional reactions, showing that "intense enjoyment of crudely disparaging jokes is chiefly an indication of repressed malice."[a]

Consequently, the preacher must be careful. His story of the ludicrous prayer made by an old Negro preacher is likely to cause his white listeners to rock with laughter. But the very process of enhancing their feeling of superiority

[x](264), 13.
[y](260), 101.
[z](276), 393.
[a](277), 81.

toward men of another race tends to nullify the good effects of his fervent sermon on Race Relations Day.

His anecdote (complete with gestures and dialect) concerning the way a small boy turned the tables on a greedy Jewish storekeeper may be very funny indeed—to his Christian listeners. But the thrust of disparaging humor may actually have greater effect than all his appeals for religious tolerance.

College students are traditionally broad-minded. But when psychologists tested groups of students they found that race jokes are definitely not funny to members of the race at which they are aimed.[b] These findings are apparently contradicted by publication of such books as Felix Mendelsohn's *Let Laughter Ring*. This volume is made up of humorous stories about Jews, and in 1941 was sponsored by the Jewish Publication Society of America. Consequently, it is actually not an example of bi-religious humor. Rather, it is a case in which members of a minority group laugh at one another. That is quite a different thing from being laughed at by members of a majority group.

In general, the preacher will do well to avoid all humor in which the foil is a member of another race or religious group. Many such stories can be revised, using the original incongruity but turning the humor upon a member of one's own group. In such cases it is always safe to direct the laugh toward the class represented by the speaker himself—making the butt of the joke a Methodist, Baptist, Congregational, Lutheran, Presbyterian, or Episcopal minister, as the case may be.

Here is a rule of thumb for measuring the suitability of humor: if it is not funny when turned upon a member of some group represented in the congregation, humor should be used with extreme caution.

[b] (263).

SOURCES OF PULPIT HUMOR

Jokes are the most abundant and available items in the field of spoken humor. At the same time, the joke is the least valuable form of laugh-getter for pulpit use.

Without qualification, situation humor is the most effective form the preacher can use. By "situation humor" is meant that which springs smoothly and spontaneously out of a real-life situation in which no false elements are introduced, but incongruity is sharpened and magnified.

For example, Harry Denman can throw an audience into hysterics with his oft-told account of discovering how many pairs of shoes a woman owns. As a bachelor, Denman assures the audience that he is quite ignorant of the ways of women. Then he describes a visit to the apartment of a business girl. Her closet door is open, and Denman stares in wonder as he notices the number and variety of shoes in the rack. He describes several types, contrasts her life with his own one-pair existence, and persuades the listener that it is absurd to be too greatly concerned with adornment of the body.

Genuine concern on the part of the speaker makes his account entertaining—and deeply meaningful as well. "The purest type of ironical humor," says Obrdlik, "is born out of sad experiences accompanied by grief and sorrow. It is spontaneously and deeply felt."[c]

Almost any type of situation introduced into a grossly inappropriate context become ludicrous. Advertisements for lipstick and nail polish are quite taken for granted when seen in magazines, heard over radio or television. But the identical advertisements, read in the course of a sermon and accented by vocal emphases, can prove hilarious.

[c](273), 715.

Humor which the preacher himself discovers in life situations is incomparably superior to any that he can get from printed sources.

This does not mean that published humor should be neglected. On the contrary, it may be used in two ways.

First, it can serve as a stimulus, leading the preacher to revise and reslant the published piece—or to use it as a springboard to devise an original application of the basic idea involved. For the latter purpose, the most fruitful source of raw material is cartoon humor published in leading mass-circulation magazines. After analyzing a comic drawing and discovering why it causes the reader to laugh, the minister frequently can adapt the laughter device to a new situation which lends itself to pulpit use.

Second, a great deal of published humor is suitable for use approximately "as is." Oral delivery of short material does not ordinarily involve infringement of copyright; if used in a sermon intended for publication, however, it is necessary to secure permission to quote. Some especially valuable forms are: anecdotes about ministers; stories about absent-mindedness; anecdotes about children; humorous epitaphs; limericks; tall tales; and boners. Some specific sources are listed by title in Chapter VI.

KEY FACTORS IN ORAL HUMOR

Listeners must be carefully considered in the selection of humor for oral use. Incongruity, suppression, superiority, and disparagement are not constant elements. Rather they vary from individual to individual and from group to group. Appeals to suppressed resentment of authority may seem staid to an ordinary congregation, but uproariously funny among cadets at a military school. Farm-linked humor may bring guffaws from a rural audience, but only polite smiles from a congregation of city dwellers.

There is no experimental evidence that there are national or racial differences in the sense of humor. Differences appear to be cultural. Americans laugh at mother-in-law jokes (though they do not always amuse mothers-in-law); Bantu tribesmen see nothing funny in such stories, for in Bantu society the mother-in-law has no authority.

Rapp holds that "a joke is, basically, a wit duel between the listener and the teller. So it naturally makes a difference who the listener is."[d] This means that one of the most important factors in oral humor is the audience. Material must be selected with specific listeners in mind. For an example of the way in which professionals fit material to the reader compare the humorous features in *Country Gentleman* with those in *The New Yorker*.

There are some general situations, such as family life, which are pertinent for any except the most specialized of audiences. But every homogeneous group has characteristics of its own; humor that is geared to the wants, likes, dislikes, and hopes of particular listeners will have maximum impact.

Audience factors may seem of no great significance to the minister who spends his life with a single congregation or with several that have very similar characteristics. Quite a different situation prevails when such a speaker addresses a group with different cultural, economic, racial, religious, or occupational background; or a highly specialized audience such as military personnel, school children, or delegates to a business convention.

Personality of the speaker is an equally important factor. No man can have real success with the use of humor that he does not himself enjoy and appreciate. There are subtle indications in voice, posture, and manner which reveal whether or not a speaker enters into an anecdote with zest. Abandon is infectious. Anticipating his own pleasure at the laugh

[d] (261), 143.

which he knows to be coming, the speaker gives unconscious signals to the audience.

Professional comedians are of the opinion that it is impossible to feign such an attitude. Telling a story out of sense of duty or necessity is like eating because a doctor has prescribed food. No matter how dainty and savory the dish, it does not really please, for appetite is lacking.

An experiment will prove the truth of this contention. Take some story that you have heard told at a gathering, and which brought a hearty laugh—in spite of your own lack of appreciation for it. Try telling that story to a group (when you do not especially care whether or not it brings a laugh). Then take some favorite story of your own, and use it with the same group.

Advance notice to the listener may be a significant factor in the reception of pulpit humor. This is especially true in the case of congregations not accustomed to regard sermon-sipping as having any entertainment value. Accustomed to pushing the mind into neutral on the last bar of the offertory music and coasting through the sermon out of gear, a listener may need to be warned that he is approaching a point of interest. Otherwise, he may roll by before he notices it.

Signals are actually radiated by a speaker who is building up to a bit of humor which he himself enjoys. But more direct action may be necessary in the case of an apathetic audience or a speaker who is just trying his hand with humor and is still not quite at ease about the matter. In such cases the situation may be met by an announcement. Simply notify the listener that he is expected to laugh: "In connection with this point, let me tell you an amusing incident that took place in Minneapolis . . ."

So warned, the listener's sense of competition is aroused. Failure to get the point will be an indication that he is either (a) too dull to recognize humor when he bumps into it face-to-face, or (b) a grumpy old sourpuss who has forgotten how to laugh. No normal person wishes to be considered a member of either category. Given advance notice, the typical listener will enter into the speech situation and actively seek to help the speaker secure a hearty response.

Use of oral style is essential for effective spoken humor. connective devices such as, "Then he said . . ." are not only superfluous, but actually detract from oral presentation. Many adjectives and adverbs, essential in written material, must be omitted and the meaning conveyed by tone, emphasis, and timing. Where written material must specify that "the boy gave a shy smile and slowly lisped . . . ," the skillful speaker will transfer the shy smile to his own face and the slow lisp to his own voice. Chapter V includes a detailed discussion of this matter.

Unlike printed humor, power of an oral laugh-getter is directly related to the explosive speed of the climax. A well-told story "cuts off clean." Nothing follows the punch line, for listeners are psychologically unable to concentrate simultaneously on the laughter element and the words currently being uttered by the speaker. After building up to a climax and taking the sudden leap with which it is actually reached, the speaker has only one duty: to be silent long enough to let listeners give undivided attention to "the point" until they grasp it fully.

CONCLUSIONS

Humor is a special communication form, serving not only to amuse but also to instruct and direct the listener. Extensive psychological analysis in recent years points to at least four bases from which laughter stems: disparagement of others, enhancement of feelings of superiority, release from suppression, and sharply-etched incongruity.

Pulpit humor helps to make sermons interesting and

entertaining—a function that is not to be belittled, in view of the fact that preachers must attract listeners and must speak to groups which include immature listeners. Polarization of the audience is effected by laughter, and the listener is given emotional conditioning that prepares him to act on the preacher's challenge. At the same time humor is a significant instrument of social control, and can be effectively directed against movements which are in conflict with Christian emphases.

Careless and slipshod selection is the chief, but not the only, danger in the use of humor. Any laugh which is won at the expense of a minority group tends to foster ill-feeling and build up tension. Unless humor can be directed toward members of the groups represented in the congregation it should be used with great care.

Books of humor are of some value to the preacher, but material found in life situations is far more effective. No matter what its source, the bid for laughter should be carefully tailored to the audience. By selecting material that he himself enjoys, then giving advance notice to listeners, it is comparatively easy for the preacher to get hearty response to humor.

Chapter X

1⌐⌐⌐⌐⌐⌐⌐⌐⌐⌐⌐⌐⌐⌐⌐⌐⌐ſ

EMOTIONAL FACTORS IN PERSUASION

AS EARLY AS THE PRE-CHRISTIAN ERA WHEN ARISTOTLE
wrote his treatise on rhetoric, it was recognized that communication includes two major elements: logical and emotional appeals. Logic is primarily concerned with information,
while emotion is closely linked with action. At extreme limits
there are communication forms which approach singularity
of function.

Thus, an unabridged dictionary has no overt emotional
goal—while lyric poetry conveys little if any information.
Information without emotion is supplied by a city directory,
scientific chart, or railroad timetable. Emotion without information is communicated by many forms of music, patriotic
symbols, purely hortatory sermons, and abstract paintings.

Most speech occasions, however, have dual orientation.
There are bids for both the mind and the will of the listener.
Factual as well as emotional elements contribute to effective
communication whose goal is to affect the idea-content and
emotional set of the listener. That is to say, the speaker bids
for the listener as a whole, and not for only one aspect of his
being.

Relative importance of the two elements will vary according to the nature of the communication situation. Typical classroom lectures are aimed chiefly at influencing the listener's stock of information. Typical sermons are largely concerned with directing or redirecting the listener's attitudes and actions.

An emotional state is an inevitable aspect of any great act of healing—whether physical or spiritual: "Leaping up he stood and walked and entered the temple with them, walking and leaping and praising God" (Acts 3:8). Emotional emphases are frequently condemned by contemporary religious leaders. Like nearly every other element in public speech, such appeals may be abused and distorted. That such misuse is prevalent no one can deny. Candidates for office, trial lawyers, advertisers, preachers, proponents of hates and 'isms frequently play on the emotions in order to secure the listener's active support of a program of action.

Many analysts are of the opinion that emotional appeals can accomplish results that mere logic is incapable of producing. Joshua Rosett points out that even such powerful stimuli as thirst may be pushed out of consciousness by emotional changes—such as the fear caused by sudden appearance of a wild animal, or grief produced by news of a tragedy in one's primary group.[a]

"An affect," declared Spinoza, "cannot be restrained or removed unless by an opposed and stronger affect."[b] Here is a somewhat more direct statement of the same conclusion, as phrased by that master of public address, Adolf Hitler: "Wrong conceptions and inferior knowledge can be abolished by instruction, but never obstacles of sentiment. Here solely an appeal to those mysterious forces themselves can be effective."[c]

If that statement were taken from its context and inserted

[a] (208), 187.
[b] (278), Bk. IV, proposition 7.
[c] (232), 706.

in one of Spurgeon's lectures it would seem quite in place. Said the great preacher-teacher, lecturing on conversion as the aim of preaching: "The class requiring logical argument is small compared to those who need to be pleaded with by way of emotional persuasion. They require not so much reasoning as heart argument, which is logic set on fire."[d]

There is no doubt that religionists have been among the most flagrant and conspicuous offenders in the use—not of Spurgeon's "logic set on fire," but of fire without logic. S. A. Nock goes so far as to say:

Oratory is the art of speaking eloquently or effectively; it is not the art of speaking intelligently, rationally, or considerately. . . . Oratory aims to inspire the hearer, to stir his emotions in one way or another. It is dynamic language. . . . *oratory, the art of speaking eloquently and effectively, is the natural language of the theologian.*[e]

Intimidated by such unqualified sneers—which gain force from the fact that intellectually honest Christians are ashamed of much that is said in the name of the faith—the modern middle-class preacher tends to shy away from anything that smacks of "emotionalism." Fosdick holds that "we modern preachers talk about psychology a great deal more than our predecessors but use it a great deal less."[f] Many, many church members of this generation have never been present in a congregation so stirred by the sermon that overt emotional displays resulted.

Granted, with St. Augustine, that "the man who cannot speak both eloquently and wisely should speak wisely without eloquence rather than eloquently without wisdom"; that the disrepute of the "sawdust trail evangelist" grows partly out of the fact that many a sermon may move uncritical listeners to dedication, without there being any intellectual content to the sermon; granted, with Angelo Pellegrini, that "the

[d] (202), II, 272.
[e] (279), 353; italics added.
[f] (242).

use of psychological techniques designed to make an audience react when it would have remained indifferent to a dispassionate, rational argument, has definite consequences for both the audience and speaker, the repeated appeal to nonrational sources of action in an individual can serve only to intensify irrationality."[g]

Nevertheless, it is high time we recognize that there is no necessary conflict between intellectual honesty and emotional fervor. One need not discard the warm heart in order to acquire the keen mind. There has been too much assent —overt and implied—to the proposition that since some preachers abuse the power of emotional appeals, all honest-thinking preachers should minimize or eliminate such factors in persuasion.

"Persuasion is unquestionably a tool of the 'propagandist' and soap-box orator," admits ethicist Charles L. Stevenson. "But it is also the tool of every altruistic reformer the world has ever known. We must not banish all doctors to rid the world of quacks."[h]

On election to his third term President Franklin D. Roosevelt was characterized in this fashion: "He had long ago learned the prime art of the Presidency—persuasion. . . . Always, eternally, he must persuade."[i] That is also the preacher's task. Provided that he has high purpose and intellectual integrity, the preacher is not only justified in using methods that will move the emotions of his listeners, he is under divine compulsion to do so.

EMOTIONS OF THE SPEAKER

Coleridge not only agreed that keen mind and warm heart are not incompatible; he went so far as to hold that

[g] (280), 27.
[h] (11), 164.
[i] *Time*, 11/18/40.

deep thinking and strong feeling are actually inseparable—
that one cannot achieve the former without the latter. In this
connection, it is significant that a great many nonreligious
thinkers mention emotion as a necessary component of genuine creativity.[j]

Only an abnormally sheltered life can escape the surge
and tug of strong emotions. Franz Werfel describes "princes
of the Church" as being "like the generals at headquarters
whither no bullet ever penetrates. Life with its harshness
comes to them in the guise of black marks on white paper."[k]
Such a person may well be chary of emotion. But his psychological state will be a large factor in his delivery of sermons;
feeling no emotion, he will engender none in his listeners.

Enthusiasm for the message is a prerequisite to vital
preaching. A speaker who has only cold detachment for his
subject is like a truck in low gear. No matter how much fuel
he has, no matter how precious the cargo he carries, no matter how fine the highway he travels, sooner or later he will
burn out his clutch.

"Remember that nothing will avail you if you go to sleep
yourself while you are preaching," warns Spurgeon. "Many
ministers are more than half asleep all through the sermon.
. . . Tame phrases, hackneyed expressions, and dreary
monotones make the staple of their discourses."[l]

So important does Spurgeon consider this question that
he places "earnestness" first on the list of qualities for success in preaching.[m] Many analysts, religious and secular,
reach similar conclusions. "Nothing great in the world is
accomplished without passion," warns Hegel.[n] Herrmann holds
that all religions have but one feature in common—the ability

[j] See Chapter XII.
[k] (281), 214.
[l] (202), I, 223.
[m] (202), II, 215.
[n] Cited, (1), 211.

to induce in believers "a sense of being possessed, so strong that a man must say, 'This is God.' Without this experience of God all else is so empty that it does not deserve to be called religion."[o]

Emerson declares that "in eloquence the great triumphs of the art are when the orator is lifted above himself." This takes place, according to the Sage of Concord, "when consciously he makes himself the mere tongue of the occasion and the hour, and says what cannot but be said. Hence the term *abandonment* to describe the self-surrender of the orator."[p]

One case history of a speaker is so significant that it deserves special treatment. Almost single-handed, and confronted by tremendous obstacles, a modern orator transformed the thinking of an entire nation. No other factor played so important a part as his power of persuasion. "Nearly always it was the case," he said later,

that in those years I stepped in front of an assembly of people who believed in the contrary of what I intended to say, and who desired the contrary of what I believed in. Then it was the task of two hours to lift two or three thousand people out of their previous conviction, to smash blow by blow the foundation of their previous opinions, and finally to lead them over to the soil of our convictions and of our way of life.[q]

His method of persuasion is frankly admitted: "Passion alone will give to him, who is chosen by her, the words that, like beats of a hammer, are able to open the doors to the heart of a people."[r] In the light of that declaration it is not strange that Hitler should have been described as a speaker who "seemed to his listeners the personification of the whole Ger-

[o] (282), 17-18.
[p] (283).
[q] (232), 701.
[r] (232), 137.

man people and their destiny—a man in a trance, from whom radiated a strange magnetism."[s]

How does one find that strange magnetism? Can the preacher use it to lead men over to the soil of the Kingdom of God and of the Christian view of life?

Der Fuehrer himself offers a hint. "Only a storm of burning passion can turn people's destinies," he declares, *"but only he who harbors passion in himself can arouse passion."*[t] Hence the magic door which leads to control of emotions is emotion itself. When a man becomes intoxicated with an idea—bad or good—it is as though he were in the grip of "a contagious evil" or "an infectious good." Surrounded by an aura, he is a walking example of a man who "has something catching."

Such a state cannot be simulated. It involves a great deal more than conventional practices. In the case of the preacher a pious tone of voice and use of right—i.e., conventionally holy—words, dress, and gestures is not enough. Any man who tries to affect holy love that he does not feel is almost certain to be detected and despised. "Please share my convictions," urges the radiant Ignatius in his *Letter to the Trallians*, "else you may be choked by what you cannot swallow!"

Preachers will do well to sip at the springs of literary criticism. It is all too easy to drift into the state of poets described by Wallace Stevens. "Choice of subject," says he,

is one of the vital factors in poetry or any art. Great numbers of poets come and go who have never had a subject at all. . . . Love is not a subject unless the writer of the song is in love. A man peddles love songs because it is easier to do than it is to peddle coconuts . . ."[u]

[s] (284), 137.
[t] (232), 137.
[u] (285), 38.

Use of that quotation is not intended to imply that any considerable number of men enter the ministry with the conscious intention of peddling sermons. That was (and is) of course a major element in recruitment of personnel for state-supported churches. It was no accident that the appointment of the 18th-century English clergyman should be termed his "living."

But in the typical Protestant denomination few men drift into the pulpit. Some are pushed in by devout parents. Most men choose the ministry, however, and it is quite exceptional when a young candidate does not have a burning sense of mission and message.

Such is the nature of man that some of the early glow tends to be lost very quickly. Caught in the ivy-covered tower of a theological seminary for three years, then pushed into the hurly-burly of administering a handed-down "program," the once fervent preacher finds it easy to degenerate into a go-getting promoter and an innocuous administrator. His task becomes, not so much the proclamation of a message radical and moving enough to turn society upside down, but rather the handling of program and people with such skill that the little local cog plays a well-oiled part in the operation of the denominational machine.

Power in handling the emotions of the listener cannot be found as an end in itself. It is always a by-product, growing out of spiritual struggles, defeats, and victories. That is why religious experience is and must remain one of the major factors in the authority of the preacher.

No hollow-sounding phrases escape the man whose desire is to share what he is convinced generates the power of speech. He is successful because he is not trying to be. He is driven to express what he cannot keep within. He is expressing a picture from within that the listener may understand what dominates his being.[v]

[v](286), 19.

In the case of the preacher that kind of eloquence is the highest goal of speech. But, like the treasure found in a field, it can be had only when one will sell all that he has in order to go and buy the field.

DYNAMIC LANGUAGE

Though some modern semanticists have passed the bounds of moderation and are up to their necks in the mire of nominalism, the movement has nonetheless borne much useful fruit. One of the distinct services rendered by semantic study is new recognition of the fact that it is not merely large communication units, but also individual words, that play dual rôles. Many a word has both factual and emotional connotations.

There have been some attempts to separate speech units into neat classes. Thus, Ogden and Richards insist that

> In strict symbolic language the emotional effects of the words, whether direct or indirect, are irrelevant to their employment. In evocative language on the other hand, all the means by which attitudes, moods, desires, feeling, emotions can be verbally incited in an audience are concerned.[w]

S. A. Nock accepts this radical dualism, going so far as to hold that "when a speaker uses words dynamically, and at the same time would have his hearers consider them as symbols, he asks too great an assumption."[x]

Such views as these, though valuable in helping to sharpen the critical faculties, are much too extreme. An attempt to classify a given word in a particular context as "informational" or "emotional" is like trying to determine whether a woman's hat is useful or beautiful. There is no valid reason why it should not be both. As Charles L. Stevenson rightly emphasizes, there are many words which have

w (31), 235.
x (279), 357.

both descriptive and emotive meaning. He cites *culture* as an example. Though the descriptive meaning is not so precise as in, say, *pineapple*, it is clearly present. But the emotional connotations of *culture* are "prizes which each man seeks to bestow on the qualities of his own choice."[y]

In precisely the same fashion the preacher can "bestow prizes" on selected ideas and modes of conduct merely by using emotion-laden words to designate them. This involves, not coining new names, but deliberate selection of terms that already tend to evoke nonreflective and emotional reactions.

"What's in a name?" Aldous Huxley has Anthony demand. "The answer is, practically everything, if the name's a good one. Freedom's a marvelous name. . . . You think that, if you call imprisonment true freedom, people will be attracted to the prison. And the worst of it is, you're quite right."[z]

It is said that the Irish patriot, William O'Brien, habitually divided all his fellow citizens into two classes on the basis of their support or opposition to his own program. Members of the former class were always referred to as "loyal comrades," and opponents as "loathsome ruffians."[a] Though his technique was crude, modern public opinion research indicates that it was probably effective.

In 1946 the Roper staff tested two carefully-matched groups of Americans, asking identical questions, with the exception that "explanation of our point of view" was used with one group, "propaganda" with the other. These questions dealt with the controversial subject of foreign broadcasts by the State Department. Persons who approved "explanation" were nearly twice as numerous as those who favored "propaganda"![b]

[y](11), 213.
[z](287).
[a](226), 54.
[b](15), 165f.

As Leonard Bloomfield points out, every person who has anything to sell—and the preacher certainly falls within this group—should be aware of the emotive potential of language. He cites the differences between *house* and *home*—respectively colorless and sentimental words that may be treated as approximately synonymous. "The speculative builder . . . uses the speech forms whose content will turn the hearer in the right direction. . . . The salesman comes to use the word 'home' for an empty shell that has never been inhabited, and the rest of us follow his style."[c]

Here are some pairs of words which illustrate the potential impact of loaded language:

> liberty—license
> Russian—Red
> news—propaganda
> housewife—mother
> fate—Providence
> lust—love

Effect of a speech on foreign relations will vary, to a more or less marked extent depending upon the critical faculties of the listeners, according to whether the speaker constantly speaks of his targets as "Russians" or "Reds." Patrick Henry would have received quite a different response had he made the challenge, "Give me license, or give me death!" And it may be of some importance whether a speaker consistently refers to the distaff side of the house as "daughters of Eve" or "mothers and mothers-to-be."

Preachers are sometimes criticized for making too extensive use of phrases such as "the blood of the Lamb," "the foot of the Cross," "the home Over Yonder," and "the company of the redeemed." It is true that such terms communicate little or no information, and should be used with care.

[c] (288), 442.

But they are powerful media for the communication of emo‐ tional overtones.

A symbol of this sort "makes use of an elaborate process of conditioning of long duration, which has given it its emotive disposition. This disposition, granted suitable attend‐ ant circumstances, enables the word to act not additively, but much more strongly, like a spark that ignites prepared tin‐ der."[d]

Obviously, the power of emotion-charged language is not a constant. It is a variable whose effect depends upon the critical threshold and emotional state of the audience. A sermon consisting largely of impassioned generalities may create a state of ecstasy in a congregation gathered in fervent expectation of seeing miracles of healing through faith. That identical message may leave a Park Avenue congregation not merely unmoved, but positively disgusted. This does not mean that the Park Avenue listener is not responsive to emotional impacts, but that a more subtle approach is indicated in his case. No matter what the intellectual and emotional level of the listener, he can be touched by the right words—which are neither more nor less than those words which are "right" for use with him.

As a rule, the sophisticated audience is more responsive to emotion-packed illustrations than to words and phrases per se. Thus, a group which would sneer at extensive play upon the virtues of "pure, old-fashioned womanhood" can be brought to the point of tears by adept handling of such a story as "The Search for the Beautiful." Mass-circulation magazines, motion pictures, radio and television programs are eloquent witnesses to the fact that people do not merely tolerate, but actually crave emotional stimulation. But no doctor would think of prescribing the same medicine for every

[d](11), 62.

patient. Just so, the preacher must tailor his emotional language and illustrations to his audience.

His task is made somewhat easier by the fact that persons of approximately similar educational, social, and cultural backgrounds tend to group themselves into congregations. Thus the difference between two urban congregations may actually be greater than that between the two extremes within a particular congregation.

There can be no rules to govern the use of communication symbols with emotional overtones. Every preaching situation is a unique case. In addition to personality of preacher and people, the major goal of a particular sermon must be taken into account.

St. Augustine points out, by direct statement and implication, that the preacher must upon occasion attempt not merely one, but two types of persuasion. In many instances, the listeners "must be persuaded not that they may know what should be done, but to do what they already know they should do."[e] This was the saint's way of anticipating modern psychology by dividing beliefs into two classes—"those that we accept and do not significantly dispute; and those that we do not accept."[f]

Sometimes preachers must deal with both types of belief. There are occasions when, for example, one might seek to persuade his listeners to act upon beliefs that they already accept in principle but have never put into practice. Almost any person attending evangelistic services will grant the fact that God is capable of bringing him into a new kind of life. In such a case, the preacher must persuade him to act upon that belief.

But quite a different situation prevails when the preacher

[e] (289), IV, 12.
[f] (290), 179.

sets out, say, to persuade his congregation to practice Christian love in their dealings with another race. Here the listener may not accept the ideal of the preacher. It then becomes the latter's task to persuade his hearers to substitute new beliefs and ideas for old ones.

Sheer word power, developed through use of loaded communication symbols, is likely to be far more useful in one type of persuasion than the other. This device may be quite effective in persuading listeners to vitalize an idea that is listlessly accepted, but not presently operative in the system of values. But supercharged words may prove completely ineffective in persuading a listener to abandon a strongly held belief in order to adopt a new and substitute purpose.

PERSUASION TOWARD DECISION

Whether it urges the listener to accept new loyalties or vitalize old ones, the effective impact of a sermon is to be measured in terms of decision. There is no decision without indecision. So long as the listener is sure of his position and firm in his movement toward a selected goal, there will be no vital change. At most, such a listener will reaffirm the allegiance he has already sworn.

"Distress of mind," says W. MacNeile Dixon, "is the great awakener of mind."[g] It is when a person faces conflict in his own attitudes that he becomes a potential "convert" to some new position. Emotional challenge is religion's most powerful tool for the awakening of a sense of crisis in the individual. Hocking goes so far as to declare that "no religion is a true religion which is not able to make men tingle, yes, even to their physical nerve tips, with the sense of an infinite hazard, a wrath to come, a heavenly city to be gained or lost in the process of time and by the use of our freedom."[h]

[g](1), 75.
[h](62), xiv.

Such a sense of hazard is produced chiefly by contrast. So long as one keeps his mind fastened upon a single alternative—no matter what its nature—he cannot see it in all its stark distinctiveness. There is no drama without a villain as well as a hero. It is by contrast with the antagonist that the heroic qualities of the protagonist become clearly apparent. Mere banal praise of a man, lauding him as a hero without making vivid the manner in which he has conquered obstacles, will persuade few persons to passionate loyalty. Sheer dramatic contrast, without overt praise, can produce such surges of admiration that many a listener yearns to follow in the footsteps of the hero.

Preaching that presents a vivid contrast between two courses of action is likely to result in decisions. When two shades of gray are placed together one will appear light and the other dark. Separate the colors, and each tends to lose the quality of "light" or "dark." Similar conditions prevail in the realm of human values. Evil always seems more somber when contrasted with goodness; goodness always shines with greater radiance when set against evil.

Sheer exhortation is not the preacher's most effective emotional challenge. Concentration on the decision, "Always follow the dictates of your conscience," will produce a sermon without contrast. It is an appeal within a one-level system of values. Quite a different situation prevails when the preacher contrasts the two attitudes of "yielding to social pressure" and "always obeying one's conscience." This is a two-value approach. Here the listener is challenged to a real decision. A sermon is like a highway; it is only when one comes to a fork in the road that he stops to think about his course.

Like the traveler confronted by a choice of roads, the listener's decision will be only as vital as the conflict which

brings it about. Given the following situations requiring
decision, only "D" involves clear-cut alternatives:

A

Weak conflict—
choice between
trail and major
highway.

B

Weak conflict—
choice between
parallel roads.

C

Weak conflict—
many alterna-
tives of approx-
imately equal
force.

D

Strong Conflict
—Choice be-
tween two
strong and def-
inite alterna-
tives.

Vital alternatives must be life-centered, not academic
or scholarly. In order to be more than a routine piece of communication, the preacher's proposition must be linked with
human wants and given its place in a scale of values.

Sharp contrast does not rule out a positive note—a
proffered conclusion by the speaker. Such a conclusion, which
is presented as a solution to the dilemma of the listener, has
force only if the listener is actually in a state of indecision.
John Dewey points out that "choice is not the emergence of
preference out of indifference. It is the emergence of unified
preference out of competing preferences."[1]

For the purposes of the preacher the order in which
"competing preferences" are presented is of major importance. Given strong conflict (situation D, above), the "wrong"
alternative should be presented first and the positive, "right"
alternative made desirable by contrast. Given a situation such
as "A" above, the contrast is comparatively weak. There is
little danger that the listener will actually take the trail in
preference to the highway. But the desirability of the highway
can become somewhat more apparent by a brief look at the
trail. In this situation it may be effective to lift up the weak,

[1](291), 193.

"wrong" alternative just before the conclusion of the sermon, in order to intensify the attractiveness of the strong, "right" alternative.

Positive, affirmative emphases always make decisions seem desirable. Notwithstanding the genius of Dante and Milton, the joys of heaven have spurred more men toward God than have the terrors of hell. Given an opportunity to repeat favorite Bible verses in a permissive atmosphere, mature Christians almost always select *promises*.

"Motivation is essentially a process of setting up a system of adequate rewards in the minds of the listeners," points out Gislason. "Show an audience that their most cherished desires and interests are involved in acting in accordance with a certain belief, or course of conduct advocated by the speaker, and they will be readily persuaded to order their behavior accordingly."[1] Basic religious appeals are positive, not negative. Hope, confidence, joy, and peace are the mainsprings of man's yearning for the divine.

There have been no great conversion experiences with largely negative content. It is true that a radical change in one's life always involves giving up one set of values in order to accept another. But the direction of the change is toward the positive. Mere emphasis upon giving up a habit will never break the hold of, say, alcohol or tobacco. Victory comes only when one develops an opposed want, so passionate that it reduces—perhaps infinitely—the attention-value of the habit.

All great religions are religions of deliverance. Conversion is a process of problem-solving—the formation of a new and higher synthesis of values. Any attempt to foster a religion of conversion without making full use of emotional factors in persuasion is like advocating art without beauty or family relationships without affection.

[1] (292).

It must be remembered, however, that no emotional appeal has a valid end in itself. Unless it leads to some type of action or decision, it may actually do harm. William James gives a classic illustration in his story of a Russian noblewoman who sat in the theater weeping over the sufferings of a fictitious hero, while her coachman sat outside literally freezing to death as he waited for her return.

After presenting an appeal with strong emotional content, the preacher should give some opportunity for decision or overt action. Use of the altar is the traditional device, but need not be the only one. There are many types of invitations that may be made to the listener:

> silent commitment during the closing hymn
> taking literature to a neighbor
> oral witness—the "testimony period"
> use of a card, checking one or more decisions
> raising the hand or remaining after the benediction
>   in order to volunteer services in some specific
>   project
> singing of a vigorous hymn with definite cathartic
>   value
> prayer at the altar
> participation in a special offering
> silent meditation with focus upon self-examination

Use of any one of these or other invitations can quickly become stereotyped, even monotonous.

Failure to provide some opportunity to decide or act may, on some occasions, greatly reduce the long-range effects of a sermon. Specific challenges must be adapted to the congregation and the occasion. But the type preachers who are likely to read this volume are far more prone to neglect than to over-emphasize opportunities to act upon specific emotional appeals.

CONCLUSIONS

Logical and emotional elements in communication are not completely separable. Most public speech bids for both the mind and the will of the listener. Since the typical sermon is aimed at producing action or decision of some sort, mastery of emotional appeals is fundamental.

Fervor on the part of the speaker is basic in arousing the enthusiasm of the listener. In the case of the preacher such an attitude is a product of religious experience; it cannot be successfully simulated.

Given a sense of mission and a genuine passion to communicate, one can add to the impact of a sermon by conscious use of dynamic language. Words and phrases with emotional overtones are, however, more useful in arousing dormant ideals than in persuading listeners to accept new ones.

After making an emotion-linked challenge, the preacher should give the listener some opportunity to act. Various types of invitations may be given; response will vary partly according to the degree of conflict produced by the sermon. For this purpose the most effective device is presentation of two definite and strong, but opposed alternatives.

Chapter XI

VISUAL ELEMENTS IN PREACHING

It is customary to think of the speech situation primarily in terms of oral communication. Prominence of this factor is indicated by the universal use of the term *audience*—which obscures the fact that the speaker also has to deal with a *"vis*-ience."

Actually, eyes play a far more important rôle in modern communication and learning than do ears. Though the spoken word is vital in teaching, entertainment, and persuasion, the stimuli which reach the brain through one's eyes are generally far more numerous than those caught by the ears.

No other organ of perception even approaches the human eye in terms of sensitivity, adaptability, and power of synthesis. It is estimated that each retina includes more than 100,000,000 separate receptors—far more than in all other human sensory organs combined. Though the dog seems to rely very heavily on his nose, and many forms of sea organisms survive by trusting their sense of touch, man depends chiefly upon his eyes. Hence a specialist in human perception concludes that "the visual messages are the most complex and the most important of all those reaching the human brain."[a]

[a] (293), 52.

Books, magazines, display advertising, scientific packaging, design of clothing and furnishings, combine with television to make the rôle of the visual increase steadily rather than decrease in modern culture. It therefore becomes more and more necessary that the preacher make maximum use of the most versatile of sensory channels, achieving direct and vital contact with his listener through appeal to his eyes.

Quantitative measurements of these factors present complex problems. Few psychologists have succeeded in making precise evaluations. Some progress has been made, however. Omwake studied auditory presentation of humor in comparison with auditory-visual, and found measurable difference in comprehension based on the dual presentation.[b] Perl analyzed humor and found that "costumes enhance the funniness by 100 per cent, business by 400 per cent, and together they enhance the funniness by 600 per cent."[c]

Studies of classroom learning, conducted by a team of psychologists, yielded conclusive proof that "when material was presented with visual aids it was more effective for immediate recall than when presented without the use of such aids."[d] Without citing laboratory findings, H. L. Hollingworth reaches a similar conclusion in his *Psychology of the Audience*.[e]

Several aspects of visual communication are related to preaching; not all are of equal importance, but each can contribute to total impact of a sermon.

POSITION, DRESS, AND EYE-CONTACT

As a general working rule, it is safe to proceed on the assumption that it is easier to gain attention through a major

[b] (294).
[c] (295), 757.
[d] (222), 87.
[e] (213), 75.

sense channel than through a minor. A moving object attracts attention quicker than a change in temperature; a sound is noticed more readily than an odor of equal intensity. At the same time, it is easier to attract attention through an unoccupied sensory channel than through one which is already receiving and transmitting stimuli at a level of intensity sufficient to influence the brain.

Both these factors enhance the significance of the preacher's initial appeal to the eyes of his congregation. Music usually occupies the ears of the listener just prior to the beginning of the sermon. Thus the initial phase of polarization—the coming to focus upon the preacher—is best accomplished through visual elements. Likewise, sensitivity of visual receptors makes the listener give his attention to such movements as walking to the pulpit and opening the Bible.

Physical arrangement of the preaching place is an important factor both at this point and throughout the sermon. If the listener cannot see the speaker—or can see only a small portion of his body—there is a sharp reduction in visual impact. Huge pulpits tend to eliminate many stimuli; occasionally an elaborate and expensive monstrosity is complete with high wings, confining the preacher's visual communication to head and facial movements, supplemented by an occasional desperate, high-flying gesture of the wig-wag variety.

Any element in the physical setting that makes a strong bid for visual attention, thereby reduces the strength of focus upon the preacher. Light is especially bad; if placed directly in the range of the listener's vision, an unshaded light source of very low intensity will draw every eye part of the time, and some eyes most of the time. Even a colorful stained-glass window, a shiny vessel of silver or brass, or a brightly colored tie worn by a member of the choir will inevitably bid for and win a portion of the attention of some listeners. Just as a formal worship center should draw all eyes in periods of silence, so the entire physical setting of the preaching occasion should help listeners focus their eyes upon the speaker.

A significant factor in this process is the dress of the minister himself. Anything slightly out of the ordinary will help focus attention. Of course, bizarre dress will draw so much attention that it is difficult for the listener to shift from looking to listening.

Dress which reduces and inhibits gesture is highly effective in screening out visual signals. This means that the preacher who wishes to make maximum use of gesture will discard his robe and alternate between two or more business suits. If local conditions demand use of a robe, one should make full use of the conventional colors that are associated with various seasons of the Christian year.

Physical setting and dress are, however, considerably less important than eye-contact. Eyes play a very important rôle in communication; consciously or unconsciously, everyone "talks with his eyes." If that seems an extreme statement, watch talk by a small child or by an adult who is in a state of high emotion. There is a persistent demand on the part of the speaker that the listener yield visual as well as auditory channels.

"Look at me when I am talking to you!" is as insistent and reasonable a command as "Listen to me!"

When a person has something vital which he wishes to communicate, he naturally insists upon reaching the eyes of his listener. On the other hand, when a person wishes to evade a question, he is likely to avert his eyes while speaking; he is afraid that the eyes will yield meaning that can be concealed in merely oral communication.

Eye contact between preacher and listener should be as intimate and continuous as possible. This does not merely help direct the listener's attention; shades of meaning are conveyed that would otherwise be lost. There are few habits more disastrous than staring at the ceiling or keeping the eyes fastened upon a manuscript.

Even a brief Scripture reading can short-circuit communication. If a passage is too long to be committed to memory, the speaker should use a small Bible. Holding it in his hand and raised close to his own eye level, he can then glance over the book into the eyes of his listeners at least half the time he is reading. In the average service of worship, listener attention is probably lower during the Scripture reading than at any other time. This is due not only to intrinsic difficulties in oral use of material prepared in written style, but also to slipshod, colorless reading without eye contact.

Good eye-contact cannot be achieved by merely acquiring the habit of looking at the listeners; something much deeper is involved. It grows out of a strong sense of communication —an urgent desire, not only to perform one's duty by filling twenty minutes with pious sounds, but to communicate, to convey a message. In its finest form, this is an aspect of sense of mission—a conviction that one has no choice; he must speak because he is unable to remain silent. Some of the emotional phases of this matter are discussed in Chapter X.

GESTURE

Many students of speech believe that gesture was an earlier form of communication than speech. Even if that hypothesis is accepted, it does not imply the conclusion sometimes drawn that gesture is an essentially "primitive" mode of communication.

All attempts to separate human bodily movement and

sound are artificial. There are special instances in which persons use only gesture: waving to a friend in the distance, blowing a kiss to a child, or silently shaking hands. Such cases are comparatively rare, and cannot serve as bases for highly complex communication. But instances of using complex sound without movement are even less frequent.

Informal speech is almost always accompanied by gesture. Varying with the personality of the speaker and the emotional content of the speech situation, the extent of gesture may range from a slight change of facial expression to complex bodily gyrations.

An angry child does not merely burst into violent noise; he screws his face into an appropriate shape and stamps his feet, beats on the nearest piece of furniture, or even bangs his head against the wall. His actions are vivid—and frequently effective—signals by which he makes it clear that he is not mildly annoyed, not righteously indignant, but absolutely furious. At the other extreme, a salesperson handing a package to a customer and thanking him for a ten-cent purchase gives signals indicating appreciation, annoyance, boredom, sheer physical weariness, or some other state.

Every part of the body clamors for a share in the speech situation. Eyes twinkle, snap, blaze, or cloud with tears. Facial muscles pull the eyebrows, forehead, lips, and cheeks into clear patterns. Indeed, scientific tests have shown that a great range of emotions may be communicated by facial expressions alone.[f] After the eyes and face, the hands are next in expressiveness. Not every speaker can have the hands of Zasu Pitts, but informal speech is nearly always accompanied by movements of the fingers, hands, and arms.

Shoulders, trunk, and head also gesture. It is natural to cower in fear, bow in humility, look up in hope, strut in

[f](213), 147.

pride, and crouch in belligerent anger. All these movements are made smoothly and naturally when one's thought is centered upon vital meaning which he wishes to convey and not upon the way in which he will express it. Even the feet rush into the speech situation when other movements are inhibited. Listeners tend to tap their feet in impatience and shuffle them in boredom. It is a revelation to stand near a row of public telephones and watch women's feet as they talk—twisting, tapping, slipping in and out of the shoes in the course of a three-minute chat.

Gesture plays a very important part in making a speaker-listener situation more flexible and compelling than a book-reader situation. Emotions, emphasis and shades of meaning that are vivid in speech disappear altogether when the same words are committed to paper.

For example, there is little in Wesley's printed sermons to suggest that these words held crowds spellbound, led men to walk miles to hear him, and frequently induced states of high emotion in listeners. Undoubtedly the spoken sermons had qualities of urgency and vitality that cannot be captured in words alone. That is to say, much of Wesley's meaning was conveyed by gesture and voice, so the printed sermon can at best transmit less-than-total meaning.

Billy Graham is a contemporary example of a preacher who uses gesture with extreme effectiveness. He speaks with his entire body, and uses as much physical effort in preaching as he would in a fast walk of the same duration. Every sentence is accompanied by movement; indeed, nearly every word is reinforced by some change in the position of the speaker's mobile body.

Not only does gesture serve as a medium of communication; it also plays a significant rôle in holding the attention of the listener. We have already noted that few other stimuli are so powerful as a single object in motion against a background which is motionless in respect to the observer. When the preacher is the only moving object in range of the listener's vision, his very movements will attract and reattract flitting attention.

By the same token, movement on the part of choir members or other listeners who fall within the same visual field as the speaker reduces the degree to which attention is focused upon him. Even such commonplace movements as waving a fan will attract the eye unless there is a more powerful stimulus bidding for the listener's attention.

Few speakers find it easy to make maximum use of gesture's power to attract attention and communicate meaning. Though a man may gesture easily and vigorously in conversation—as all persons actually do, to some extent—he tends to "freeze" when he steps before an audience. His movements are reduced in frequency and extent; sometimes he clutches the pulpit with both hands, as though fearful that high winds will blow him off the rostrum. When he attempts a gesture he finds his movements clumsy and jerky. Hands seem inordinately large and conspicuous; every muscle in the body is tense.

This condition, which is accompanied by some degree of conscious "stage fright," is an almost universal experience. Even veteran speakers sometimes find themselves gripped in an icy hand which inhibits normal movement, at the same time serving as a barrier between speaker and listener. Few quantitative tests have been made, but in one study of 789 college students taking communication courses only eleven per cent reported themselves free of stage fright.[g]

Acute cases are accompanied by marked physiological disturbances: perspiration, acceleration of heartbeat, ab-

[g] (296), 329.

dominal tension, tremors in arms and legs, dry mouth, and stuttering or stammering. Basing his conclusions on a number of medical studies, Lomas concludes that there is no significant physiological difference between states of rage, fear, high emotional tension, and vigorous physical action. In each instance, "emergency concentrations" of adrenalin and thyroxin are believed to produce part of the physical effect. But there are other factors which have not yet been successfully isolated for measurement.[h]

Certain clearly defined aspects of stage fright point, however, toward a plausible hypothesis. There is no doubt whatever that the body is prepared for vigorous action. Inhibition of gesture, with accompanying failure to give the physiological potential a normal outlet, may cause it to be shunted into abnormal channels. It is as though the body were an electric motor. Current is sent charging through the circuit, but the motor is overloaded to the point that it turns very slowly if at all. If this condition prevails past the maximum point of resistance, the current will force a new outlet and the motor will be burned out.

Stage fright is a condition in which muscles of abdomen, throat, legs, arms, and face are in a state of tension. So the real problem in stage fright—severe or mild—is closely related to use of gesture. If tense muscles can give way to a state of natural and relatively vigorous gesture, there ensues a comparatively relaxed physiological state, which is marked by effective mastery of visual communication.

There is strong evidence that in both stuttering and stage fright, "the basic disturbance may be designated as anxiety-tension occasioned by misevaluative reactions to speech situations."[1] That is a technical way of saying that the goal of the speaker is not communication, but approbation.

[h](297), 35ff.
[1](296), 330.

In the case of the stuttering child there is a desire to win the approval of some listener, such as a parent. Much of the child's attention is centered upon the idea: "I must please daddy! I must do what he will like! I must not make him scold!" Of course, these thoughts are not usually formulated so clearly by the child—but he concentrates so strongly on them that he gives only marginal attention to the speech act, and quickly develops habitual motor aberrations.

In the case of a speaker who freezes as he faces the audience there is a strong desire to "make a successful speech"—i.e., win overt approval of the listeners. Much of the speaker's attention is directed to such thoughts as: "This is a crucial occasion; I must make good. If I fail, I will be disgraced." Concentrating on the goal of winning approval, he cannot simultaneously give full attention to the speech act. Valued only as a sorry second-rate goal, the act of communication is crowded out of the center of mental activity. Under such circumstances co-ordination is poor and tension is high; mild or severe stage fright ensues, and gestures are awkwardly stiff if not altogether inhibited.

John L. Casteel, of Union Theological Seminary, found theological students markedly inferior to lay students in their use of gesture. This situation he concluded to be related to speech goals—one of which is "fear of becoming sawdust-trail evangelists."[j] That is simply a negative way of recognizing that these students had as a major purpose the wish to win approval of the listeners—presumed to disapprove of "the platform spellbinder."

"Abandonment," says St. Augustine, "is the precious fruit of love." In the case of the preacher love of God and of fellow men must be the motive power behind effective speech. Love that is directed inward produces self-conscious-

[j] (298), 76.

ness. Brooks, Abbott, Jefferson, and other Yale lecturers warn against egocentricity in preaching.[k] Winans points out that "we can forget only by turning our attention to something else. Stand behind your speech, and embarrassment will disappear."[l]

Numerous speakers—of whom Lincoln was one—almost invariably suffer stage fright as they begin a talk. Frequently this condition diminishes very rapidly; as the speaker becomes more and more absorbed in his message he withdraws attention from ego-linked goals and acquires poise and ease.

Many teachers advise the tense speaker to seek relaxation by some motor activity such as deep breathing, tapping the foot, or chewing. This is sometimes held to release some of the excess energy mobilized by the body.[m] Such a hypothesis is hardly tenable; such action as chewing or tapping can at most "burn" very little energy. It appears far more likely that the beneficial results are due to redirected attention rather than from use of "excess energy." Concentrating on some motor activity, the speaker cannot simultaneously think about his own success or failure. Attention being directed away from the ego, tension is relaxed.

It follows that the most important method of developing forceful use of gesture is to have something vital to say.

When attention is focused upon the act of communication—conveying a message to one or more listeners—gesture is natural and easy. A housewife wishes the produce clerk to understand that she wants this bunch of bananas, not that one; she points with vigor and complete clarity. Cheer leaders at an athletic meet wish to encourage a runner; with no inhibitions whatever, they signal for speed and even go through motions which imitate those of the athlete. Handed

[k] (225), 93ff.
[l] (299), 24.
[m] (301), 492.

an unexpected bonus check, a preacher does not restrict his reaction to words. By facial expression, movement of the hands and body, he signals his gratitude.

In all such cases the speaker is not concerned with causing the listener to approve of him as a person. Rather, he wishes to convey a message and produce appropriate action on the part of the listener. When that is the primary purpose of the public speaker he will gesture as freely and effectively as in face-to-face conversation.

Even a sense of prophecy—the wish to impart a vital message—will not give all preachers equal fluency in gesture. Profound differences in temperament and personality cause some persons to be naturally phlegmatic and stolid, others to be fluid and volatile. There is no reason to believe that reserved and undemonstrative persons can achieve mobility in gesture without some profound personality change, which may or may not come as a by-product of a soul-shaking religious experience.

Even the naturally reserved speaker can, however, achieve considerable skill in using his body to communicate meaning. Manuals of gesture, such as those which were current in the Chautauqua Era, are worse than useless. Directions concerning specific gestures may be suited for some but never for all personality types. A stereotyped gesture is like a spoken cliché. It doesn't say anything. All the meaning has been squeezed out of it and there is nothing left but rind and pulp. Though it fills an interval in the communication situation, it conveys no meaning.

Good gestures and good words are alike in that both are real vehicles of communication. No set of directions can have general validity. But there is one simple way in which a speaker can cultivate proficiency: by practicing telling stories to small children.

In order to hold the attention of a group of five-year-olds, the speaker must use eyes, face, hands, and body. When he tells about Peter Rabbit's journey to Mr. MacGregor's garden he must show Peter walking. It is not enough to say that the old gentleman grows angry at the sight of the rabbit boy; that anger must be exhibited in the face of the story-teller. And when Peter is caught in the gooseberry bush his reactions must be shown as well as told.

A preacher who doesn't have small children of his own can always practice on a few listeners from the church school nursery. Besides informal practice with children, it helps to pick out youngsters in the congregation and address portions of the sermon to them. Extra emphasis, added naturally in conversation with children, becomes a "plus" which heightens the impact upon adult listeners.

VISUAL AIDS AND ILLUSTRATIONS

Recognizing the tremendous "pull" of visual stimuli, it appears reasonable that the preacher should use illustrations and aids with eye appeal to reinforce and supplement his spoken message. In practice, however, such communication methods are rare in pulpits of middle- and upper-class denominations.

One does not have to look far to find the reason. It is the same factor which inhibited Casteel's theological students: fear of criticism for use of "spectacular" methods.

Many authorities have nothing but condemnation for anything that smacks of the unusual. Without reaching a standard definition of the sensational, no less than ten Yale lecturers on preaching have warned against "sensational preaching."[n]

Such a view is somewhat too narrow. It fails to take into

[n] (225), 138f.

account the rôle of purpose in the preaching situation—whether "sensational methods" are used to draw attention to the speaker or merely to make his message memorable and arresting. If a scalpel of sedate purism were used to cut all spectacular elements from the body of Jewish-Christian prophecy the spineless and bloodless remnant—no longer sturdy and virile—would be fit for nothing but continued post-mortem dissection.

If vivid and unconventional methods make preaching worthless some very familiar names must head the list of homiletical failures. Moses used sleight-of-hand to attract and to convince his listeners. Elijah disdained the conventional and made the most of an appearance so startling that it must have been deliberately adopted. Isaiah and Jeremiah undoubtedly cause many tongues to wag. Amos saw no impropriety in capturing the eyes of his countrymen in order to gain their ears. John the Baptist affected a striking costume that must have been criticized by many a suave Levite. And our Saviour helped make His message real by laying His hand upon the sick and crippled so that they might be visible illustrations of the changes wrought by acceptance of His sensational sermons.

A certain staid and dignified Oxford scholar was once in a situation that demanded a love that transcended fear of carping criticism. Denied a pulpit, John Wesley led his congregation to the adjacent graveyard, mounted the tombstone of his own father, and launched into a sermon. His friend and associate Whitefield—one of the most powerful preachers of all time—caused many a staid curate to look down his nose. In order to make vivid a sermon on hell, the evangelist once donned the black cap worn by judges when pronouncing the death sentence on condemned criminals. He frequently preached from tombs, roadside signs, and even gibbets.

Though Spurgeon was somewhat less unconventional, he can hardly be considered as colorless as a cup of tea brewed by a cautious old lady. He once told his students of an aged saint who found it hard to remain awake in church. She confessed her sin to her preacher, and asked for forgiveness and a remedy. He recommended that she try taking snuff. Righteously indignant, she snorted that she wouldn't need it if the minister would put more snuff into his message.

"We must plentifully cast snuff into the sermon," urged Spurgeon, "or something yet more awakening. . . . [We must give the listeners] something striking, something that a man would get up in the middle of the night to hear, and which is worth his walking fifty miles to listen to. . . . To wake people up, we must astonish them with something unawares. Let your thunderbolt drop out of a clear sky. When all is calm and bright, let the tempest rush up, and by contrast make its terrors all the greater."[o]

James A. Winans, writing for secular speakers, points out that it is ridiculous to make a blanket denunciation of all unconventional methods. He holds that "even rather extreme forms are at times justified." Such methods are especially valuable, says he, when speaking to listeners who are present under coercion. Preachers will be first amused, then challenged by the list of situations which this veteran teacher of speech considers especially difficult. Though he does not use the term, Winans holds that the "captive audience" is found chiefly in classrooms, prisons, and churches.[p]

Other secular analysts agree that the compelling speaker, like it or not, must find courage to plunge—"to get out of your everyday self and find a self that is willing to dash into the limelight and offer itself as a target for others. The advice, 'Be yourself' . . . is for homebodies."[q]

[o](202), I, 207, 211, 223.
[p](299), 160.
[q](300), 49.

No small part of the self-righteous criticism of "sensational" preaching originates with preachers who have not themselves found the courage and sense of message to speak with abandon. Most of the rest comes from laymen who are dreadfully afraid that vigorously unconventional sermons might cause them to be half as greatly moved in church as at a football game. Any method is valid, provided that a speaker conscientiously uses it, not to gain personal praise but to interest his listeners in his message and persuade them to act upon it for their own eternal good.

Actual use of visual aids in preaching takes two major forms.

First, one may exhibit some object (or person) that has illustrative force or adds reality to the exposition of a theme. Beecher's use of the ex-slave freed by the Underground Railway falls into this category.

Perhaps the preacher wishes to illustrate the curse of nourishing resentment. He selects Maupassant's classic story, "The Piece of String," and summarizes the action. Instead of merely describing how the old farmer found and hid a piece of string, he may show the action—actually using a piece of string.

Or suppose he wishes to help his listeners understand how wholehearted love of God will push bad habits out of one's life. It is helpful to refer to "the natural man" as like a glass filled with the air of self-love. No matter how hard one tries to pour out that air, he has no success. Even if he turns the glass upside down it remains full of air. But when he pours water into the glass, air is forced out little by little until at last the glass is practically free of air. That sort of illustration is incomparably more vivid and compelling when actually demonstrated—effectively making the metaphor real through the eyes as well as ears of the listener.

Examples might be multiplied almost endlessly. There is hardly a sermon which could not include some bid for eye-attention, if only exhibiting a book from which a quotation is read.

Second, many ideas lend themselves to presentation in diagram form. Using stiff poster paper and India ink, one need not be an artist to make use of the visual. Charts and diagrams may be made with no equipment but a straight edge. Frequently the text itself may be given a visual interpretation, reinforcing and supplementing the oral bid for conviction.

Here are my own visualizations of two famous texts.

DIAGRAM OF JOHN 3:16

Each side of the triangle represents a segment of the verse. Beginning at the top, it shows God's downward overture toward man: "God so loved the world that he gave his only Son." Then, following the diagram, we see the flow of movement in human life: "that whoever believes in him should not perish . . ." Finally there is an abrupt turning upward as the newborn spirit, radiant in victory, recognizes that he shall not merely "not perish," *but have eternal life*, which brings him up to the presence of God.

The following diagram shows the radical nature of the change that must take place in the life of one who finds Christ. Proceeding through life in his own strength, man goes forward but not upward. There is a radical break between the natural and the newborn man; there are no connecting links. Man cannot bridge this gap in his own power; he must be lifted up. And once having found the new life, he must continue to climb upward and not merely stop on the lowest step.

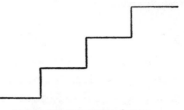

DIAGRAM OF JOHN 3:7B
"YOU MUST BE BORN ANEW..."

There is nothing definitive about a diagram of this sort; other analysts might well arrive at quite different representations of the same texts. By the same token, there are few passages that do not lend themselves to some sort of visual interpretation.

Whether diagrams and charts or actual physical objects are used as visual aids, they should not dominate the preaching situation. Introduced in order to make an emphasis clear and vivid, they should be removed from sight when their function has been served. A diagram left in front of the pulpit during an entire sermon becomes a competitor, bidding for the attention of the listener at times when the visual stimuli are irrelevant.

Neither should any type of visual appeal—gesture, dress, facial expression, physical object or chart—be regarded as capable of serving an end in itself. These stimuli are valid and effective only when used as communication devices. Their purpose is to convey meaning, not call attention to themselves. Unless a visual illustration actually illuminates, it is rightly regarded as cheap and phoney.

Within these limits it is ridiculous to be afraid of the unconventional merely because it is unconventional. No matter how unusual or even "sensational" a device may be, it is valid and effective provided that in practice it serves to implement the preacher's spirit-led urge to communicate and to persuade.

CONCLUSIONS

Modern communication employs the eyes to a much greater extent than the ears. As a result, persons are conditioned to visual learning; this element cannot be neglected in preaching.

Several physical factors are significant. Even the preacher's dress and physical position may help attract and hold the attention of the listener. Far more important is the matter of eye-contact—which grows, not out of mere adoption of desirable habits, but out of an urge to deliver a message that is regarded as vital.

This factor also affects one's freedom in use of gesture. A natural phase of genuine communication, gesture becomes stiff and awkward when one's attention is directed to some goal other than conveying ideas and emotions to listeners. When freed of self-consciousness through dedication to an idea a speaker can usually gain genuine abandon. He then employs gesture naturally and easily, to whatever degree may be in keeping with his personality.

In addition to gesture, communication may be effected through use of visual aids and illustrations. These may be of two types: physical objects and charts or diagrams. Such materials should never be used in such fashion that they call attention to themselves. But the preacher whose chief goal is communication need not be afraid to step outside the bounds of traditional practices. Use of off-trail techniques may actually contribute to both interest-value and persuasive power of preaching.

Chapter XII

PLAGIARISM AND THE DEVELOPMENT
OF ORIGINALITY

ANY MINISTER CAN CONSISTENTLY PRODUCE ORIGINAL sermons. Yet there is a steady stream of instances in which plagiarism is detected in published works. Many more cases go undetected, especially among sermons that are preached but never published. This chapter presents a brief history and a positive solution to the problem of plagiarism in preaching and in writing.

No one knows what writer first borrowed from another without permission or acknowledgment. This technique was in wide use at least as early as 405 B.C., however, for Aristophanes satirized it in *The Frogs*. At this period there seems to have been no standard name for the writer with light fingers. Nearly three centuries passed before Martial termed such a person *plagiarus*—a title formerly reserved for the abductor of a child or slave. As an apt designation for the kidnaper of one's brain child, the name stuck. It entered 16th-century English as *plagiarist,* and was given currency by Ben Jonson in his *Poetaster*.

At this period there was almost complete lack of scruples

concerning use of another's work. Literary rights, as such, had not existed before the invention of printing. Only when mass production was developed did it become possible to treat a story or treatise as a profitable piece of property. There were no copyright laws. Writers and publishers, eager to exploit the market for all it was worth, were shameless in their tactics.

It was inevitable that this attitude should affect the pulpit.

Relatively few original sermons were produced from the days of the early Church until the Reformation began to bear fruit. For many generations, priests had tended to follow the advice of Gregory I and read the homilies of the Fathers from the pulpit. But the flowering of dissent brought new interest in the Bible as the source-book of all religious thought. In order that the people might understand Scripture it was necessary that portions of it be expounded on every Lord's Day. And the doctrines of the Reformers had to be interpreted.

Consequently, the pulpit assumed an importance it had not known in the medieval Church. Ministers were not only expected to preach; increasingly, congregations demanded original sermons. James I of England required his divines to deliver four sermons each month—and stipulated that at least one should be written for the occasion. Charles I frowned on the reading of classic sermons by any preacher, and actually forbade it among the doctors at the universities.[a]

Strong pressure for original sermons produced a crisis in clerical circles. It was made more acute by the scarcity of well-educated preachers. If the brilliant Jeremy Taylor was forced to borrow from Europeans, how could the average country parson hope to stand on his own feet?

[a] (162), 91, 338.

Remember that this was a period when few persons hesitated to claim borrowed material as their own. Confronted with a demand which they felt incapable of meeting, preachers began to beg, borrow, and steal sermons. Printers and Grub Street hacks saw their opportunity and quickly seized it. "Would you think it, gentlemen," says such a fellow in Goldsmith's *Citizen of the World*, "I have actually written last week sixteen prayers, twelve bawdy jests, and three sermons, all at the rate of sixpence apiece."[b]

No less a person than the great Samuel Johnson wrote numerous sermons for sale.[c] And Milton became so alarmed that he denounced "the multitude of sermons ready printed and piled up on every text that is not difficult. . . . [Printers] have not within their hallowed limits more vendible ware of all sorts ready made."[d]

This trade flourished throughout the 18th and 19th centuries. In 1769, the Rev. Dr. John Trusler achieved a record, of sorts. He sent a notice to ministers throughout Great Britain, offering a series of 150 sermons. Priced at one shilling each, they were printed in script type that imitated handwriting.[e] Though one enlightened critic pronounced this clerical almanac to be "the most unspeakable trash that can be conceived," it seems to have met considerable success.[f] It was Trusler, incidentally, who anticipated Dale Carnegie by a century and a half with *The Way to Be Rich and Respectable* —which passed through seven editions.

Extent of the commerce in sermons is indicated by an advertisement in the London *Courier*, May 9, 1807. Printed in Latin so that the laity could not read the piece, it offered a set of sixty sermons printed in a new type which was

[b] (163).
[c] (164), III, 22, 206; V, 75.
[d] (165), 41.
[e] (166), LVII, 268.
[f] (167); Oct. 30, 1875; p. 345.

described as "an accurate imitation of handwriting."[g] Sixty years later *St. Paul's Magazine* devoted a long article to the flourishing trade in sermons. By that time publishers were promising that no duplicates would be sent to towns. In return, the purchaser was expected to refrain from preaching any of his purchases outside his own parish. According to the author of the study, which was limited to the Church of England, some 1,200 bought sermons were being preached every Sunday.[h]

A few enterprising sermon publishers even saved the cost of employing writers. They sent clerks into the churches of prominent preachers and had them take down their messages. Known to the trade as "cat's meat sermons," they were produced in such quantity that a purchaser could find almost any type discourse he wanted. As an added attraction, many of them were advertised as "beautifully written and legible to the weakest eyes."[i]

Modern copyright laws, enacted late in the 19th century, gradually brought an end to the open theft and sale of religious discourses. Meanwhile, the literary conscience had become much more sensitive. By 1900 it was generally acknowledged that extensive use of another person's ideas and/or language, without permission or acknowledgement, is best described by the blunt word, *theft*.

A MATTER OF CONSCIENCE

Except in very rare instances, plagiarism is a matter for the conscience rather than the courts. Even in cases of overt violation of copyright, few publishers of sermons will take action. (That is not true of such literary properties as short stories, novels, motion pictures, stage plays, radio and television plays.)

[g](168), 103.
[h](162), 97.
[i](167), June 15, 1895; p. 468.

There are no hard and fast rules by which to govern one's use of material from printed sources. Courts have consistently held to a policy of judging each case on its own merits. "Fair usage" is the rule of thumb.

Oral delivery of copyrighted material seldom involves legal rights, no matter how flagrant the violation of ethics. And in the case of material prepared for publication, two simple steps will prevent the possibility of an embarrassing situation. Simply give credit where credit is due, and in the case of long or especially vivid quotations, write for permission before using them.

How long must a quotation be in order to require a letter of permission?

In preaching, such permission is seldom needed. However, there have been some recent cases in which sermons published posthumously were attacked by authors whose rights were violated. So even in preparing manuscripts for one's own pulpit, it is well to make notations concerning sources used. And in writing for publication it is routine to secure permission to use any quotation of more than three or four sentences—or two lines of poetry. If a copyright notice reads, "No part of this work may be reproduced in any form without permission in writing," it is necessary to secure permission for even one-sentence quotations. Most publishers and other copyright owners readily grant permission to make reasonable use of their material.

Part of our modern dilemma arises from false ideas concerning the nature and worth of originality. There seems to be a widespread opinion among ministers that one who borrows from others is somehow guilty. This feeling is vague and undefined, but real.

It fails to take into account the true meaning of originality. Major General J. G. Harbord, chairman of the board, Radio Corporation of America, once defined originality as "the ability to put two things together, not to make a third thing equal to the sum of the other two, but superior to the sum."[j] Note that this entire definition rests upon putting together ideas and materials taken from others. There are few really new ideas. It has been estimated that if the Cinderella story were to be excised from the literature of the world, "more than fifty per cent of dramatic literature would be wiped out with it."[k]

If originality were defined as the creation of entirely new products or ideas, without dependence upon the work of others, few if any of the world's masterpieces could be termed original. Sterne borrowed most of the best passages in *Tristram Shandy;* he imitated Rabelais and took material bodily from Pope and Swift.[l] According to Alfred Einstein, Handel leaned heavily upon Erba, Urio, Stradella, and numerous others.[m] Shakespeare boldly appropriated ideas from Chaucer, Boccaccio, North, Holinshed, Lodge, and no one knows how many others.

Disraeli was perpetually borrowing; his famous funeral oration over Wellington was taken almost entirely from an article by Thiers.[n] *Faust,* especially in its first part, has been described as "a patchwork of plagiarisms."[o] And when Jack London sued the Biograph Company for alleged theft of his story "Just Meat," said to have been used in producing the picture *Love of Gold,* the learned judge handed down a significant decision. He pointed out that both plots rested upon Kipling's *The King's Ankus,* which was adapted from Chaucer's *Pardoner's Tale.* Chaucer, said the jurist, probably got the idea from a long line of Oriental tales.[p]

[j](169), 168.
[k](170), 76.
[l](171), 898.
[m](172), 127.
[n](171), 892.
[o](173), 100.
[p](170), 77.

An obscure contemporary of Shakespeare attacked him for alleged borrowing from him, and described the bard of Avon as "an upstart crowe beautified with our feathers that with his Tyger's heart wrapt in a player's hide supposes he is as well able to bumbast out a blank verse as the best of you."[q] Shakespeare may have borrowed from Robert Greene, as he certainly did from many others. But, says E. R. Richardson, "he was not a plagiarist, for by subtle alchemy ideas passed through him and were converted into gold that was his own."[r] Einstein points out that neither Bach nor Mozart nor Handel was entirely original; then he adds: "Handel *made* something out of his thefts. . . . Even where he copied, so to speak, word for word, the copy became *in* and *through* the new context, his property."[s] Kipling, bolder than most who commit words to paper, put it like this:

> When 'Omer smote 'is bloomin' lyre,
>   He'd 'eard men sing by land an' sea;
> An' what 'e thought 'e might require,
>   'E went an' took—the same as me![t]

In that saucy verse we may discover a positive approach to the problem. No man need be ashamed of giving credit to those from whom he has gained ideas or material. But any man is rightly ashamed when he is detected preening himself before an admiring audience, adorned with feathers which he claims are his own, but are not.

Few congregations will think less of a minister who frankly states that the outline of a sermon was adapted from Wesley, or one of its major points from Spurgeon. Failure to make such acknowledgment is a way of claiming complete originality. And when a supposedly original sermon is found

[q] (174), I, 49.
[r] (175), 19.
[s] (172), 127.
[t] (176), 776; used by permission.

in a book, the minister descends in the estimation of his people.

Sydney Smith frankly announced that he preached Channing's sermon on war in St. Paul's. "I thought I could not write anything half as good," he said, "so I preached Channing."[u] Southey advised James White, a young minister, to adapt the best sermons of pulpit giants to his own congregation.[v] Addison put it even more bluntly: "I could heartily wish that more of our clergy (would read sermons of others) and instead of wasting their spirits in laborious compositions of their own, preach those penned by great masters."[w]

Such advice may or may not appeal to the modern preacher. Certainly, he will wish to be honest with himself and his congregation if he follows it. But if he decides to produce most or all of his own sermons, he can develop originality to such a degree that he does not need to stoop to plagiarism. There are only three major aspects to the enhancement of one's creative power: work, time, and vital concern.

NO SUBSTITUTE FOR SPADE WORK

After a long period of active association with writers of many types, George H. Doran concluded that intellectual indolence is the chief cause of "assimilation or plagiarism."[x]

Several investigators have reached independent conclusions that echo such a verdict. After spending years in analysis of Shakespeare's creative genius, Edward Armstrong concluded: "Inspiration frequently comes suddenly and unexpectedly, but not gratuitously. Those who seek, find; their reward is usually the outcome of much travail."[y] Basing his

[u](177), II, 528.
[v](178), 306.
[w](179), No. 106.
[x](180), 121.
[y](181), 174.

judgment upon study of numerous great inventors, Ribot declares that "invention is prepared for by accumulating as much material as possible, living in it, and preparing one's self for psychological unity by great efforts of analysis and synthesis."[z] Henri Poincare, James H. Leuba, and Joseph Montmasson reached similar conclusions in their studies of originality.[a]

It is well known that Coleridge regarded his *Kubla Khan* as having been produced by "inspiration." He actually composed nearly three hundred lines while in a profound sleep; upon awakening, he was unable to recall all the poem, but remembered more than two hundred lines of it. A literary critic has studied large numbers of books to which Coleridge referred in his diary, and has concluded that words, phrases, and sentences in *Kubla Khan* were unconsciously borrowed from many sources. When the poet read, "the mind moved, like the passing of a magnet, over pages to all seeming as bare of poetic implications as a parallelogram, and drew and held fixed whatever was susceptible of imaginative transmutation."[b]

Many ministers are under pressure to prepare two sermons a week. Even under the best of circumstances it is all but impossible to maintain high quality with such an output. Since much corn that goes into the grist mill of the mind is reduced to chaff and lost, it is always necessary to put in more than one expects to get out. A high level of productivity demands an even greater rate of intake. Without wide reading, "inspiration" could not have produced *Kubla Khan.*

A major factor contributing to sermonic dishonesty is, without doubt, extensive reading of published sermons. These volumes, however noble they may be, resemble precooked

[z] (182), 338.
[a] (183), 56f; (184), 699; (125), 17ff.
[b] (185), 34.

baby food, from which all the lumps have been carefully removed. Such food requires no chewing. One may ingest it almost without effort, and digest it with equal ease.

James W. Bridges declares, "All that is necessary for creative imagination is past experience and the ability to make new combinations."[c] Obviously, the richer and more varied one's mental and spiritual experiences, the more dynamic his new combinations will be.

Creativity demands mental exercise; it never comes until one begins to stretch the muscles of his mind. Hence comparatively difficult books will yield richer results than easy ones. Effective and original sermons grow from reading history, theology, philosophy, biography, psychology, and allied works. Biography and history are of course especially fruitful in illustrative materials. Every minister should spend some time every week in the company of the early Fathers, the saints, and the Reformers. Great souls and keen minds necessarily affect all who touch them, however remotely.

Narrow specialization should be avoided. Ideas transplanted from one field to another frequently take root and bear rich fruit. So, without attempting to be an amateur commentator on the advance of science, the minister should read in such fields as physics, biology, astronomy, geology, and related disciplines.

Unless your memory is phenomenal, you will find it best not to rely too heavily on it. Read with a pencil in hand. If a volume is your own, do not hesitate to mark it. Should it be borrowed, make notes as you read and copy significant passages when you have completed the book. (In making such extracts, be sure to note the source.) Should you be struck by an idea or statement from which you have a flash of insight, take care to note its application; hours or days

[c](186), 237.

later you may prod your memory in vain—the particular combination of circumstances under which the inspiration came cannot be duplicated.

As with reading, so with thinking, playing, eating, traveling. Creative giants have testified to the importance of a notebook or sketch book in which to record flashes of inspiration. In the midst of a conversation Mozart would say: "Do not speak to me. Do not disturb me. There is a song in my ears. I must set it down."[d]

No matter how fresh and vivid a thought, it can be lost unless it is immediately committed to writing, even though in sketchy form. Modern literature has no more vivid expression of this psychological phenomenon than that which Lewis Carroll places on the lips of the Queen in *Jabberwocky*:

"The horror of that moment," the King went on, "I shall **never, never** forget."

"You will, though," the Queen said, "if you don't make a memorandum of it."

Once you have accumulated a quantity of notes from your reading and observation of life they must be arranged in such fashion that you can find the material you want when you want it. There are many different systems, based upon files, scrapbooks, and notebooks. One system is discussed in Chapter VI; any method is of value if it works. Enriched by a quantity of diverse material, one may find the bones of a sermon in a published work; place new flesh upon the skeleton and it emerges so stalwart and vigorous that it deserves to be called your own.

FROM INCUBATION TO ILLUMINATION

Ideas tend to be more like oaks than gourds. With rare exceptions, they do not mature fully until they are given a

[d](187), 44.

considerable period for unhurried growth. Psychologists are
generally of the opinion that the subconscious mind—whatever that may be!—is a significant, even an essential, factor
in true creativity.

"A good subconscious that has handled ideas long
enough emits them in forms that their parents can scarcely
recognize," says a literary analyst.[e] Voronoff points out that
there is often "a kind of collaboration between the conscious
and the subconscious . . . [and] subconscious work is usually
produced only after a long period of conscious incubation."[f]

Basing his conclusion upon the matchless mind of Shakespeare, Armstrong says, "Memory is so allied with other
functions that it does more than record. . . . Its products
can become so changed from what they were when registered
that in comparison they may be described as imaginative."[g]

When ideas emerge from the subconscious they are likely
to startle the mind. Ancient poets, feeling themselves incapable of having produced their own verse, attributed their
work to the Muses. Socrates attributed many of his ideas to
a familiar spirit. Emerson testified to his conviction that his
mind "could not possibly be the source of the ideas that came
to him in his creative moments."[h] Stevenson credited his most
brilliant work to "the brownies."[i] Joel Chandler Harris re-
peatedly said he had no literary skill, and that his "other
fellow" did the work, while he got credit.[j]

"Unconscious rumination" was deliberately practiced
by such diverse craftsmen as Lafcadio Hearn, Holmes, Tolstoy, Schopenhauer, Condorcet, and Coleridge.[k] Goethe de-
pended heavily upon "the subconscious activity within us,

[e] (175), 364.
[f] (187), 60.
[g] (181), 110.
[h] (188), 354.
[i] (189), 250-65.
[j] (190), 384-5.
[k] (191), I, 140-1; (181), 108; (187), 62.

which unites in a free understanding with our consciousness in such a way as to produce a unity which surprises the world."[1] When Haydn found himself unable to produce, he would slip into the chapel with his rosary, turn his mind from his work and say a prayer. "Immediately ideas came to me," he testified.[m] Bertrand Russell early adopted the practice of thinking intensively on a topic for some time, then shifting his mind to another problem. After some time elapsed, he would "return consciously to the topic and find that the work has been done."[n]

Scientific discoveries tend to be more clear-cut in their originality than most literary works. As a result, it is in this field that we find the most spectacular evidence concerning the value of committing ideas to the mind in order that they may be mellowed by time.

It is of course clear that time is not a substitute for work, but a supplement. Most of the men discussed in this chapter have been marked by great productivity. Einstein once told a friend, "I think and think, for months, for years. Ninety-nine times the conclusion is false. The hundredth time, I am right."[o] Faraday worked for twenty-three years on his hypothesis that magnetism and light are related, before devising the first experiment that led to a positive result.[p]

Once one has paid the price by performing intense labor, he may reap a harvest when time has done its work. Many of Newton's mathematical discoveries actually came to him during his sleep or immediately upon awakening.[q] August Kekule solved the problem of the constitution of the benzene molecule while drowsing on top of a London bus.[r] Frederick

[1] (187), 60.
[m] (192), 228.
[n] (193), 75-6.
[o] N. Y. *Times*, 4/1/34.
[p] (194), 587.
[q] (192), 221.
[r] (195), 125ff.

Banting discovered insulin as a direct result of a "hunch" that awakened him at 2:00 A.M. on October 30, 1920. It is significant that he had read two medical works, apparently unrelated, before going to bed. He saw no connection between the data in the two studies—but his mind continued to work on the problem after he fell asleep.[s]

Examination of a few literary case histories will reveal that this mysterious "illumination" is not limited to scientists and mathematicians. Gilbert Chesterton's *Ballad of the White Horse,* considered by many to be his greatest work, was on his mind for five years. When it finally took form in 1911, large sections of the verse came to him in his sleep.[t] Longfellow's diary gives a brief account of the birth of "The Wreck of the Hesperus." After an evening of routine work, he sat by the fire until midnight. He went to bed, but was unable to sleep because the poem was forcing itself into his mind. "It hardly cost me an effort," he noted. "It did not come into my mind by lines, but by stanzas."[u]

Beecher once preached a new sermon daily for eighteen months. He did it by keeping numerous themes in his thinking; several days ahead, he would select one, work on it, then put it aside. On the morning he expected to use it he would produce the finished version very rapidly. It is significant that dabblers and dilettantes seldom report illumination. Persons of great productivity can work on many ideas concurrently, taking each out when it "ripens," and quickly putting it in finished form.

There is no precise understanding of the mechanics of inspiration. William H. Easton concludes that it is "evoked by intense deliberate thinking, which forms new combinations of ideas after the thinking has ceased."[v] He hastens to add

[s] (196), 59f.
[t] (197), 282.
[u] (198), 13.
[v] (199), 29.

that "illumination is not incited by easy-going thinking, but it prepares for action whenever the mind struggles with some obstacle."

This process is not without its dangers; the history of religion is replete with trances and visions that proved barren. And even in the field of science at least one observer has noted that inspiration does not necessarily lead to outstanding work, "for it may even result in the production of illusory values which for others are not values at all."[▼]

Consequently, the seeker for originality must be aware of the dangers associated with "inspiration." He must recognize that knowledge of the process is too limited to provide precise directions by which it may be used. At the same time, it is impossible to escape the conclusion that there is no true originality without some degree of illumination. An alert mind confronted with a problem, supplied with materials more or less vitally related to it, and given ample time to do its work, is likely to yield something quite fresh.

DYNAMIC POWER OF GREAT DEVOTION

Hard work, stretched over a long period of time, does not always result in creativity. There is at least a third element which in some respects is more difficult to analyze than the other two. If that element must bear a label, the most suitable is "devotion."

Perhaps a physical analogy will make clear the rôle of devotion. Suppose you are given iron filings and powdered sulphur; from these raw materials you must create something new. You get an adequate supply, mix the substances thoroughly and let the mixture stand for an indefinite time. At intervals you look to see whether anything new will be produced. Despairing, you place the unchanged mixture into a

▼ (200), 88.

spoon and expose it to a flame. Under the impact of heat the ingredients become iron sulphide. Nothing remains of the original ingredients; a new product has been formed. Its qualities could not possibly be predicted from a knowledge of the properties of iron and sulphur.

Intense emotion frequently causes raw materials in the mind to unite in a totally unpredictable fashion. Shakespeare's imagination was undoubtedly affected by emotional factors.[x] In the process of making a notable discovery Newton sometimes felt "a sense of ecstasy—a wave of emotion so intense that he was forced to stop work for a time."[y] Voronoff points out that Wagner's love for Mathilda Wesendonck was the flame that fused gross ingredients into *Tristan and Isolde*. He concludes that Dante's adoration of Beatrice was an important element in creation of the *Divine Comedy*, and shows that Goethe's *Faust* was thirty years in the writing because it had to be sustained by "various and violent passions."[z]

Lange-Eichbaum goes so far as to declare that creative activity cannot result from intellectual effort alone. "It is, rather," he says, "intimately connected with feelings, moods, affects, impulses, conations. It is permeated by these, and, indeed, receives its first impetus from them."[a]

Poincaré is emphatic in linking feeling with mathematical discovery, as is Hadamard. Says the latter, "I should agree with this curious statement of Daunou: 'In Sciences, even the most rigid ones, no truth is born of the genius of an Archimedes or a Newton without a poetical emotion.' "[b] Beethoven once described a moment of what he felt to be typical of proffered illumination: "I pursue it, I grasp it, I see it fly from me and lose itself in the seething mass. I seize

[x](181), 110.
[y](192), 221.
[z](187), 114-15.
[a](200), 77.
[b](124), 10.

it again with renewed passion; I can no longer separate myself from it. I have to multiply it in a spasm of ecstasy."[c] Russell describes the moment of insight as "exciting, like quick motoring."[d]

If emotion is an element in secular creativity, how much more can pure love of God contribute to the originality of the preacher! It is perhaps at this very point that the heaviest casualties occur. Absorbed with the material—with an institution, its building, congregation, and program—one *cannot* achieve and maintain a kindling passion that is pure and undefiled.

It was holy love, no less than zealous cultivation of the mind, that produced the originality of the great pioneers of religion. To the degree that the modern minister succeeds in finding such a passion he will enhance his development of originality.

CONCLUSIONS

Ministerial plagiarism developed as a by-product of the Reformation, and still flourishes widely. It has been fostered by a strong, but perhaps unjustified demand for "complete originality." More important as a matter of conscience than law, it may be completely eliminated by common-sense application of two rules: (1) give credit where credit is due; (2) secure permission to use any material about which there is doubt as to your right to borrow.

Originality may be cultivated through intensive and extensive reading, careful observation, unhurried assimilation of ideas and problems, and zealous attention to spiritual health. Here are a few specific suggestions:

(1) Read the Scriptures regularly, with an open mind.

[c](123), 9.
[d](123), 134.

It is preferable to devote the last waking hour of the day to this discipline, in order that great ideas of the faith may permeate the subconscious mind.

(2) Read much; hunt, fish, and play golf in moderation —if at all. Pay great attention to history, biography, philosophy, devotional classics, and the humanities in general. Do not neglect the physical sciences; avoid excessive reading of contemporary sermons.

(3) Keep your ideas, problems, and homiletical gear in such form that nothing will be permanently lost. Read with pencil in hand; carry a notebook at all times.

(4) Never force the development of an idea. Give it time to mature, with the certainty that you will receive insight and the possibility that inspiration will be given you.

BIBLIOGRAPHY

Footnotes employ the following code:

Numbers in parentheses refer to corresponding numbers in the bibliography; capital Roman numerals refer to volumes; small letter Roman numerals and Arabic numerals refer to page numbers.

(1) W. MacNeile Dixon, *The Human Situation.* New York: Longmans, Green and Co., n. d. (Gifford Lectures, 1935-37).

(2) James H. Leuba, *The Reformation of the Churches.* Boston: Beacon Press, 1950.

(3) Reinhold Niebuhr, *Reflections on the End of an Era.* New York: Scribners, 1934.

(4) C. G. Jung, *Modern Man in Search of a Soul.* New York: Harcourt, Brace & Co., 1934.

(5) Henry Nelson Wieman and Bernard Eugene Meland, *American Philosophies of Religion.* New York: Harper & Brothers, 1936.

(6) Charles T. Brown, "What do You Want to Hear?" *Education,* Vol. 65 (1944).

(7) St. Augustine, "The Advantage of Believing," trans. by Luanne Meagher. In *The Fathers of the Church,* Vol. II. New York: Cima Pub. Co., 1947.

(8) Marian Castle, "Some Private Thoughts on Public Speaking," *Harper's,* Vol. 176 (1938).

(9) Stuart Chase, *The Tyranny of Words.* New York: Harcourt, Brace & Co., 1938.

(10) Edwin DuBose Mouzon, *Preaching with Authority.* Garden City, New York: Doubleday, Doran and Co., 1929.

(11) Charles L. Stevenson, *Ethics and Language*. New Haven: Yale University Press, 1944.

(12) William James, *The Will to Believe*. New York: Longmans, Green & Co., 1908.

(13) Josiah Royce, *The Religious Aspect of Philosophy*. New York: Houghton-Mifflin Co., 1885.

(14) John Dewey, *The Quest for Certainty*. New York: Minton, Balch & Co., 1929.

(15) Stuart Chase, *The Proper Study of Mankind*. New York: Harper & Brothers, 1948.

(16) Samuel Butler, *Selected Essays*. New York: J. Cape and H. Smith, 1929.

(17) Philip B. Ballard, *Thought and Language*. London: University of London Press, 1934.

(18) W. A. Sinclair, *Introduction to Philosophy*. London: Oxford University Press, 1944.

(19) Edward L. Thorndike, "Reading as Reasoning," *Journal of Educational Psychology*; Vol. 8 (1917).

(20) Harry E. Bartow, "A Layman Looks at the Sermon," *The Pastor*; Vol. 15, No. 9 (May, 1952).

(21) Brand Blanshard, *The Nature of Thought*; 2 vols. New York: The Macmillan Co., 1940.

(22) Paul S. Yates, *Reading Recognition Vocabulary and Hearing Recognition Vocabulary*. Unpublished Master's thesis, Washington University, 1937.

(23) W. E. Young, *Relations of Reading Comprehension and Retention to Hearing Comprehension and Retention*. Unpublished Doctor's thesis, University of Iowa, 1930.

(24) Mary Burton, "The Hearing and Reading Comprehension of Vocabulary Among High-School Seniors," *School Review*; Vol. 52 (1944).

(25) Robert P. Larsen and D. D. Fedar, "Common and Differential Factors in Reading and Hearing Comprehension," *Journal of Educational Psychology*, Vol. 31 (1940).

(26) Francis Bacon, *Novum Organum*.

(27) Wendell Johnson, "General Semantics and the Science Teacher," *American Journal of Physics*; Vol. 15 (1947).

(28) Irving J. Lee, editor, *The Language of Wisdom and Folly*. New York: Harper & Brothers, 1949.

(29) Douglas L. Oliver, "Human Relations and Language in a Papuan-Speaking Tribe of Southern Bougainville, Solomon Islands"; *Papers of the Peabody Museum of American Archaeology and Ethnology;* Harvard University; Vol. 29 (1949), No. 2.

(30) Grace de Laguna, "Perception and Language," *Human Biology;* Vol. 1, No. 4 (December, 1929).

(31) C. K. Ogden and I. A. Richards, *The Meaning of Meaning.* New York: Harcourt, Brace & Co., 1946.

(32) Edward Sapir, "Conceptual Categories in Primitive Languages," *Science;* Vol. 74 (1931).

(33) Gustav le Bon, *The Crowd;* London: T. Fisher Unwin, 1896.

(34) James J. Gibson, *The Perception of the Visual World.* Cambridge: Riverside Press, 1950.

(35) Leonard Bloomfield, "Linguistic Aspects of Science," *International Encyclopedia of Unified Science;* Vol. 1, No. 4. Chicago: Univ. of Chicago Press, 1939.

(36) Susanne K. Langer, "The Lord of Creation," *Fortune;* Vol. 29 (1944).

(37) Helen Keller, *Story of My Life.* New York: Doubleday, Page & Co., 1903.

(38) Carl Britton, *Communication.* New York: Harcourt, Brace & Co., 1939.

(39) Borden P. Bowne, *Theory of Thought and Knowledge.* New York: American Book Co., 1897.

(40) Edward L. Thorndike, "Psychology of Semantics," *American Journal of Psychology;* Vol. 59 (1946).

(41) G. W. Cunningham, "On the Meaningfulness of Vague Language," *Philosophical Review;* Vol. 58 (1949).

(42) Ernst Cassirer, "Influence of Language on Development of Scientific Thought," *Journal of Philosophy;* Vol. 39 (1942).

(43) John Oman, *Honest Religion.* Cambridge: University Press, 1941.

(44) John Oman, *Vision and Authority;* revised ed. New York: Harper & Brothers, 1929.

(45) S. I. Hayakawa, *Language In Action.* Madison, Wis.: College Typing Co., 1939.

(46) Anton T. Boisen, *The Exploration of the Inner World.* Chicago: Willett, Clark & Co., 1936.

(47) J. R. P. Sclater, "Preaching and Prophesying," *Religion In Life;* Vol. 12 (1943).

(48) William Peter King, address at S. C. Methodist Pastors' School, Columbia, S. C., 1941.

(49) E. Jerome Johnson, "What Is Christian Preaching?" *The Pastor;* Vol. 15, No. 8 (April, 1952). An exposition of Wingren's untranslated *Preaching: A Study of Its Basic Character.*

(50) Samuel L. Terrien, "The Old Testament and the Christian Preacher Today," *Religion in Life;* Vol. 15 (1946).

(51) George Boas, *Our New Ways of Thinking.* New York: Harper & Brothers, 1930.

(52) Leo Postman and J. S. Bruner, "Multiplicity of Set as a Determinant of Perceptual Behavior," *Journal of Experimental Psychology;* Vol. 39, 1949.

(53) Alfred Korzybski, *The Manhood of Humanity.* Lakeville, Conn.: Non-Aristotelian Library Publishing Co., 1950.

(54) Alfred Korzybski, *Science and Sanity.* Lakeville, Conn.: Non-Aristotelian Library Publishing Co., 1948.

(55) Irving J. Lee, *Language Habits in Human Affairs.* New York: Harper & Brothers, 1941.

(56) Hans Vaihinger, *The Philosophy of "As If."* New York: Harcourt, Brace & Co., 1925.

(57) R. M. Eaton, *Symbolism and Truth.* Cambridge: Harvard University Press, 1925.

(58) Guy T. Buswell, *How People Look at Pictures.* Chicago: Univ. of Chicago Press, 1935.

(59) F. A. Philbrick, *Understanding English.* New York: The Macmillan Co., 1944.

(60) Edward L. Thorndike, *Studies in the Psychology of Language.* Archives of Psychology, No. 231 (1938).

(61) Charles T. Brown, "The Speaker Approach to Speech," *Education;* Vol. 64 (1943).

(62) W. E. Hocking, *The Meaning of God in Human Experience.* New Haven: Yale University Press, 1912.

(63) St. Augustine, "The Magnitude of the Soul," trans. by John J. McMahon. In *The Fathers of the Church,* Vol. II. New York: Cima Pub. Co., 1947.

(64) R. H. Strachan, *The Authority of Christian Experience*. Nashville: Cokesbury Press, 1931.

(65) Esta A. Berg, "Technique for Measuring Flexibility in Thinking," *Journal of General Psychology*; Vol. 39 (1948).

(66) Auguste Sabatier, *Religions of Authority and the Religion of the Spirit*. New York: McClure, Phillips & Co., 1905.

(67) *The Nature of Religious Experience*; a symposium. New York: Harper & Brothers, 1937.

(68) Henry Nelson Wieman, *The Wrestle of Religion with Truth*. New York: The Macmillan Co., 1927.

(69) C. H. Dodd, *The Authority of the Bible*. New York: Harper & Brothers, 1929.

(70) J. S. Mill, *Utilitarianism*. London: Parker, Son, and Bourne, 1863.

(71) P. T. Forsyth, *The Principle of Authority*. London: Hodder & Stoughton, n. d. (c. 1915).

(72) J. H. Leckie, *Authority in Religion*. Edinburgh: T. & T. Clark, 1909.

(73) *Dogma in History and Thought*, a symposium. London: Nisbet & Co., 1929.

(74) John Henry Newman, "Essay on Private Judgment," in *Essays, Critical and Historical*. London: Longmans, Green & Co., 1895.

(75) Adolf von Harnack, *History of Dogma*; Vol. I. London: Williams and Norgate, 1896.

(76) Adolf von Harnack, *What Is Christianity?* New York: G. P. Putnam's Sons, 1903.

(77) Reinhold Niebuhr, *Faith and History*. New York: Charles Scribner's Sons, 1949.

(78) George Wobbermin, *The Nature of Religion*; T. Menzel and D. S. Robinson, trans. New York: Thomas Y. Crowell, 1933.

(79) James Martineau, *The Seat of Authority in Religion*; second ed., rev. London: Longmans, Green & Co., 1890.

(80) Bertrand Russell, Mysticism and Logic. New York: W. W. Norton and Co., 1929.

(81) Warren N. Nevius, *Religion as Experience and Truth*. Philadelphia: Westminster Press, 1941.

(82) Henry C. Sheldon, *History of Christian Doctrine;* fourth ed.;
2 vols. New York: Eaton & Mains, 1906.

(83) Gerald Kennedy, "Preaching Effectively to College Students,"
Religion in Life; Vol. 15 (1946).

(84) Paul Arthur Schilpp, ed., *The Philosophy of Ernst Cassirer.*
Evanston: Library of Living Philosophers, 1949.

(85) Edgar S. Brightman, *A Philosophy of Religion.* New York:
Prentice-Hall, Inc., 1940.

(86) *Action, Perception and Measurement;* a symposium. London:
Harrison & Smith, 1938.

(87) Albert C. Knudson, *The Validity of Religious Experience.*
New York: Abingdon-Cokesbury Press, 1937.

(88) Theodor Reik, *Dogma and Compulsion.* New York: International Univ. Press, 1951.

(89) Thomas M. Lindsay, *History of the Reformation;* 2 vols.
New York: Charles Scribner's Sons, 1906-7.

(90) Rupert E. Davies, *The Problem of Authority in the Continental Reformers.* London: Epworth Press, 1946.

(91) Preserved Smith, *Life and Letters of Martin Luther.* Boston:
Houghton-Mifflin Co., 1911.

(92) B. B. Warfield, *Calvin and Calvinism.* London: Oxford University Press, 1931.

(93) L. E. Elliott-Binns, *The Reformers and the Bible.* Cambridge:
W. Heffner & Sons, 1923.

(94) P. F. Wiener, *Martin Luther: Hitler's Spiritual Ancestor.* Universal Distributors, 1945.

(95) Eric S. Waterhouse, *The Philosophy of Religious Experience.*
London: Epworth Press, 1923.

(96) Philip Schaff, *History of the Christian Church;* Vol. II. New
York: Charles Scribner's Sons, 1916.

(97) G. H. Gilbert, *Interpretation of the Bible: A Short History.*
New York: The Macmillan Co., 1908.

(98) Alfred E. Garvie, *The Christian Preacher.* New York: Charles
Scribner's Sons, 1923.

(99) J. S. Bruner and Leo Postman, "Symbolic Value as an Organizing Factor in Perception," *Journal of Social Psychology;*
Vol. 27 (1948).

(100) F. E. D. Schleiermacher, *Uber die Religion;* 2 vols. Berlin: G.
Reimer, 1831.

(101) F. Darwin, ed., *Life and Letters of Charles Darwin*; 2 vols. New York: D. Appleton & Co., 1911.

(102) Emile Durkheim, *Elementary Forms of the Religious Life*; J. W. Swain, trans. New York: The Macmillan Co., 1911.

(103) Sigmund Freud, *Totem and Taboo*. New York: Moffatt, Yard & Co., 1918.

(104) Sigmund Freud, *Future of an Illusion*. London: L. & V. Woolf, 1928.

(105) F. A. Lange, *The History of Materialism*; third ed. London: K. Paul, et. al., 1895.

(106) H. W. Schneider, "Radical Empiricism and Religion," *Essays in Honor of John Dewey*. New York: Henry Holt & Co., 1929.

(107) Karl Barth, *Epistle to the Romans*. London: Oxford Univ. Press, 1933.

(108) Th. Haecker, *Sören Kierkegaard*. London: Oxford Univ. Press, 1937.

(109) Emile Brunner, *The Word and the World*. New York: Chas. Scribner's Sons, 1931.

(110) Emile Brunner, *Doctrine of the Word of God*. Edinburgh: T. & T. Clark, 1936.

(111) James H. Leuba, *A Psychological Study of Religion*. New York: The Macmillan Co., 1912.

(112) John Wood Oman, *The Natural and the Supernatural*. New York: The Macmillian Co., 1931.

(113) F. R. Tennant, *Philosophical Theology*. Cambridge: Univ. Press, 1928.

(114) William James, *Varieties of Religious Experience*. New York: Longmans, Green & Co., 1902.

(115) Rudolph Otto, *Idea of the Holy*. London: Oxford Univ. Press, 1923.

(116) Rufus Jones, *Religious Foundations*. New York: The Macmillan Co., 1923.

(117) Charles A. Bennett, *A Philosophical Study of Mysticism*. New Haven: Yale Univ. Press, 1923.

(118) Rufus M. Jones, *Studies in Mystical Religion*. London: The Macmillan Co., 1909.

(119) Edward Taylor, *Jacob Boehme's Theological Philosophy*. London: 1691.

(120) Douglas Clyde MacIntosh, *The Problem of Religious Knowledge*. New York: Harper & Brothers, 1940.
(121) *Christian Science Journal.*
(122) Eric T. Bell, *The Search for Truth*. New York: Reynal & Hitchcock, 1934.
(123) Eliot D. Hutchinson, *How to Think Creatively*. New York: Abingdon-Cokesbury Press, 1939.
(124) Jacques Hadamard, *Essay on the Psychology of Invention in the Mathematical Field*. Princeton: Princeton Univ. Press, 1949.
(125) J. M. Montmasson, *Invention and the Unconscious*. London: K. Paul, et. al., 1931.
(126) Rudolf Flesch, *The Art of Readable Writing*. New York: Harper & Brothers, 1949.
(127) James H. Leuba, *Psychology of Religious Mysticism*. New York: Harcourt, Brace & Co., 1925.
(128) George A. Coe, *The Psychology of Religion*. Chicago: University of Chicago Press, 1916.
(129) Graham Wallas, *The Art of Thought*. New York: Harcourt, Brace & Co., 1926.
(130) Henry Suso, *Life of the Blessed Henry Suso*. Leipzig: Inselverlag, 1937.
(131) Anatol Rapaport, *Science and the Goals of Man*. New York: Harper & Brothers., 1950.
(132) Bertrand Russell, *Authority and the Individual*. New York: Simon and Schuster, 1949.
(133) W. P. Montague, *The Ways of Knowing*. London: Allen & Unwin, 1925.
(134) J. R. Howard, ed., *Beecher's Patriotic Addresses*. New York: Fords, Howell, & Hulbert, 1887.
(135) Middleton Murry, *The Necessity of Art.*
(136) Albert Schweitzer, *Christianity and the Religions of the World*, New York: George H. Doran Co., 1923.
(137) F. G. Henke, "The Gift of Tongues and Related Phenomena," *American Journal of Theology*; Vol. 13 (1909).
(138) John M. Moore, *Theories of Religious Experience*. New York: Round Table Press, 1938.
(139) Douglas Clyde MacIntosh, *Theology as an Empirical Science*. New York: The Macmillan Co., 1919.

(140) P. W. Bridgman, *The Logic of Modern Physics*. New York: The Macmillan Co., 1927.

(141) Charles Silvester Horne, *The Romance of Preaching*. New York: Fleming H. Revell Co., 1914.

(142) Henri Bergson, *The Two Sources of Morality and Religion*. New York: Henry Holt & Co., 1935.

(143) Harold Hoffding, *History of Modern Philosophy*; 2 vols. London: The Macmillan Co., 1900.

(144) Percy Bysshe Shelley, "Adonais."

(145) W. M. Horton, *A Psychological Approach to Theology*. New York: Harper & Brothers, 1930.

(146) S. A. Nock, "Sound and Symbol," *Philosophy of Science*; Vol. 8 (1941).

(147) Max C. Otto, "Authoritarianism and Supernaturalism," in *Scientific Spirit and Democratic Faith*. New York: King's Crown Press, 1944.

(148) *Journal of Philosophy*; Vol. 7 (1910).

(149) Eric T. Bell, *The Magic of Numbers*. New York: McGraw-Hill, Inc., 1946.

(150) Arthur Eddington, *The Philosophy of Physical Science*. New York: The Macmillan Co., 1939.

(151) Tobias Dantzig, *Aspects of Science*. New York: The Macmillan Co., 1937.

(152) Ernst Cassirer, "Influence of Language on Development of Scientific Thought," *Journal of Philosophy*, Vol. 39 (1942).

(153) Eric T. Bell, *Mathematics: Queen and Servant of Science*. New York: McGraw-Hill Book Co., 1951.

(154) *Sören Kierkegaard: The Journals*; A. Dru, ed. London: Oxford Univ. Press, 1938.

(155) Herbert W. Schneider, "The Power of Free Religion," in *Scientific Spirit and Democratic Faith*. (See 147).

(156) Brand Blanshard, "Theology and the Individual," in *Scientific Spirit and Democratic Faith*. (See 147).

(157) Horace M. Kallen, "Freedom and Authoritarianism in Religion," in *Scientific Spirit and Democratic Faith*. (See 147).

(158) Wolfgang Kohler, *Dynamics in Psychology*. New York: Liveright Pub. Co., 1940.

(159) Morris R. Cohen and Nagel, *Logic and Scientific Method*. New York: Harcourt-Brace & Co., 1934.

(160) Bernard Shaw, *St. Joan*. London: Constable & Co., 1924.

(161) Rudolf Flesch, *The Art of Clear Thinking*. New York: Harper & Brothers, 1951.

(162) H. M. Paull, *Literary Ethics*. New York: E. P. Dutton & Co., 1929.

(163) Oliver Goldsmith, *Citizen of the World*. Washington: M. W. Dunne; c. 1901.

(164) *Boswell's Life of Johnson;* G. B. Hill, ed. New York: Bigelow, Brown and Co., n.d.

(165) John Milton, *Areopagitica* (1644). Oxford: Clarendon Press, 1917.

(166) *Dictionary of National Biography.*

(167) *Notes and Queries.*

(168) Robert Southey, *Common-Place Book;* Second series; J. W. Warter, ed. London: Longman, Brown, Green, and Longmans, 1849.

(169) *American Magazine*, February, 1937.

(170) Levy Newman, "They've Stolen My Plot!" *Atlantic;* Vol. 184 (1949).

(171) William S. Walsh, *Handy-Book of Literary Curiosities*. Philadelphia: J. B. Lippincott, 1892.

(172) Alfred Einstein, *Greatness in Music*. London: Oxford Univ. Press, 1941.

(173) Charles L. Moore, "The Highest Type of Originality in Literature," *Current Literature;* Vol. 50 (1911).

(174) *Plays and Poems of Robert Greene*. Oxford: Clarendon Press, 1905.

(175) E. R. Richardson, "The Ubiquitous Plagiarist," *Bookman;* Vol. 73 (1931).

(176) Rudyard Kipling, "When 'Omer Smote 'is Bloomin' Lyre," in *Rudyard Kipling's Verse*. Garden City, N. Y.: Doubleday, Page & Co., 1923.

(177) Sydney Smith, *Memoir of the Rev. Sidney Smith*. New York: Harper & Brothers, 1855.

(178) Robert Southey, *Life and Correspondence;* C. C. Southey, ed. New York: Harper & Brothers, 185–.

(179) *The Spectator.*

(180) George H. Doran, *Chronicles of Barabbas*. New York: Harcourt, Brace & Co., 1935.

(181) Edward A. Armstrong, *Shakespeare's Imagination*. London: Lindsay Drummond, Ltd., 1946.

(182) Th. Ribot, *Essay on the Creative Imagination*. Chicago: Open Court, 1906.

(183) Henri Poincare, *Science and Method*. Paris: E. Flammarion, 1908.

(184) James H. Leuba, "Intuition," *Forum;* Vol. 79 (1928).

(185) John L. Lowes, *Road to Xanadu*. New York: Houghton-Mifflin Co., 1927.

(186) James W. Bridges, *Psychology, Normal and Abnormal*. Toronto: Isaac Pitman & Sons, n.d.

(187) Serge Voronoff, *From Cretin to Genius*. New York: Alliance Book Corp., 1941.

(188) John M. Fletcher, *Psychology in Education*. Garden City, N. Y.: Doubleday, Doran & Co., 1934.

(189) Robert L. Stevenson, chapter on dreams in *Travels and Essays of Robert L. Stevenson*. New York: Chas. Scribner's Sons, 1909.

(190) Julia C. Harris, *Life and Letters of Joel Chandler Harris*. New York: Houghton-Mifflin Co., 1918.

(191) Elizabeth Bisland, *The Life and Letters of Lafcadio Hearn*. New York: Houghton-Mifflin Co., 1906.

(192) T. B. Hyslop, *The Great Abnormals*. London: Philip Allan & Co., 1925.

(193) Bertrand Russell, *The Conquest of Happiness*. New York: Garden City Pub. Co., 1930.

(194) William S. Jevons, *Principles of Science*. New York: The Macmillan Co., 1892.

(195) C. E. K. Mees, *The Path of Science*. New York: John Wiley & Sons, 1946.

(196) Paul De Kruif, *Men Against Death*. New York: Harcourt, Brace & Co., 1932.

(197) Maisie Ward, *Gilbert Keith Chesterton*. New York: Sheed & Ward, 1943.

(198) Henry Wadsworth Longfellow, *Complete Poetical Works of Henry Wadsworth Longfellow*. Boston: Houghton-Mifflin Co., 1893.

(199) William H. Easton, "Illumination." *Science Digest*, December, 1946.

(200) Wilhelm Lange-Eichbaum, *The Problem of Genius*. New York: The Macmillan Co., 1932.

(201) H. A. Overstreet, *Influencing Human Behavior*. New York: Peoples' Institute Pub. Co., 1925.

(202) Charles H. Spurgeon, *Lectures To My Students*; First and Second Series. New York: American Tract Society, n. d.

(203) Leo Postman and J. S. Bruner, *Journal of Experimental Psychology*, Vol. 39 (1949).

(204) John P. Hyland, *The Fluctuation of Attention. Psychological Review*, Supplement II (1898).

(205) W. B. Pillsbury, *Attention*. London: Swan Sonnenschein & Co., 1908.

(206) Irwin Edman, "Under Whatever Sky," *American Scholar*, Vol. 20 (1951).

(207) F. W. Lambertson, "Hitler, the Orator," *Quarterly Journal of Speech*, Vol. 28 (1942).

(208) Joshua Rosett, *The Mechanism of Thought, Imagery, and Hallucination*. New York: Columbia University Press, 1939.

(209) J. Calvin Callaghan, "Social Facilitation in Persuasion," *Quarterly Journal of Speech*, Vol. 26 (1940).

(210) Henry Ward Beecher, *Yale Lectures on Preaching*; Series I.

(211) Henry Ward Beecher, *Yale Lectures on Preaching*; Series II.

(212) Henry Ward Beecher, *Yale Lectures on Preaching*; Series III.

(213) H. L. Hollingworth, *The Psychology of the Audience*. New York: American Book Co., 1935.

(214) Charles G. Finney, *Revival Lectures*. New York: Leavitt, Lord & Co., 1835.

(215) Hugo Munsterberg, *Psychology and Industrial Efficiency*. Boston: Houghton-Mifflin Co., 1913.

(216) George W. Hartman, *Gestalt Psychology*. New York: Ronald Press, 1935.

(217) Joseph E. Barmack, *Boredom and Other Factors in the Physiology of Mental Effort*. Archives of psychology, No. 218 (1937).

(218) David Katz, *Gestalt Psychology*; Robert Tyson, trans., New York: Ronald Press, 1950.

(219) Wendell White, *The Psychology of Making Life Interesting*. New York: The Macmillan Co., 1939.

(220) Clarence E. Macartney, *Preaching Without Notes*. New York: Abingdon-Cokesbury Press, 1946.

(221) Alan H. Monroe, *Measurement and Analysis of Audience Reaction to Student Speakers*. Bulletin of Purdue University, Lafayette, Indiana, 1937.

(222) Franklin H. Knower, Phillips and Keoppel, "Studies in Listening to Informative Speaking," *Journal of Abnormal and Social Psychology*, Vol. 40 (1945).

(223) Donald E. Soper and W. F. Braasch, "Effect of Distraction on Test Results," *Journal of Educational Psychology*, Vol. 38 (1947).

(224) W. H. D. Rouse, "Style," in *Essays and Studies by Members of the English Association;* Vol. 27. Oxford: Clarendon Press, 1941.

(225) Batsell B. Baxter, *The Heart of the Yale Lectures*. New York: The Macmillan Co., 1947.

(226) *Edinburgh Review*, 1802.

(227) Thorstein Veblen, *The Theory of the Leisure Class*. New York: The Macmillan Co., 1902.

(228) Robert P. Larsen and D. D. Fedar, "Common and Differential Factors in Reading and Hearing Comprehension," *Journal of Experimental Psychology*, Vol. 31 (1940).

(229) Ernest C. Colwell, *An Approach to the Teaching of Jesus*. New York: Abingdon-Cokesbury Press, 1947.

(230) Lionel Crocker, "The Rhetorical Training of Henry Ward Beecher," *Quarterly Journal of Speech*, Vol. 19 (1933).

(231) William Hazlitt, "On the Difference Between Writing and Speaking," in *The Writer's Art;* Rollo Walter Brown, ed. Cambridge, Mass.: Harvard University Press, 1921.

(232) Adolf Hitler, *Mein Kampf*. New York: Reynal & Hitchcock, 1940.

(233) Ralph G. Nichols, "Listening: Questions and Answers," *Quarterly Journal of Speech*, Vol. 33 (1947).

(234) Benjamin C. Leeming, *Imagination*. New York: The M. H. Schroeder Co., 1926.

(235) Walter A. Steigleman, *Writing the Feature Article*. New York: The Macmillan Co., 1950.

(236) Gilbert K. Chesterton, quoted, *Reader's Digest*, June, 1939.

(237) George Bernard Shaw, *Sixteen Self Sketches*. London: Longmans.

(238) Clovis G. Chappell, *Sermons on the Lord's Prayer*. Nashville: Cokesbury Press, 1934.

(239) *Studies in Rhetoric and Public Speaking*, by pupils and colleagues of James A. Winans. New York: The Century Co., 1925.

(240) Oscar F. Green, "The Three Factors in Preaching," *Religion in Life*, Vol. 13 (1944).

(241) W. Norwood Brigance, "Effectiveness of the Public Platform," *Annals of the American Academy*, Vol. 250 (1947).

(242) Harry Emerson Fosdick, "What Is the Matter with Preaching?" *Harper's*, Vol. 157 (1928).

(243) Harold Sonberg, "A Study of the Relative Effectiveness of Climax and Anti-Climax in an Argumentative Speech," *Speech Monographs*, Vol. 13 (1946).

(244) F. H. Lund, "The Psychology of Belief," *Journal of Abnormal Psychology*, Vol. 20 (1925).

(245) Joseph Schiffman, "Observations on Roosevelt's Literary Style," *Quarterly Journal of Speech*, Vol. 35 (1949).

(246) Arthur Jersild, "Modes of Emphasis in Public Speaking," *Journal of Applied Psychology*, Vol. 12 (1928).

(247) Lionel G. Crocker, *Henry Ward Beecher's Art of Preaching*. Chicago: University of Chicago Press, 1934.

(248) Isaac Goldberg, *The Wonder of Words*. New York: D. Appleton-Century Co., 1938.

(249) Alexander Bain, *Study of Character*. New York: D. Appleton & Co., 1873.

(250) Joshua C. Gregory, "Metaphor and Analogy," *Fortnightly Review*, Vol. 165, (1949).

(251) James E. Creighton, *An Introductory Logic*; 5th edition. New York: The Macmillan Co., 1926.

(252) Benjamin W. Robinson, *Some Elements of Forcefulness in the Comparisons of Jesus*. Chicago: Univ. of Chicago Press, 1904.

(253) Vincent Van Gogh, *Letters of a Post Impressionist*. Boston: Houghton-Mifflin Co., 1913.

(254) Wilbur M. Urban, *Language and Reality*. London: George Allen & Unwin, 1939.

(255) Henry Ward Beecher, *Eyes and Ears*. Boston: Tishmor & Fields, 1863.

(256) Andrew L. Drummond, *Story of American Protestantism.* Edinburgh: Oliver and Boyd, 1949.

(257) John A. Sawhill, *The Use of Athletic Metaphors in the Biblical Homilies of St. John Chrysostom.* Princeton University Press, 1928.

(258) J. H. Jowett, *The Preacher: His Life and Work.* New York: Hodder & Stoughton, 1912.

(259) Raymond B. Cattell and Lester B. Luborsky, "Personality Factors in Response to Humor," *Journal of Abnormal and Social Psychology,* Vol. 42 (1947).

(260) William L. Stidger, *Planning Your Preaching.* New York: Harper & Brothers, 1932.

(261) Albert Rapp, *The Origins of Wit and Humor.* New York: E. P. Dutton & Co., 1951.

(262) Stephen Leacock, *Humour and Humanity.* London: Thornton Butterworth, 1947.

(263) H. A. Wolff, Smith and Murray, "A Study of Responses of Race-Disparagement Jokes," *Journal of Abnormal and Social Psychology,* Vol. 28 (1934).

(264) Russell Maloney, "The Laugh's On You," *Saturday Review of Literature,* Oct. 9, 1948.

(265) Thomas Hobbes, *On Human Nature,* 1650.

(266) Charles M. Diserens and Mabel Bonifield, "Humor and the Ludicrous," *Psychological Bulletin,* Vol. 27 (1930).

(267) T. Gaylord Andrews, "A Factorial Analysis of Responses to the Comic as a Study in Personality," *Journal of General Psychology,* Vol. 28 (1943).

(268) Max Eastman, "What We Laugh At—And Why," *Reader's Digest,* April, 1943.

(269) Helen K. Mull, "A Study of Humor in Music," *American Journal of Psychology,* Vol. 62 (1949).

(270) Ernest Harms, "The Development of Humor," *Journal of Abnormal and Social Psychology,* Vol. 38 (1943).

(271) Bernard DeVoto, *Mark Twain in Eruption,* reviewed, *Saturday Review of Literature,* Oct. 18, 1941.

(272) Sydney Smith, *Sketches of Moral Philosophy.* New York: Harper & Brothers, 1856.

(273) Antonin J. Obrdlik, "Gallows Humor—A Sociological Phe-

nomenon," *American Journal of Sociology*, Vol. 47 (1941-42).

(274) K. M. Wilson, "Sense of Humor," *Contemporary Review*, Vol. 131 (1922).

(275) Harold Hoffding, *Den Store Humor*. Copenhagen: Gyldendal, 1916.

(276) Kimball Young, *Source Book for Social Psychology*. New York: Alfred A. Knopf, 1927.

(277) Henry A. Murray, "The Psychology of Humor," *Journal of Abnormal and Social Psychology*, Vol. 29 (1934).

(278) Baruch Spinoza, *Ethics*. New York: D. Van Nostrand, 1876.

(279) S. A. Nock, "Sound and Symbol," *Philosophy of Science*, Vol. 8 (1941).

(280) Angelo M. Pellegrini, "Argumentation and Personal Success," *Quarterly Journal of Speech*, Vol. 29 (1943).

(281) Franz Werfel, *Song of Bernadette*. New York: Viking Press, 1942.

(282) Wilhelm Herrmann, *Communion With God*. London: Williams & Norgate, 1906.

(283) Ralph Waldo Emerson, "Lecture on Art." New York: Houghton-Mifflin Co., 1904.

(284) Otto D. Tolischus, *They Wanted War*. New York: Reynal & Hitchcock, 1940.

(285) Wallace Stevens, "Effects of Analogy," *Yale Review*, Vol. 38 (1948-49).

(286) Charles T. Brown, "The Speaker Approach to Speech," *Education*, Vol. 64 (1943).

(287) Aldous Huxley, *Eyeless in Gaza*. London: Harper & Brothers, 1936.

(288) Leonard Bloomfield, *Language*. New York: Henry Holt & Co., 1933.

(289) St. Augustine, "Christian Instruction," in *Writings of St. Augustine*, Vol. IV. New York: Cima Publishing Co., 1947.

(290) H. B. Gislason, "An Approach to Persuasion," *Quarterly Journal of Speech*, Vol. 19 (1933).

(291) John Dewey, *Human Nature and Conduct*. (Modern Library Edition). New York: 1930.

(292) H. B. Gislason, *The Art of Effective Speaking*. New York: D. C. Heath & Co., 1934.

(293) E. D. Adrian, *The Physical Background of Perception.* Oxford: Clarendon Press, 1947.

(294) L. Omwake, "Factors Influencing the Sense of Humor," *Journal of Social Psychology,* Vol. 10 (1939).

(295) Ruth E. Perl, "A Review of Experiments on Humor," *Psychological Bulletin,* Vol. 30 (1933).

(296) Floyd I. Greenleaf, "An Exploratory Study of Stage Fright," *Quarterly Journal of Speech,* Vol. 38 (1952).

(297) C. L. Lomas, "Psychology of Stage Fright," *Quarterly Journal of Speech,* Vol. 23 (1937).

(298) John L. Casteel, "College Speech Training and the Ministry," *Quarterly Journal of Speech,* Vol. 31 (1945).

(299) James A. Winans, *Speech-Making.* New York: D. Appleton-Century Co., 1938.

(300) Charles H. Woolbert and Severina E. Nelson, *The Art of Interpretative Speech.* New York: F. S. Crofts, 1938.

(301) G. L. Freeman, "Dr. Hollingworth on Chewing as a Technique of Relaxation," *Psychological Review,* Vol. 47 (1940).

Date Due